Thrilling Adventures Among the Early Settlers

THRILLING ADVENTURES
AMONG THE EARLY SETTLERS

EMBRACING

DESPERATE ENCOUNTERS WITH INDIANS, TORIES, AND
REFUGEES; DARING EXPLOITS OF TEXAN RANGERS
AND OTHERS, AND INCIDENTS OF GUERILLA
WARFARE; FEARFUL DEEDS OF THE
RAMBLERS AND DESPERADOES,
RANGERS AND REGULATORS
OF THE WEST AND SOUTH-
WEST; HUNTING STORIES,
TRAPPING ADVENTURES,
ETC., ETC., ETC.

BY WARREN WILDWOOD, ESQ.

LITTLE FROG HILL
LF ANTELOPE HILL PUBLISHING A H

Republished 2022 by Little Frog Hill, the children's imprint of Antelope Hill Publishing.
First printing 2022.

Originally published by John E. Potter and Company, Philadelphia, 1861.

Cover art by Swifty.
Edited by Malta and Margaret Bauer.
Formatted by Margaret Bauer.

Antelope Hill Publishing
www.antelopehillpublishing.com

Paperback ISBN-13: 978-1-956887-39-6
EPUB ISBN-13: 978-1-956887-40-2

PUBLISHER'S NOTE

Note that some edits have been made to update more archaic word choices and phrasing, but most of the charm of the original remains, along with intentional misspellings in speech to indicate pronunciation. Parental guidance is advised for children under ten both due to the violent nature of many of these stories, which report the whole truth of these historical accounts, and due to the advanced vocabulary and sentence structure, which may not be accessible to younger readers. These stories represent a time in our nation's history when men were much more daring and adventurous, cunning and noble, and we thoroughly hope you enjoy these tales and are inspired by them as much as we are.

"In a great crisis, one brave, clear-headed man is worth many timid statesmen or cowardly rhetoricians."

CONTENTS

PREFACE

But a brief period has elapsed since this continent was peopled by a new and daring race, a race who sought a refuge from tyranny and oppression among these American wilds, for civil and religious liberty, for liberty of conscience to worship their Creator according to their own conceptions of heaven's revealed will. Among savage beasts and more savage men, liable at any moment to meet death in its most appalling forms, they yet shrunk not from the burdens they had assumed, until their efforts were crowned by a glorious and final triumph.

And now, from the old world and the new, a vast tide of emigration swept in upon the immense prairies of the west and the fertile fields of the south, a heterogeneous mass of elements, the enterprising and virtuous seeking to improve their condition, the vicious of all grades desiring to escape from the terrors and trammels of the law. Between such opposing interests and passions, collisions were inevitable, and fearful have been some of the deeds that stain the history of these localities.

In every new country, there is an era of strife, turbulence, and general combat, a state of nature which is always a state of war, when sanguinary crimes provoke still more sanguinary punishments, and savage fury, and brutal force inaugurate a reign of universal terror. It is peculiar to no geographical section, but applies with more force to the west and southwest than elsewhere. Petty villains and noted criminals—gamblers, counterfeiters, murderers, and others—who have outraged the laws of older localities, have here sought a comparatively secure retreat and inviting fields in which to continue the perpetration of their crimes. But happily, in all instances, the phenomenon is of brief duration; the evil soon runs its course. In the absence of legitimate authority and regular organizations, lynch law usurps its place and often visits a swift and terrible retribution upon the offenders. Anarchists and desperadoes are either exterminated, or driven farther west, and the beautiful spirit of order and progress emerges from the chaos of confusion and blood.

While therefore we can never sufficiently admire those noble founders of the republic, who were ready and willing to sacrifice their all for their country's good, we yet dwell with an intense and living interest upon the bold and daring, though sometimes unscrupulous deeds of the men of a later day, who have made "the wilderness to blossom as the rose." For no more in the petty contests of life on the frontier, than in the mightiest shock of adverse nations and races, will humanity or civilization ever suffer permanent check, or lose a single important battle.

No efforts of the imagination can equal these startling realities—these lights and shadows of life among the early settlers—some of which the editor has presented in the following pages. He claims no originality in the work, having gleaned his subjects from a variety of sources and simply seeking to admit none but those he believed reliable and truthful. The facts of each are common property, some of which have been given by a variety of parties, but in all cases where there was a choice, he has adopted the one which seemed to him best and most truthfully told, without regard to whom should be the narrator. To many of our readers, therefore, some of the tales may not be new, but he believes all are worthy of preservation. The aid of the artist has been invoked, who has added largely to the force and beauty of the text, by many graphic delineations of the more important points in the various stories.

With the hope that the public generally may be as deeply interested in its perusal as has been the author in its preparation, the volume is left in their hands to be dealt with as to them shall be deemed meet and proper.

Warren Wildwood

McCULLOCH'S FEARFUL LEAP

General Putnam's bold plunge on horseback down the steep declivity at Horseneck, in his escape from the British troops, has passed into general history, and there are but few who are ignorant of its details. This exploit, however, is by no means a solitary example of desperate daring, as the narrative which we subjoin will abundantly attest.

Fort Henry was situated about a quarter of a mile above Wheeling Creek, on the left bank of the Ohio River, and was erected to protect the settlers of the little village of Wheeling, which, at the time of its investment, consisted of about twenty-five cabins. In the month of September, 1775, it was invested by about four hundred warriors, on the approach of whom the settlers had fled into it, leaving their cabins and their contents to the torch of the savages. The whole force comprising the garrison consisted of forty-two fighting men all told, but there were among them men who knew the use of the rifle and who were celebrated throughout the borders as the implacable enemies of the Red man and as the best marksmen in the world. Of these, however, more than one-half perished in an ill-advised sortie before the siege commenced, and when the fort was surrounded by the foe, but sixteen men remained to defend it against their overwhelming numbers. But their mothers, wives, and daughters were there, and nerved the little band to deeds of heroism to which the records of the wars of ancient and modern history present no parallel. Here it was that Elizabeth Zane passed through the fire of the whole body of redskins in the effort to bring into the fort the ammunition so necessary to its defense. Here it was, also, that the wives and daughters of its noble defenders marched to a spring in point-blank range of the ambushed Indians, in going back and forth, for the purpose of bringing water for the garrison.

Messengers had been dispatched at the earliest alarm to the neighboring settlements for aid, and in response to the call Captain Van Swearingen, with fourteen men, arrived from Cross Creek and fought his way into the fort without the loss of a man. Soon afterwards, a party of forty horsemen, led by the brave and intrepid Major Samuel McCulloch, were seen approaching and endeavoring to force their way through the dense masses of Indians which nearly surrounded the station. Their friends within the fort made every preparation to receive them, by opening the gates and organizing a sortie to cover their attempt. After a desperate hand-to-hand conflict, in which they made several of the Indians bite the dust, they broke through the lines and entered the fort in triumph, without the loss of an individual. All except their daring leader succeeded in the effort. He was cut off and forced to fly in an opposite direction. McCulloch was as well-known to the Indians as to the Whites for his deeds of prowess, and his name was associated in their minds with some of the bloodiest fights in which the White and Red men had contended. To secure him alive, therefore, that they might enact their vengeance upon him, was the earnest desire of the Indians, and to this end they put forth the most superhuman exertions. There were very few among their number who had not lost a relative by the unerring aim and skill of the fearless woodsman, and they cherished toward him an almost frenzied hatred, which could only be satisfied in his tortures at the stake.

With such feelings and incentives, they crowded around him as he dashed forward in the rear of his men and succeeded in cutting him off from the gate. Finding himself unable, after the most strenuous exertions, to accomplish his entrance, and seeing the uselessness of a conflict with such a force opposed to him, he suddenly pivoted his horse and fled in the direction of Wheeling Hill at his utmost speed. A cloud of warriors started up at his approach and cut off his retreat in this direction, driving him back upon another party who blocked up the path behind, while a third closed in upon him on one of the other sides of the square. The fourth and open side was in the direction of the brow of a precipitous ledge of rocks, nearly one hundred and fifty feet in height, at the foot of which flowed the waters of Wheeling Creek. As he momentarily halted and took a rapid survey of the dangers which surrounded him on all sides, he felt that his chance was indeed a desperate one. The Indians had not fired a shot, and he well knew what this portended, as they could easily have killed him had they chosen to do so. He appreciated the feeling of hatred felt towards him by the foe and saw at a glance the intention to take him alive, if possible, that his ashes might be offered up as a sacrifice to the spirits of their departed friends slain by his hand. This was to die a thousand deaths, in preference to which he determined to run the risk of being dashed in pieces, and he struck his heels against the sides of his steed, which sprang forward toward the precipice.

The encircling warriors had rapidly lessened the space between them and their intended victim and, as they saw him so completely within their toils, raised a yell of triumph, little dreaming of the fearful energy which was to baffle their expectations. As they saw him push his horse in the direction of the precipice, which they had supposed an insurmountable obstacle to his escape, they stood in wonder and amazement, scarcely believing that it could be his intention to attempt the awful leap, which was, to all appearances, certain death. McCulloch still bore his rifle, which he had retained in his right hand, and carefully gathering up the bridle in his left, he urged his noble animal forward, encouraging him by his voice, until they reached the edge of the bank, when, dashing his heels against his sides, they made the fearful leap into the air. Down, down they went, with fearful velocity, without resistance or impediment, until one-half of the space was passed over, when the horse's feet struck the smooth, precipitous face of the rock, and the remainder of the distance was slid and scrambled over until they reached the bottom, alive and uninjured. With a shout which proclaimed his triumphant success to his foe above him, McCulloch pushed his steed into the stream, and in a few moments horse and rider were seen surmounting the banks on the opposite side.

No pursuit was attempted, nor was a shot fired at the intrepid rider. His enemies stood in awe-struck silence upon the brow of the bank from whence he had leaped, and as he disappeared from their view they returned to the investment of the fort. They did not long continue their unavailing efforts, however, for its capture; the numerous additions it had received to its garrison, the fearless-ness exhibited in its defense, together with the feat they had witnessed, disheartened them, and they beat a hasty retreat the next morning—not, however, until they had reduced to ashes the cabins outside of the stockade, and slaughtered some three hundred head of cattle belonging to the settlers.

THE BLOODY BLOCKHOUSE

While Louisiana was yet a French province, Asa Nolens, with his three brothers, his brother-in-law, a cousin, and their wives, tired of their settlement on the Ohio, floated down the Mississippi and squatted on the banks of the Red River. There they become involved in a quarrel with certain Creoles about a horse-trade and Asa, the leader of the party, advised the erection of a blockhouse, as a means of defense against any attack which the Creoles might make. An attack was attempted, with what result this narrative given by Nathan Strong, one of the attacked, will disclose:

One morning we were working in the bush and circling trees, when Righteous, a brother of Asa, rode up full gallop.

"They're coming!" cried he. "A hundred of them at least!"

"Are they far off?" said Asa, quite quietly, as if he had been talking of a herd of deer.

"They are coming over the prairie. In less than half an hour they will be here."

"How are they marching? With van and rear guard? In what order?"

"No order at all, but all of a heap together."

"Good!" said Asa. "They can know but little about bush-fighting or soldiering of any kind. Now then, the women into the blockhouse."

Righteous galloped up to our fort to be there first in case the enemy should find it. The women soon followed, carrying what they could with them. When we were all in the blockhouse, we pulled up the ladder, made the gate fast, and there we were.

We felt somehow strange when we found ourselves shut up inside the Palisades and only able to look out through the slits we left for our rifles. We weren't used to being confined in a place, and it made us right down wolfish. There we remained, however, as still as mice. Scarce a whisper was to be heard. Rachel tore up old shirts and greased them for wadding for the guns, we changed our flints and fixed everything about the rifles properly, while the women sharpened our knives and axes, all in silence. Nearly an hour had passed in this way when we heard shouting and scream-ing and a few musket-shots. We saw through our loopholes some Spanish soldiers running backward and forward on the crest of the slope on which our houses stood. Suddenly a great pillar of smoke arose, then a second, then a third.

"God be good to us!" said Rachel. "They are burning our houses."

We were all trembling, and quite pale with rage. When men have been slaving and sweating for four or five months to build houses for their wives and for the poor worms of children, and then a parcel of devils come and burn them down like maize stalks in a stubble-field, it is no wonder that their teeth should grind together and their fists clench of themselves. So, it was with us; but we said nothing, for our rage would not let us speak. But presently, as we strained our eyes through the loopholes, the Spaniards showed themselves at the opening of the forest yonder, coming toward the blockhouse. We tried to count them, but at first it was impossible, for they came on in a crowd, without any order. They thought little enough of those they were seeking or they would have been more prudent. However, when they came within five hundred paces, they formed ranks and we were able to count them. There were eighty-two foot-soldiers with muskets and carbines, and three officers on horseback with drawn swords in their hands. The latter dismounted, and their example was followed by seven other horsemen, among whom we recognized three of the rascally Creoles who had brought all this trouble upon us. He they called Croupier was among them. The other four were also Creoles, Acadians or Canadians. We had seen lots of their sort on the Upper Mississippi, and fine hunters they were, but mostly wild, drunken, debauched barbarians.

The Acadians came on in front and they set up a whoop when they saw the blockhouse and stockade, but finding we were prepared to receive them, they retreated upon the main body. We saw them speaking to the officers, as if advising them, but the latter shook their heads, and the soldiers continued moving on. They were in uniforms of all colors: blue, white, and brown, but each man dirtier than his neighbor. They marched in good order, nevertheless, the captain and officers coming on in front, and the Acadians keeping the flanks. The latter, however, edged gradually off toward the cotton trees and presently disappeared among them.

"Them be the first men to pick off," said Asa, when he saw this maneuver of the Creoles. "They've steady hands and sharp eyes, but if we get rid of them, we need not mind others."

The Spaniards were now within a hundred yards of us.

"Shall I let fly at the thievin' incendiaries?" said Righteous.

"God forbid!" replied Asa, quite solemn-like. "We will defend ourselves like men, but let us wait till we are attacked, and may the blood that is shed lie at the door of the aggressors."

The Spaniards now saw plainly that they would have to take the stockade before they could get at us, and the officers were seen consulting together.

"Halt!" cried Asa, suddenly.

"*Messieurs les Américains*," said the captain, looking up at our loopholes.

"What's your pleasure?" demanded Asa.

Upon this the captain stuck a dirty pocket-handkerchief upon the point of his sword, and laughing with his officers, moved some twenty paces forward, followed by the troops. Thereupon Asa again shouted to him to halt.

"This is not according to the customs of war," said he. "The flag of truce may advance, but if it is accompanied, we fire."

It was evident that the Spaniards never dreamed of our attempting to resist them, for there they stood in line before us, and if we had fired, every shot must have told. The Acadians, who kept themselves all this time snug behind the cotton-trees, called more than once to the captain to withdraw his men into the wood, but he only shook his head contemptuously. When, however, he heard Asa threaten to fire, he looked puzzled, as if he thought it just possible, we might do as we said. He ordered his men to halt and called out to us not to fire till he had explained what they came for.

"Then cut it short," cried Asa, sternly. "You'd have done better to explain before you burned down our houses, like a pack of Mohawks on the war-path."

As he spoke three bullets whistled from the edge of the forest and struck the stockades within a few inches of the loophole at which he stood. They were fired by the Creoles, who, although they could not possibly distinguish Asa, had probably seen his rifle barrel glitter through the opening. As soon as they had fired, they sprang behind their trees again, craning their heads forward to hear if there was a groan or a cry. They'd have done better to have kept quiet, for Righteous and I caught sight of them and let fly at the same moment. Two of them fell and rolled from behind the trees, and we saw that they were the Creole called Croupier, and another of our horse-dealing friends.

When the Spanish officer heard the shots, he ran hark to his men and shouted out, "Forward! To the assault!" They came on like mad for a distance of thirty paces and then, as if they thought we were wild geese, to be frightened by their noise, they fired a volley against the blockhouse.

"Now then!" cried Asa. "Are you loaded, Nathan and Righteous? I take the captain—you, Nathan, the lieutenant—Righteous, the third officer—James, the sergeant. Mark your men and waste no powder."

The Spaniards were still some sixty yards off, but we were sure of our mark at a hundred and sixty—and that if they had been squirrels instead of men. We fired; the captain and lieutenant, the third officer, two sergeants, and another man, writhed for an instant upon the grass. The next moment they stretched themselves out—dead.

All was now confusion among the musketeers, who ran in every direction. Most of them took to the wood, but about a dozen remained and lifted up their officers to see if there was any spark of life left in them.

"Load again—quick!" said Asa, in a low voice. We did so and six more Spaniards tumbled over. Those who still kept their legs ran off as if the soles of their shoes had been of red-hot iron. We set to work to pick out our touch-holes and clean our rifles, knowing that we might not have time later, and that a single misfire might cost us all our lives. We then loaded and began calculating what the Spaniards would do next. It is true they had lost their officers, but there were five Acadians with them and those were the men we had most reason to fear. Meantime, the vultures and turkey buzzards had already begun to assemble and presently hundreds of them were circling and hovering over the carcasses, which they as yet feared to touch.

Just then, Righteous, who had the sharpest eye of us all, pointed to the corner of the wood just yonder, where it joins the bushwood thicket. I made a sign to Asa, and we all looked and saw there was something creeping and moving through the underwood. Presently we distinguished two Acadians heading a score of Spaniards and endeavoring, under cover of the bushes, to steal across the open ground to the east side of the forest.

"The Acadians for you, Nathan and Righteous—the Spaniards for us," said Asa. The next moment two Acadians and four Spaniards lay bleeding in the brushwood. But the bullets were scarcely out of our rifles when a third Acadian, whom we had not seen, started up.

"Now's the time," shouted he, "before they have loaded again. Follow me, we will have their blockhouse yet!"

And he sprang across, followed by the Spaniards. Although we had killed and disabled a score of our enemies, those who remained were more than ten to one of us, and we were even worse off than at first, for then they were altogether, and now we had them on each side of us. But we did not let ourselves be discouraged, although we could not help feeling that the odds against us were fearfully great.

We had now to keep a sharp lookout, for if one of us showed himself at a loophole, a dozen bullets rattled about his ears. There were many shot holes through the palisades, which were covered with white streaks where the splinters had been torn off by the lead. The musketeers had spread themselves all along the edge of the forest and had learned by experience to keep close to their cover. We now and then got a shot at them, and four or five more were killed, but it was slow work and the time seemed very long.

Suddenly the Spaniards set up a loud shout. At first, we could not make out what was the matter, but presently we heard a hissing and crackling on the roof of the blockhouse. They had wrapped tow around their cartridges, and one of the shots had set light to the fir-boards. Just as we found it out, they gave three more hurrahs and we saw the dry planks begin to flame, and the fire to spread.

"We must put that out and at once," said Asa, "if we don't wish to be roasted alive. Someone must get up the chimney with a bucket of water. I'll go myself."

"Let me go, Asa," said Righteous.

"You stop here. It don't matter who goes. The thing will be done in a minute."

He put a chair on the table and got upon it, seizing a bar which was fixed across the chimney to hang hams upon. He drew himself up by his arms and Rachel handed him a pail of water. All this time the flame was burning brighter and the Spaniards getting louder in their rejoicings and hurrahs. Asa stood upon the bar, and raising the pail above his head, poured the water out of the chimney upon the roof.

"More to the left, Asa," said Righteous, "the fire is strongest to the left."

"Tarnation seize it!" cried Asa. "I can't see. Hand me another pail-ful."

We did so, and when he had got it, he put his head out at the top of the chimney to see where the fire was and threw the water over the exact spot. But at the very moment that he did, the report of a dozen muskets was heard.

"Ha!" cried Asa, in an altered voice. "I have it." The hams and bucket came tumbling down the chimney and Asa after them, all covered with blood.

"In God's name, man, are you hurt?" cried Rachel.

"Hush, wife!" replied Asa. "Keep quiet. I have enough for the rest of my life, which won't be long, but never mind. Lads, defend yourselves well, and don't fire two at the same man. Save your lead, for you will want it all. Promise me that."

"Asa, my beloved Asa!" shrieked Rachel. "If you die, I shall die too."

"Silence, foolish woman, think of our child and the one yet unborn! Hark! I hear the Spaniards! Defend yourselves—Nathan, be a father to my children."

I had barely time to press his hand and promise. The Spaniards, who had guessed our loss, rushed like mad wolves up the mound, twenty on one side and thirty or more on the other.

"Steady!" cried I. "Righteous, here with me, and you, Rachel, show yourself worthy to be Hiram Strong's daughter and Asa's wife, load this rifle for me while I fire my own."

"O God! O God!" cried Rachel. "The hellhounds have murdered my Asa!"

She clasped her husband's body in her arms and there was no getting her away. I felt sad enough myself, but there was scanty time for grieving. For a party of Spaniards, headed by one of the Acadians, was close up to the mound on the side which I was defending. I shot the Acadian but another, the sixth and last but one, took his place.

"Rachel!" cried I. "The rifle, for God's sake, the rifle! A single bullet may save all our lives."

But no Rachel came. The Acadian and Spaniards, who from the cessation of our fire guessed that we were either unloaded or had expended our ammunition, now sprang forward, and by climbing, scrabbling, and getting on one another's shoulders managed to scale the side of the mound, almost perpendicular as it then was. And in a minute the Acadian and half a dozen Spaniards with axes were chopping away at the palisades and severing the wattles which bound them together. To give the devil his due: if there had been three like that Acadian, it would have been all up with us. He handled his axe like a real backwoodsman, but the Spaniards were left wanting of either the skill or the strength of arm and made little impression. There were only Righteous and myself to oppose them, for a dozen more soldiers, with the seventh of those cursed Acadians, were attacking the other side of the stockade.

Righteous shot down one of the Spaniards, but just as he had done so the Acadian tore up a palisade by the roots—how he did it I know not to this hour—and held it with the wattles and branches hanging round it like a shield before him, guarding off a blow I aimed at him, then hurled it against me with such force that I staggered backward and he sprang past me. I thought it was all over with us. It is true that Righteous, with the butt of his rifle, split the skull of the first Spaniard who entered and drove his hunting knife into the next, but the Acadian alone was man enough to give us abundant occupation—now he had got in our rear. Just then there was a crack of a rifle as the Acadian gave a leap into the air and fell dead. At the same moment my son Godsend, a boy ten years old, sprang forward. In his hand Asa's rifle, still smoking from muzzle and touch-hole. The glorious boy had loaded the piece when he saw that Rachel did not do it, and in the very nick of time had shot the Acadian through the heart. This brought me to myself again, and with axe in one hand and knife in the other, I rushed in among the Spaniards, hacking and hewing right and left. It was a real butchery, which lasted a good quarter of an hour—as it seemed to me—but certainly some minutes until at last the Spaniards got sick of it—and would have done so sooner had they known that their leader was shot. They jumped off the mound and ran away, such of them as were able. Righteous and I put the palisade in its place again, securing it as well as we could, and then telling my boy to keep watch, ran over to the other side, where a desperate fight was going on.

Three of our party, assisted by the women, were defending the stockade against a score of Spaniards who kept poking their bayonets between the palisades, till all our people were wounded and bleeding. But Rachel had now recovered from her first grief at her husband's death—or rather it had turned to rage and re-venge—and there she was like a furious tigress, seizing the bayonets as they were thrust through the stockade and wrenching them off the muskets, and sometimes pulling the muskets themselves out of the soldiers' hands. But all this struggling had loosened the palisades, and there were one or two openings in them through which the thin-bodied Spaniards, pushed on by their comrades, were able to pass. Just as we came up, two or three of these copper-colored Dons had squeezed themselves through, without their muskets, but with their short sabers in their hands— they are active and dangerous fellows, those Spaniards, in a hand-to-hand tussle. One of them sprang at me, and if it had not been for my hunting knife, I was done for, for I had no room to swing my axe. But as he came on, I dealt him a blow with my fist, which knocked him down, and then ran my knife into him. Jumping over his body, I snatched a musket out of Rachel's hand and began laying about me with the butt end of it. I was sorry not to have my rifle, which was handier than those heavy Spanish muskets. The women were now in the way—we hadn't room for so many—so I called out to them to get into the blockhouse and load the rifles. There was still another Acadian alive, and I knew that the fight wouldn't end till he was one four. But while we were fighting, Godsend and the women loaded the rifles and brought them out, and firing through the stockade, killed three or four. And as luck would have it, the Acadian was one of the numbers. So, when the Spaniards, who are just like hounds—they only come on if led and encouraged—saw their leader had fallen, they sprang off the mound with a *"Carajo! Malditos!"* and ran away as if a shell had burst among them.

I couldn't say how long the fight lasted; it seemed short—we were so busy—and yet long, deadly long. It is no joke to have to defend one's life and the lives of those one loves best against fourscore blood-thirsty Spaniards, and that with only half a dozen rifles for arms and a few palisades for shelter. When it was over, we were so dog-tired that we fell down where we were, like over-driven oxen, and without minding the blood which lay like water on the ground. Seven Spaniards and two Acadians lay dead within the stockade. We ourselves were all wounded and hacked about, some with knife-stabs and saber-cuts, others with musket-shots; ugly wounds enough, but none mortal. If the Spaniards had returned to the attack, they would have made short work of us, for as soon as we left off fighting and our blood cooled, we became stiff and helpless. But now came the women with rags and bandages, washing our wounds and binding them up, and we dragged ourselves to the blockhouse and lay down upon our mattresses of dry leaves. Godsend loaded the rifles and a dozen Spanish muskets that were lying about, to be in readiness for another attack, and the women kept watch while we slept. But the Spaniards had had enough, and we saw no more of them. Only the next morning, when Jonas went down the ladder to reconnoiter, he found thirty dead and dying, and a few wounded who begged hard for a drink of water, their comrades having deserted them. We got them up into the blockhouse and had their wounds dressed, and after a time they were cured and left us.

POE'S DESPERATE ENCOUNTER WITH BIG FOOT

About the middle of July, 1782, seven Wyandottes crossed the Ohio a few miles above Wheeling and committed great depredations upon the southern shore, killing an old man whom they found alone in his cabin and spreading terror throughout the neighborhood. Within a few hours after their retreat, eight men assembled from different parts of the small settlement and pursued the enemy with great expedition. Among the most active and efficient of the party were two brothers, Adam and Andrew Poe. Adam was particularly popular. In strength, action, and hardihood, he had no equal, being finely formed and inured to all the perils of the woods.

They had not followed the trail far before they became satisfied that the depredators were conducted by Big Foot, a renowned chief of the Wyandotte tribe, who derived his name from the immense size of his feet. His height considerably exceeded six feet, and his strength was represented as Herculean. He had also five brothers, but little inferior to himself in size and courage, and as they generally went in company, they were the terror of the whole country. Adam Poe was overjoyed at the idea of measuring his strength with that of so celebrated a chief and urged the pursuit with a keenness that quickly brought him into the vicinity of the enemy.

For the last few miles, the trail had led them up the southern bank of the Ohio, where the footprints in the sand were deep and obvious, but, when within a few hundred yards of the point at which the Whites as well as the Indians were in the habit of crossing, it suddenly diverged from the stream and stretched along a rocky ridge, forming an obtuse angle with its former direction. Here Adam halted for a moment and directed his brother and the other young men to follow the trail with proper caution, while he himself still adhered to the river path, which led through clusters of willows directly to the point where he supposed the enemy to lie. Having examined the priming of his gun, he crept cautiously through the bushes until he had a view of the point of embarkation. Here lay two canoes, empty and apparently deserted. Being satisfied, however, that the Indians were close at hand, he relaxed nothing of his vigilance and quickly gained a jutting cliff, which hung immediately over the canoes.

Hearing a low murmur below, he peered cautiously over and beheld the object of his search. The gigantic Big Foot lay below him in the shade of a willow and was talking in a low deep tone to another warrior, who seemed a mere pigmy by his side. Adam cautiously drew back and cocked his gun. The mark was fair—the distance did not exceed twenty feet—and his aim was unerring. Raising his rifle slowly and cautiously, he took a steady aim at Big Foot's breast and drew the trigger. His gun flashed. Both Indians sprung to their feet with a deep interjection of surprise, and for a single second all three stared upon each other. This inactivity, however, was soon over. Adam was too much hampered by the bushes to retreat, and setting his life upon a cast of the die, he sprung over the bush that had sheltered him and, summoning all his powers, leaped boldly down the precipice and alighted upon the breast of Big Foot with a shock that bore him to the earth. At the moment of contact, Adam had also thrown his right arm around the neck of the smaller Indian, so that all three came to the earth together.

At that moment a sharp firing was heard among the bushes above, announcing that the other parties were engaged, but the trio below were too busy to attend to anything but themselves. Big Foot was for an instant stunned by the violence of the shock, and Adam was enabled to keep them both down. But the exertion necessary for that purpose was so great, that he had no leisure to use his knife. Big Foot quickly recovered and, without attempting to rise, wrapped his long arms around Adam's body and pressed him to his breast with the crushing force of a boa constrictor. Adam, as we have already remarked, was a powerful man and had seldom encountered his equal, but never had he yet felt an embrace like that of Big Foot. He instantly relaxed his hold of the small Indian, who sprung to his feet. Big Foot then ordered him to run for his tomahawk, which lay within ten steps, and kill the White man, while he held him in his arms. Adam seeing his danger, struggled manfully to extricate himself from the folds of the giant, but in vain. The lesser Indian approached with his uplifted tomahawk, but Adam watched him closely, and as he was about to strike, gave him a kick so sudden and violent as to knock the tomahawk from his hand and send him staggering back into the water. Big Foot uttered an exclamation in a tone of deep contempt at the failure of his companion and, raising his voice to its highest pitch, thundered out several words in the Indian tongue, which Adam could not understand but supposed to be a direction for second attack. The lesser Indian now again approached, carefully shunning Adam's heels, and making many motions with his tomahawk, in order to deceive him as to the point where the blow would fall. This lasted for several seconds, until a thundering exclamation from Big Foot compelled his companion to strike.

Such was Adam's dexterity and vigilance, however, that he managed to receive the tomahawk in a glancing direction upon his left wrist, wounding him deeply but not disabling him. He now made a sudden and desperate effort to free himself from the arms of the giant and succeeded. Instantly snatching up a rifle (for the Indian could not venture to shoot for fear of hurting his companion), he shot the smaller Indian through the body. But scarcely had he done so when Big Foot arose and, placing one hand upon his collar and the other upon his hip, pitched him ten feet into the air, as he himself would have pitched a child. Adam fell upon his back at the edge of the water, but before his antagonist could spring upon him he was again upon his feet, and stung with rage at the idea of being handled so easily, he attacked the gigantic antagonist with a fury that for a time compensated for inferiority of strength. It was now a fair fist fight between them, for in the hurry of the struggle neither had leisure to draw their knives.

Adam's superior activity and experience as a pugilist gave him great advantage. The Indian struck awkwardly, and finding himself rapidly dropping to leeward, he closed with his antagonist and again, hurled him to the ground. They quickly rolled into the river, and the struggle continued with unabated fury, each attempting to drown the other. The Indian being unused to such violent exertion, and having been much injured by the first shock in his stomach, was unable to exert the same powers which had given him such a decided superiority at first. Adam, seizing him by the scalp lock, put his head under water and held it there, until the faint struggles of the Indian induced him to believe that he was drowned when he relaxed his hold and attempted to draw his knife. The Indian, however, to use Adam's own expression, "had only been possuming!" He instantly regained his feet, and in his turn put his adversary under.

In the struggle, both were carried out into the current beyond their depth, and each was compelled to relax his hold and swim for his life. There was still one loaded rifle upon the shore, and each swam hard in order to reach it, but the Indian proved the most expert swimmer, and Adam seeing that he should be too late, turned and swam out into the stream, intending to dive and thus frustrate his enemy's intention. At this instant, Andrew, having heard that his brother was alone in a struggle with two Indians, and in great danger, ran up hastily to the edge of the bank above, in order to assist him. Another White man followed him closely and, seeing Adam in the river, covered with blood, and swimming rapidly from shore, mistook him for an Indian and fired upon him, wounding him dangerously in the shoulder. Adam turned and, seeing his brother, called loudly upon him to "shoot the big Indian upon the shore." Andrew's gun, however, was empty, having just been discharged. Fortunately, Big Foot had also seized the gun with which Adam had shot the lesser Indian, so that both were upon an equality.

The contest now was who could load first. Big Foot poured in his powder first, and drawing his ramrod out of its sheath in too great a hurry threw it into the river, and while he ran to recover it, Andrew gained an advantage. Still the Indian was but a second too late, for his gun was at his shoulder, when Andrew's ball entered his breast. The gun dropped from his hands, and he fell forward upon his face upon the very margin of the river. Andrew, now alarmed for his brother, who was scarcely able to swim, threw down his gun and rushed into the river in order to bring him ashore, but Adam, more intent upon securing the scalp of Big Foot as a trophy than upon his own safety, called loudly on his brother to leave him alone and scalp the big Indian, who was now endeavoring to roll himself into the water, from a romantic desire, peculiar to the Indian warrior, of securing his scalp from the enemy. Andrew, however, refused to obey and insisted upon saving the living, before attending to the dead. Big Foot, in the meantime, had succeeded in reaching the deep water before he expired, and his body was borne off by the waves, without being stripped of the ornament and pride of an Indian warrior.

Not a man of the Indians had escaped. Five of Big Foot's brothers, the flowers of the Wyandotte nation, had accompanied him in the expedition, and all perished. It is said that the news of this calamity threw the whole tribe into mourning. Their remarkable size, their courage, and their superior intelligence gave them immense influence, which, greatly to their credit, was generally exerted on the side of humanity. Their powerful interposition had saved many prisoners from the stake and had given a milder character to the warfare of the Indians in that part of the country. A chief of the same name was alive in that part of the country so late as 1792, but whether a brother or a son of Big Foot is not known.

Adam Poe recovered of his wounds and lived many years after his memorable conflict, but never forgot the tremendous "hug" that he sustained in the arms of Big Foot.

ADVENTURES OF DANIEL BOONE

In 1769, Boone left his family at their home upon the Yadkin river in North Carolina and set out, in company with five others, to explore the country of Kentucky.

On the 7th of June they reached Red River and, from a neighboring eminence, were enabled to survey the vast plain of Kentucky. Here they built a cabin in order to afford them a shelter from the rain which had fallen in immense quantities on their march, and remained in a great measure stationary until December, killing a great quantity of game immediately around them. Immense herds of buffalo ranged through the forest in every direction, feeding upon the leaves of the cane or the rich and spontaneous fields of clover.

On the 22nd of December, Boone and John Stuart, one of his companions, left their encampment and, following one of the numerous paths which the buffalo had made through the cane, they plunged boldly into the interior of the forest. They had as yet seen no Indians, and the country had been reported as totally uninhabited. This was true in a strict sense, for although the southern and northwestern tribes were in the habit of hunting here as upon neutral ground, yet not a single wigwam had been erected, nor did the land bear the slightest mark of having ever been cultivated. The different tribes would fall in with each other, and from the fierce conflicts which generally followed these casual encounters, the country had been known among them by the name of "the dark and bloody ground"! The two adventurers soon learned the additional danger to which they were exposed. While roving carelessly from canebrake to canebrake, and admiring the rank growth of vegetation and the variety of timber which marked the fertility of the soil, they were suddenly alarmed by a party of Indians, who, springing from their place of concealment, rushed upon them with a rapidity which rendered escape impossible.

They were almost immediately seized, disarmed, and made prisoners. Their feelings may be readily imagined. They were in the hands of an enemy who knew no alternative between adoption and torture, and the numbers and fleetness of their captors rendered escape by open means impossible, while their jealous vigilance seemed equally fatal to any secret attempt. Boone, however, was possessed of a temper admirably adapted to the circumstance in which he was placed. Of a cold and saturnine, rather than an ardent disposition, he was never either so much elevated by good fortune or depressed by bad, as to lose for an instant the full possession of all his faculties. He saw that immediate escape was impossible, but he encouraged his companion, and constrained himself, to accompany the Indians in all their excursions, with so calm and contented an air, that their vigilance insensibly began to relax.

On the seventh evening of their captivity, they encamped in a thick canebrake, and having built a large fire, lay down to rest. The party whose duty it was to watch were weary and negligent, and about midnight Boone, who had not closed an eye, ascertained from the deep breathing all around him that the whole party, including Stuart, was in a deep sleep. Gently and gradually extricating himself from the Indians who lay around him, he walked cautiously to the spot where Stuart lay and, having succeeded in awakening him without alarming the rest, he briefly informed him of his determination and exhorted him to arise, make no noise, and follow him. Stuart, although ignorant of the design and suddenly roused from sleep, fortunately obeyed with equal silence and celerity, and within a few minutes they were beyond hearing.

Rapidly traversing the forest by the light of the stars and the barks of the trees, they ascertained the direction in which the camp lay, but upon reaching it on the next day, to their great grief, they found it plundered and deserted with nothing to show the fate of their companions—and even to the day of his death, Boone knew not whether they had been killed or taken or had voluntarily abandoned their cabin and returned. Here, in a few days, they were accidentally joined by Boone's brother and another man who had followed them from Carolina and fortunately stumbled upon their camp. This accidental meeting in the bosom of a vast wilderness gave great relief to the two brothers, although their joy was soon overcast.

Boone and Stuart, in a second excursion, were again pursued by savages, and Stuart was shot and scalped, while Boone fortunately escaped. Within a few days they sustained another calamity, if still more distressing. Their only remaining companion was benighted in a hunting excursion and, while encamped in the woods alone, was attacked and devoured by the wolves.

The two brothers were thus left in the wilderness alone, separated by several hundred miles from home, surrounded by hostile Indians, and destitute of everything but their rifles. After having had such melancholy experience of the dangers to which they were exposed, it might be supposed that their fortitude would have given way and that they would instantly have returned to the settlements. But the most remarkable feature in Boone's character was calm and cold equanimity, which rarely rose to enthusiasm and never sunk to despondence.

His courage undervalued the danger to which he was exposed and his presence of mind, which never forsook him, enabled him on all occasions to take the best means of avoiding it. The wilderness with all its danger and privations had a charm for him, which is scarcely conceivable by one brought up in a city—and he determined to remain alone, while his brother returned to Carolina for an additional supply of ammunition, as their original supply was nearly exhausted. His situation would seem in the highest degree gloomy and dispiriting. The dangers which attended his brother on his return were nearly equal to his own, and each had left a wife and children, which Boone acknowledged cost him many an anxious thought.

But the wild and solitary grandeur of the country around him, where not a tree had been cut nor a house erected, was to him an inexhaustible source of admiration and delight, and he tells himself that some of the most rapturous moments of his life were spent in those lonely rambles. The utmost caution was necessary to avoid the savages, and scarcely less to escape the ravenous hunger of the wolves that prowled nightly around him in immense numbers. He was compelled frequently to shift his lodgings and, by undoubted signs, saw that the Indians had repeatedly visited his hut during his absence. He sometimes lay in canebrakes, without fire, and heard the yells of the Indians around him. Fortunately, however, he never encountered them.

On the 27th of July, 1770, his brother returned with a supply of ammunition, and with a hardihood which appears almost incredible, they ranged through the country in every direction and without injury until March, 1771. They then returned to North Carolina, where Daniel rejoined his family after an absence of three years, during nearly the whole of which time he had never tasted bread or salt, nor seen the face of a single White man, with the exception of his brother and the two friends who had been killed. He here determined to sell his farm and remove, with his family, to the wilderness of Kentucky.

Accordingly, on the 25th of September, 1771, having disposed of all the property which he could not take with him, he took leave of his friends and commenced his journey to the west. A number of milk cows and horses, laden with a few necessary utensils, formed the whole of his baggage. His wife and children were mounted on horseback and accompanied him, everyone regarding them as devoted to destruction. In Powell's Valley they were joined by five more families and forty men well-armed. Encouraged by this accession of strength, they advanced with additional confidence but had soon a severe warning of the further dangers which awaited them. When near Cumberland Mountain, their rear was suddenly attacked with great fury by a scouting party of Indians and thrown into considerable confusion.

The party, however, soon rallied and, being accustomed to Indian warfare, returned the fire with such spirit and effect that the Indians were repulsed with slaughter. Their own loss, however, had been severe. Six men were killed upon the spot and one wounded. Among the killed was Boone's eldest son, to the unspeakable affliction of his family. The disorder and grief occasioned by this rough reception seems to have affected the emigrants deeply, as they instantly retraced their steps to the settlements on Clinch River, forty miles from the scene of action. Here they remained until June 1774, probably at the request of the women who must have been greatly alarmed at the prospect of plunging more deeply into a country upon the skirts of which they had witnessed so keen and bloody a conflict.

At this time Boone, at the request of Governor Dunmore of Virginia, conducted a number of surveyors to the falls of Ohio, a distance of eight hundred miles. After his return, he was engaged under Dunmore until 1775 in several affairs with the Indians, and at the solicitation of some gentlemen of North Carolina, he attended at a treaty with the Cherokees for the purpose of purchasing the lands south of the Kentucky River.

It was under the auspices of Col. Richard Henderson that Boone's next visit to Kentucky was made. Leaving his family on Clinch River, he set out at the head of a few men to mark out a road for the pack horses or wagons of Henderson's party. This laborious and dangerous duty he executed with his usual patient fortitude until he came within fifteen miles of the spot where Boonesborough afterwards was built. Here, on the 22nd of March, his small party was attacked by the Indians and suffered a loss of four men killed and wounded. The Indians, although repulsed with loss in this affair, renewed the attack with equal fury on the next day and killed and wounded five more of his party. On the 1st of April, the survivors began to build a small fort on the Kentucky River, afterwards called Boonesborough, and on the 4th they were again attacked by the Indians and lost another man. Notwithstanding the harassing attacks to which they were constantly exposed (for the Indians seemed enraged to madness at the prospect of their building houses on their hunting ground), the work was prosecuted with indefatigable diligence and on the 14th was completed.

Boone instantly returned to Clinch River for his family, determined to bring them with him at every risk. This was done as soon as the journey could be performed, and Mrs. Boone and her daughters were the first White women who stood upon the banks of the Kentucky river, as Boone himself had been the first White man who ever built a cabin upon the borders of the state.

Within a few weeks after the arrival of Mrs. Boone and her

daughters, the infant colony was reinforced by three more families. Boonesborough, however, was the central object of Indian hostilities, and scarcely had his family become domesticated in their new possession, when they were suddenly attacked by a party of Indians and lost one of their garrison. This was on the 24th of December, 1775.

In the following July, however, a much more alarming incident occurred. One of his daughters, in company with a Miss Calloway, were amusing themselves in the immediate neighborhood of the fort when a party of Indians suddenly rushed out of a canebrake and, intercepting their return, took them prisoners. The screams of the terrified girls quickly alarmed the family. The small garrison was dispersed in their usual occupations, but Boone hastily collected a small party of eight men and pursued the enemy. So much time, however, had been lost that the Indians had got several miles the start of them. The pursuit was urged through the night with great keenness by woodsmen capable of following a trail at all times, and on the following day, they came up with them.

The attack was so sudden and furious that the Indians were driven from their ground before they had leisure to tomahawk their prisoners, and the girls were recovered without having sustained any other injury than excessive fright and fatigue. Nothing but a barren outline of this interesting occurrence has been given. The Indians lost two men, while Boone's party was uninjured.

From this time until the 15th of April, 1777, the garrison was incessantly harassed by flying parties of Indians. While ploughing their corn, they were waylaid and shot; while hunting, they were chased and fired upon; and sometimes a solitary Indian would creep up near the fort in the night and fire upon the first of the garrison who appeared in the morning. They were in a constant state of anxiety and alarm, and the most ordinary duties could only be performed at the risk of their lives.

On the 15th of April the enemy appeared in large numbers, hoping to crush the infant settlement at a single blow. Boonesborough, Logan's Station, and Harrodsburg were attacked at one and the same time. But destitute as they were of artillery, scaling ladders, and all the proper means of reducing fortified places, they could only distress the men, alarm the women, and destroy the corn and cattle. Boonesborough sustained some loss, as did the other stations, but the enemy being more exposed suffered so severely as to retire with precipitation.

No rest, however, was given to the unhappy garrison. On the 4th of July following, they were again attacked by two hundred warriors, and again repulsed the enemy with loss. The Indians retreated but a few days afterwards fell upon Logan's Station with great fury, having sent detachments to alarm the other stations, so as to prevent the appearance of reinforcements to Logan's. In this last attempt they displayed great obstinacy, and as the garrison consisted of only fifteen men, they were reduced to extremity. Not a moment could be allowed for sleep. Burning arrows were shot upon the roofs of the houses, and the Indians often pressed boldly up to the gates and attempted to hew them down with their tomahawks. Fortunately, at this critical time, Colonel Bowman arrived from Virginia with one hundred men well-armed, and the savages precipitately withdrew, leaving the garrison almost exhausted with fatigue and reduced to twelve men.

A brief repose now followed, in which the settlers endeavored to repair the damages done to their farms. But a period of heavy trial to Boone and his family was approaching. In January 1778, accompanied by thirty men, Boone went to the Blue Licks to make salt for the different stations, and on the 7th of February following while out hunting, he fell in with one hundred and two Indian warriors on their march to attack Boonesborough. He instantly fled, but being upwards of fifty years old, was unable to contend with the fleet young men who pursued him and was a second time taken prisoner. As usual, he was treated with kindness until his final fate was determined and was led back to the Licks where his men were still encamped. Here his whole party, to the number of twenty-seven, surrendered themselves upon the promise of life and good treatment, both of which conditions were faithfully observed.

Had the Indians prosecuted their enterprise, they might, perhaps, by showing their prisoners and threatening to put them to torture, have operated so far upon the sympathies of the garrisons as to have obtained considerable results. But nothing of the kind was attempted. They had already been unexpectedly successful, and it is their custom, after good or bad fortune, immediately to return home and enjoy their triumph or lament their ill success. Boone and his party were conducted to the old town of Chillicothe, where they remained until the following March. No journal was written during this period by either Boone or his party. We are only informed that his mild and patient equanimity wrought so powerfully upon the Indians that he was adopted into a family and uniformly treated with the utmost affection. One fact is given us which shows his acute observation and knowledge of mankind. At the various shooting matches to which he was invited, he took care not to beat *too* often. He knew that no feeling is more painful than that of inferiority, and that the most effectual way of keeping them in a good humor with *him* was to keep them in a good humor with themselves. He, therefore, only shot well enough to make it an honor to beat him, and thus found himself a universal favorite.

On the 10th of March, 1778, Boone was conducted to Detroit, where Governor Hamilton himself offered £100 for his ransom, but so strong was the affection of the Indians for their prisoner that it was positively refused. Several English gentlemen, touched with sympathy for his misfortunes, made pressing offers of money and other articles, but Boone steadily refused to receive benefits which he could never return. The offer was honorable to them, and the refusal was dictated by rather too refined a spirit of independence. Boone's anxiety on account of his wife and children was incessant and the more intolerable as he dared not excite the suspicion of the Indians by any indication of a wish to rejoin them.

Upon his return from Detroit, he observed that 150 warriors of various tribes had assembled, painted and equipped for a raid against Boonesborough. His anxiety at this sight became ungovernable, and he determined, at every risk, to effect his escape. During the whole of this agitating period, however, he permitted no symptoms of anxiety to escape him. He hunted and shot with them, as usual, until the morning of the 10th of June when, taking an early start, he left Chillicothe and directed his route to Boonesborough. The distance exceeded 160 miles, but he performed it in four days, during which he ate only one meal. He appeared before the garrison like one risen from the dead.

His wife, supposing him killed, had transported herself, children, and property to her father's house in North Carolina; his men, suspecting no danger, were dispersed in their ordinary avocations, and the works had been permitted to go to waste. Not a moment was to be lost. The garrison worked day and night upon the fortifications. New gates, new flanks, and double bastions were soon completed. The cattle and horses were brought into the fort, ammunition prepared, and everything made ready for the approach of the enemy within ten days after his arrival. At this time, one of his companions in captivity arrived from Chillicothe and announced that his escape had determined the Indians to delay the invasion for three weeks.

During this interval, it was ascertained that numerous spies were traversing the woods and hovering around the station, doubtless for the purpose of observing and reporting the condition of the garrison. Their report could not have been favorable. The alarm had spread very generally and all were upon the alert. The attack was delayed so long that Boone began to suspect that they had been discouraged by the report of the spies, and he determined to invade them. Selecting nineteen men from his garrison, he put himself at their head and marched with equal silence and celerity against the town of Paint Creek on the Scioto. He arrived without discovery within four miles of the town and there encountered a party of thirty warriors on their march to unite with the grand army in the expedition against Boonesborough.

Instantly attacking them with great spirit, he compelled them to give way with some loss and without any injury to himself. He then halted and sent two spies in advance to ascertain the condition of the village. In a few hours they returned with the intelligence that the town was evacuated. He instantly concluded that the grand army was upon its march against Boonesborough, whose situation, as well as his own, was exceedingly critical. Retracing his steps, he marched day and night hoping still to elude the enemy and reach Boonesborough before them. He soon fell in with their trail, and making a circuit to avoid them, he passed their army on the sixth day of their march and on the seventh reached Boonesborough.

On the eighth, the enemy appeared in great force. There were nearly five hundred Indian warriors, armed and painted in their usual manner, and what was still more formidable, they were conducted by Canadian officers, well skilled in the usages of modern warfare. As soon as they were arrayed in front of the fort, the British colors were displayed, and an officer with a flag was sent to demand the surrender of the fort with a promise of quarter and good treatment in case of compliance and threatening "the hatchet" in case of a storm. Boone requested two days for consideration, which, in defiance of all experience and common sense, was granted. This interval, as usual, was employed in preparation for an obstinate resistance. The cattle were brought into the fort, the horses secured, and all things made ready against the commencement of hostilities.

Boone then assembled the garrison and represented to them the condition in which they stood. They had not now to deal with Indians alone, but with British officers, skilled in the art of attacking fortified places, sufficiently numerous to direct but too few to restrain their savage allies. If they surrendered, their lives might and probably would be saved but they would suffer much inconvenience and must lose all their property. If they resisted and were overcome, the life of every man, woman, and child would be sacrificed. The hour was now come in which they were to determine what was to be done. If they were inclined to surrender, he would announce it to the officer. If they were resolved to maintain the fort, he would share their fate, whether in life or death. He had scarcely finished when every man arose and, in a firm tone, announced his determination to defend the fort to the last.

Boone then appeared at the gate of the fortress and communicated to Captain Duquesne the resolution of his men. Disappointment and chagrin were strongly painted upon the face of the Canadian at this answer, but endeavoring to disguise his feelings, he declared that Governor Hamilton had ordered him not to injure the men if it could be avoided and that if nine of the principal inhabitants of the fort would come out into the plain and treat with them, they would instantly depart without further hostility. The insidious nature of this proposal was evident, for they could converse very well from where they then stood, and going out would only place the officers of the fort at the mercy of the savages, not to mention the absurdity of supposing that this army of warriors would "treat" but upon such terms as pleased them, and no terms were likely to do so short of a total abandonment of the country.

Notwithstanding these obvious objections, the word "treat" sounded so pleasantly in the ears of the besieged that they agreed at once to the proposal and Boone himself, attended by eight of his men, went out and mingled with the savages who crowded around them in great numbers with countenances of deep anxiety. The treaty then commenced and was soon concluded. Duquesne, after many pretty periods about the kindness and humanity which should accompany the warfare of civilized beings, at length informed Boone that it was a custom with the Indians, upon the conclusion of a treaty with the Whites, for two warriors to take hold of the hand of each White man.

Boone thought this rather a singular custom, but there was no time to dispute about etiquette, particularly as he could not be more in their power than he already was, so he signified his willingness to conform to the Indian mode of cementing friendship. Instantly two warriors approached each White man with the word "brother" upon their lips but a very different expression in their eyes and, grappling him with violence, attempted to bear him off. They expected such a consummation and all at the same moment sprung from their enemies and ran to the fort under a heavy fire, which fortunately only wounded one man.

The attack instantly commenced by a heavy fire against the picketing and was returned with fatal accuracy by the garrison. The Indians quickly sheltered themselves, and the action became more cautious and deliberate. Finding but little effect from the fire of his men, Duquesne next resorted to a more formidable mode of attack. The forest stood on the south bank of the river within yards of the water. Commencing under the bank, where their operations were concealed from the garrison, they attempted to push a mine into the fort. Their object, however, was fortunately discovered by the quantity of fresh earth which they were compelled to throw into the river and by which the water became muddy for some distance below. Boone instantly cut a trench within the fort in such a manner as to intersect the line of their approach and thus frustrated their design.

The enemy exhausted all the ordinary artifices of Indian warfare but were steadily repulsed in every effort. Finding their numbers daily thinned by the deliberate but fatal fire of the garrison and, seeing no prospect of final success, they broke up on the ninth day of the siege and returned home. The loss of the garrison was two men killed and four wounded. On the part of the savage, thirty-seven were killed and many wounded, who, as usual, were all carried off. This was the last siege sustained by Boonesborough. The country had increased so rapidly in numbers and so many other stations lay between Boonesborough and the Ohio, that the savages could not reach it without leaving enemies in the rear.

In the autumn of this year, Boone returned to North Carolina for his wife and family, the former having, as already observed, supposed him dead and returned to her father.

In the summer of 1780, he returned to Kentucky with his family and settled at Boonesborough. Here he continued, busily engaged upon his farm until the 6th of October, when, accompanied by his brother, he went to the Lower Blue Licks for the purpose of providing himself with salt. This spot seemed fatal to Boone. Here he had once been taken prisoner by the Indians, and here he was destined, within two years, to lose his youngest son and to witness the slaughter of many of his dearest friends. His present visit was not free from calamity. Upon their return, they were encountered by a party of Indians, and his brother, who had accompanied him faithfully through many years of toil and danger, was killed and scalped before his eyes.

Unable either to prevent or avenge his death, Boone was compelled to fly and, by his superior knowledge of the country, contrived to elude his pursuers. They followed his trail, however, by the scent of a dog that pressed him closely and prevented his concealing himself. This was one of the most critical moments of his life, but his usual coolness and fortitude enabled him to meet it. He halted until the dog, baying loudly upon his trail, came within gunshot, when he deliberately turned and shot him dead. The thickness of the woods and the approach of darkness then enabled him to effect his escape.

A PERILOUS ADVENTURE IN A CANOE

One morning in September, 1817, Solomon Sweatland of Conneaut on the Ohio shore of Lake Erie had risen at the earliest dawn to enjoy his favorite amusement of hunting deer. This exciting sport he had been accustomed to follow in connection with a friend and neighbor who, by the aid of dogs, would drive the deer into the lake where Sweatland would pursue them in his canoe and shoot them without difficulty. On the present occasion he had left his cabin without his coat or waistcoat to listen for the baying of the dogs as they drove the deer. The welcome sound soon greeted his ears, and he was surprised to find that a noble buck had already taken the water and was some little distance out in the lake. In the enthusiasm of the moment, he threw his hat upon the beach, jumped into his canoe, and put off after the animal with every nerve thrilling with intense interest in the pursuit. The wind, which had been blowing steadily from the south during the night, had now increased to a gale, but he was too intent upon securing the valuable prize, which was breasting the waves in advance to heed the dictates of prudence. The race promised to be a long one, for the deer was a powerful animal and was not to be easily beaten by a log canoe and a single paddle. A considerable distance from the land had been attained, and the canoe had shipped a heavy sea before he overtook the deer, who turned and made for the shore.

Upon tacking to pursue him, Sweatland was at once apprised of his danger by the fact that, with his utmost exertions, he not only made no progress in the desired direction but, on the contrary, was drifting further out to sea. He had been observed in his outward progress by his neighbor, as well as by his own family, and as he disappeared from sight, considerable apprehension was felt for his safety. The alarm was soon given in the neighborhood, and it was decided by those competent to judge that his return would be impossible and, unless help could be afforded him, that he was doomed to perish at sea. Actuated by those generous impulses which often induce men to risk their own lives to save those of others, three neighbors, Messrs. Gilbert, Cousins, and Belden, took a light boat and started in search of the wanderer. They met the deer returning but could see nothing of their neighbor and friend. They made stretches off shore in the probable range of the fugitive, until they reached a distance of five or six miles from the land, when, meeting with a heavy sea in which they deemed it impossible for a canoe to live and seeing no signs of it on the vast expanse of waters, they reluctantly, and not without difficulty and danger, returned to shore, and Sweatland was given up as lost. Meantime, the object of their search was laboring at his paddle in the vain hope that the wind might abate or that aid might reach him from the shore. One or two schooners were in sight in the course of the day, but notwithstanding, he made every effort to attract the attention of their crews but failed to do so.

For a long time, the shore continued in sight, and as he traced its dim and fast-receding outline and recognized the spot where stood his cabin—within whose precincts were the cherished objects of his affections, now doubly dear from the prospect of losing them forever—he felt that the last tie which united him in companionship with his fellow-men was about to be dissolved and the world, with all its busy interests, forever hidden from his sight. Fortunately, he possessed a cool head and a stout heart, which, united with a considerable share of physical strength and power of endurance, eminently fitted him for any emergency. He was a good sailor, and his experience taught him that while there was life there was hope. That experience taught him also, as the outline of the far-off shore disappeared from his sight, that his only expedient was to endeavor to reach the Canada side, a distance of fifty miles. It was now blowing a gale, and the sea was evidently increasing, so that it required the most incredible exertion on his part to trim his uncouth vessel to the waves. He was obliged to stand erect and move cautiously from one end to the other, well aware that one lost stroke of the paddle, or a tottering movement, would bring his voyage to a sudden termination. Much of his attention was likewise required in bailing out the canoe, which he managed to do with one of his substantial shoes. Hitherto he had been blessed with the light of day, but to add to his distress, night was fast approaching when he could only depend upon a kind Providence to guide him over the dark waste of waters. The sky, too, began to be overcast, and an occasional star which glistened through the haze was all the light afforded him through that long and fearful night. Wet to the skin by the constant dashing spray, part of the time in water half up to the knees, so cold that his blood seemed chilled in his veins, and almost famished with hunger, he felt that death was preferable to such long-continued suffering, and nothing but the thought of his family sustained him in his exertions to keep his boat trimmed and headed for the land.

When morning dawned, the outline of the Canada shore greeted his eyes, and he found he had made land in the vicinity of Long Point. Here he met with another difficulty, in an adverse wind and heavy breakers, but the same hand which had sustained him thus far guided him in this emergency, and after thirty hours of unremitting and incredible exertions, he succeeded in landing in safety. What his emotions were on again treading the green and solid earth, we shall not attempt to inquire, but his trials were not yet ended. He found himself faint with hunger and exhausted with fatigue at the distance of forty miles from any human habitation, while the country that intervened was a desert filled with marshes and tangled thickets from which nothing could be obtained to supply his wants. These difficulties, together with the reduced state of his strength, made his progress toward the settlement slow and toilsome. On his way he found a quantity of goods which had been thrown ashore from the wreck of some vessel, which, although they afforded him no immediate relief, were afterward of material service. After a long and weary march through the wilderness, he arrived at length at the settlement where he was received and treated with great kindness and hospitality by the people.

When his strength was sufficiently recruited, he procured a

boat and went in search of his goods. These he found and brought off. He started overland for Buffalo, where he disposed of part of his treasure and with the proceeds furnished himself with a complete outfit, and finding the *Traveler*, Captain Charles Brown, from Conneaut in the harbor, he engaged passage on board of her. The captain and crew had heard of his disappearance and looked upon him as one risen from the grave. His story was so astonishing as scarcely to be credible, but as he was there in person to verify it, it could not be doubted. Within a day or two he was on his way to join his family, who, he was informed by the captain, had given him up for dead and were wrapped in the deepest despair. His feelings can be easily imagined as he approached the vicinity of that home which he had never expected again to behold. When the packet arrived opposite the house, the crew gave three long, loud, and hearty cheers and fired guns from the deck in token of joy, which led his family to anticipate his return. On landing, he found that his funeral sermon had been preached, and he had the rare privilege of seeing his own *widow*, clothed in the habiliments of deep mourning.

THE MYSTERY AT LANCASTER

The American authorities found much difficulty in disposing of their prisoners. They had no posts regularly fitted for the purpose and they could suggest no better means for securing them than to place them under guard in a thickly settled part of the country where the inhabitants were most decidedly hostile to the English. The town of Lancaster, in Pennsylvania, was one of those selected for this purpose. The prisoners were confined in barracks, enclosed with a stockade, and vigilantly guarded. But in spite of all precautions, they often disappeared in an unaccountable manner and nothing was heard of them till they had resumed their places in the English army. Many and various were the conjectures as to the means of their escape; the officers inquired and investigated in vain, the country was explored to no purpose, the soldiers shook their heads and told of fortune-tellers, peddlers, and such characters who had been seen at intervals, and sundry of the more credulous could think of nothing but supernatural agency, but whether man or spirit was the conspirator, the mystery was unbroken.

When this became known to Washington, he sent General Hazen to take this responsible charge. This energetic officer, after exhausting all resources, resorted to stratagem. He was convinced that, as the nearest British post was more than a hundred miles distant, the prisoners must be aided by Americans, but where the suspicion should fall, he could not even conjecture, the reproach of Toryism being almost unknown in that region. Having been trained to meet exigencies of this kind in a distinguished career as colonel in the British army, his plan was formed at once and communicated to an officer of his own upon whose talent he relied for its successful execution. This was Captain Lee, whose courage and ability fully justified the selection.

The secret plan concocted between them was this. It was to be given out that Lee was absent on furlough or command. He, meanwhile, was to assume the dress of a British prisoner and, having provided himself with information and a story of his capture, was to be thrown into the barracks where he might gain the confidence of the soldiers and join them in a plan of escape. How well Captain Lee sustained his part may be inferred from the fact that when he had disappeared and placed himself among the prisoners, his own officers and soldiers saw him every day without the least suspicion. The person to whom the author of this sketch is indebted for these particulars was the attendant of the prisoners and familiar with Lee, but though compelled to see him often in the discharge of his duty, he never penetrated the disguise. Well it was for Lee that his disguise was so complete. Had his associates suspected his purpose to betray them, his history would have been embraced in the proverb, "dead men tell no tales."

For many days he remained in this situation, making no discoveries whatsoever. He thought he perceived, at times, signs of intelligence between the prisoners and an old woman who was allowed to bring fruit for sale within the enclosure. She was known to be deaf and half-witted and was therefore no object of suspicion. It was known that her son had been disgraced and punished in the American army, but she had never betrayed any malice on that account and no one dreamed that she could have had the power to do injury if she possessed the will. Lee watched her closely, but saw nothing to confirm his suspicions. Her dwelling was about a mile distant, a wild retreat where she shared her miserable quarters with a dog and cat, the former of which mounted guard over her mansion while the latter encouraged superstitious fears that were equally effectual in keeping visitors away.

One dark, stormy night in autumn, he was lying awake at midnight, meditating on the enterprise he had undertaken, which, though in the beginning it had recommended itself to his romantic disposition, had now lost all its charms. It was one of those tempests which in our climate so often hang upon the path of the departing year. His companion slept soundly, but the wind, which shook the building to its foundation and threw heavy splashes of rain against the window, conspired with the state of his mind to keep him wakeful. All at once, the door was gently opened and a figure moved silently into the room. It was too dark to observe its motions narrowly, but he could see that it stooped towards one of the sleepers who immediately arose. Next, it approached and touched him on the shoulder. Lee immediately started up; the figure then allowed a slight gleam from a dark lantern to pass over his face and, as it did so, whispered impatiently, "Not the man, but come!" It then occurred to Lee that this was the opportunity so much desired. The unknown then whispered to him to keep his place till another man was called, but just at that moment some noise disturbed him and, making a sign to Lee to follow, he moved silently out of the room.

They found the door of the house unbarred and a small part of the fence removed, where they passed out without molestation; the sentry had retired to a shelter where he thought he could guard his post without suffering from the rain, but Lee saw that his conductors put themselves in preparation to silence him if he should happen to address them. Just outside the fence appeared a stooping figure, wrapped in a red cloak and supporting itself with a large stick which Lee at once perceived could be no other than the old fruit woman. But the most profound silence was observed; a man came out of a thicket at a little distance and joined them, and the whole party moved onward under the guidance of the old woman. At first, they frequently stopped to listen, but having heard the sentinels cry, "All's well," they seemed reassured and moved with more confidence than before.

They soon came near to her cottage under an overhanging bank where a bright light was shining out from a little window upon the wet and drooping boughs that hung near it. The dog received them graciously, and they entered. A table was spread with some coarse provisions upon it and a large jug, which one of the soldiers was about to seize when the man who conducted them withheld him.

"No," said he, "we must first proceed to business." He then went to a small closet from which he returned with what seemed to have been originally a Bible, though now it was worn to a mahogany color and a spherical form. While they were doing this, Lee had time to examine his companions, one of whom was a large, quite good-looking soldier, the other a short, stout man with much the aspect of a villain. They examined him in turn, and as Lee had formerly been obliged to punish the shorter soldier severely, he felt some misgivings when the fellow's eye rested upon him. Their conductor was a middle-aged, harsh-looking man whom Lee had never seen before.

As no time was to be lost, their guide explained to them in a few words that, before he should undertake his dangerous enterprise, he should require of them to swear upon the scriptures not to make the least attempt to escape and never to reveal the circumstances or agents in the proceeding, whatever might befall them. The soldiers, however, insisted on deferring this measure till they had formed some slight acquaintance with the contents of the jug and expressed their sentiments on the subject rather by actions than words. In this they were joined by Lee, who, by this time, had begun to contemplate the danger of the enterprise in a new and unpleasant point of view. If he were to be compelled to accompany his party to New York, his disguise would at once be detected and it was certain that he would be hanged as a spy. He had supposed, beforehand, that he should find no difficulty in escaping at any moment, but he saw that their conductor had arms for them which they were to use in taking the life of any one who should attempt to leave them—and then the oath. He might possibly have released himself from its obligations when it became necessary for the interests of his country, but no honorable man can well bear to be driven to an emergency in which he must violate an oath, however reluctantly taken. He felt that there was no retreating when there came a heavy shock, as of something falling against the sides of the house; their practiced ears at once detected the alarm gun and their conductor, throwing down the old Bible which he had held all the while impatiently in his hand, directed the party to follow him in close order and immediately quitted the house, taking with him his dark lantern.

They went on with great dispatch but not without difficulty. Sometimes their footing would give way on some sandy bank or slippery field, and when their path led through the woods, the wet boughs dashed heavily in their faces. Lee felt that he might have deserted his precious companions while they were in this hurry and alarm, but he felt that, as yet, he had made no discoveries and however dangerous his situation was, he could not bear to confess that he had not nerve to carry it through. On he went, therefore, for two or three hours and was beginning to sink with fatigue, when the barking of a dog brought the party to a stand. Their conductor gave a low whistle, which was answered at no great distance, and a figure came forward in the darkness who whispered to their guide and then led the way up to a building which seemed, by the shadowy outline, to be a large stone barn. They entered it and were severally placed in small nooks where they could feel that the hay was all around them except on the side of the wall. Shortly after, some provisions were brought to them with the same silence, and it was signified to them that they were to remain concealed through the whole of the coming day.

Through a crevice in the wall, Lee could discover, as the day came on, that the barn was attached to a small house. He was so near the house that he could overhear the conversation which was carried on about the door. The morning rose clear, and it was evident from the inquiries of horsemen, who occasionally galloped up to the door, that the country was alarmed. The farmer gave short and surly replies, as if unwilling to be taken off from his labor, but the other inmates were eager in their questions, and, from the answers, Lee gathered that the means by which he and his companions had escaped were as mysterious as ever.

The next night, when all was quiet, they resumed their march and explained to Lee that, as he was not with them in their conspiracy and was accidentally associated with them in their escape, they should take the precaution to keep him before them, just behind the guide. He submitted without opposition, though the arrangement considerably lessened the chances in favor of his escape. He observed, from the direction of the stars, that they did not move in a direct line toward the Delaware, but they changed their course so often that he could not conjecture at what point they intended to strike the river. He endeavored, whenever any peculiar object appeared, to fix it in his memory as well as the darkness would permit and succeeded better than could have been expected, considering the agitated state in which he traveled.

For several nights they went on in this manner, being delivered over to different persons from time to time, and as Lee could gather from their whispering conversation, they were regularly employed on occasions like the present and well rewarded by the British for their services. Their employment was full of danger, and though they seemed like desperate men, he could observe that they never remitted their precautions. They were concealed by day in barns, cellars, and caves made for the purpose and similar retreats, and one day was passed in a tomb, the dimensions of which had been enlarged and the inmates, if there had been any, banished to make room for the living. The burying grounds were a favorite retreat, and on more occasions than one they were obliged to resort to superstitious alarms to remove intruders upon their path; their success fully justified the experiment, and unpleasantly situated as he was, in the prospect of soon being a ghost himself, he could not avoid laughing at the expedition with which old and young fled from the fancied apparitions under clouds of night, wishing to meet such enemies, like Ajax, in the face of day.

Though the distance to the Delaware was not great, they had now been twelve days on the road, and such was the vigilance and suspicion prevailing throughout the country that they almost despaired of effecting their object. The conductor grew impatient, and Lee's companions, at least one of them, became ferocious. There was, as we have said, something unpleasant to him in the glance of this fellow toward him, which became more and more fierce as they went on, but it did not appear whether it was owing to circumstances or actual suspicion. It so happened that, on the twelfth night, Lee was placed in a barn while the rest of the party sheltered themselves in the cellar of a little stone church, where they could talk and act with more freedom, both because the solitude of the place was not often disturbed, even on the Sabbath, and because even the proprietors did not know that illegal hands had added a cellar to the conveniences of the building.

The party were seated here as the day broke, and the light which struggled in through crevices opened for the purpose showed a low room about twelve feet square with a damp floor and large patches of white mold upon the walls. Finding, probably, that the pavement afforded no accommodation for sleeping, the worthies were seated each upon a little cask which seemed like those used for gunpowder. Here they were smoking pipes with great diligence and, at intervals not distant, applying a huge canteen to their mouths from which they drank with upturned faces, expressive of solemn satisfaction. While they were thus engaged, the short soldier asked them in a careless way if they knew whom they had in the party. The others started and took their pipes from their mouths to ask him what he meant.

"I mean," said he, "that we are honored with the company of Captain Lee, of the rebel army. The rascal once punished me, and I never mistook my man when I had a debt of that kind to pay. Now I shall have my revenge."

The others hastened to express their disgust at his ferocity, saying that if, as he said, their companion was an American officer, all they had to do was to watch him closely. They said that, as he had come among them uninvited, he must go with them to New York and take the consequences; but, meantime, it was their interest not to seem to suspect him, otherwise he might give an alarm, whereas it was evidently his intention to go with them till they were ready to embark for New York. The other persisted in saying that he would have his revenge with his own hand, upon which the conductor, drawing a pistol, declared to him that if he saw the least attempt to injure Captain Lee, or any conduct which would lead him to suspect that his disguise was discovered, he would that moment shoot him through the head. The soldier put his hand upon his knife with an ominous scowl upon the conductor, but seeing that he had to do with one who was likely to be as good as his word, he restrained himself and began to arrange some rubbish to serve him for a bed. The other soldiers followed his example, and their guide withdrew, locking the door after him.

The next night they went on as usual, but the manner of their conductor showed there was more danger than before; in fact, he explained to the party that they were now not far from the Delaware and hoped to reach it before midnight. They occasionally heard the report of a musket, which seemed to indicate that some movement was going on in the country. Thus warned, they quickened their steps, and it was not long before they saw a gleam of broad, clear light before them, such as is reflected from calm waters even in the darkest nights. They moved up to it with deep silence, and there were various emotions in their breasts; Lee was hoping for an opportunity to escape from an enterprise which was growing too serious, and the principal objects of which were already answered; the others were anxious lest some accident might have happened to the boat on which they depended for crossing the stream.

When they came to the bank, there were no traces of a boat on the waters. Their conductor stood still for a moment in dismay, but recollecting himself, he said it was possible it might have been secured lower down the stream, and forgetting everything else, he directed the larger soldier to accompany him, and giving a pistol to the other, he whispered, "If the rebel officer attempts to betray us, shoot him; if not, you will not, for your own sake, make any noise to show where we are." In the same instant they departed, and Lee was left alone with the ruffian.

He had before suspected the fellow knew him, and now doubts were changed to certainty at once. Dark as it was, it seemed as if fire flashed from his eye now that he felt revenge was in his power. Lee was as brave as any officer in the army, but he was unarmed, and though he was strong, his adversary was still more powerful. While he stood uncertain what to do, the fellow seemed to be enjoying the prospect of revenge as he looked upon him with a steady eye. Though the officer stood in appearance unmoved, the sweat rolled in heavy drops from his brow. He soon took his resolution and sprang upon his adversary with the intention of wresting the pistol from his hand, but the other was upon his guard and aimed with such precision that, had the pistol been charged with a bullet, that moment would have been his last. But it seemed that the conductor had trusted to the sight of his weapons to render the use of them unnecessary and had therefore loaded them only with powder; as it was, the shock threw Lee to the ground, but fortunately as the fellow dropped the pistol, it fell where Lee could reach it, and as his adversary stooped and was drawing his knife from his bosom, Lee was able to give him a stunning blow. He immediately threw himself upon the assassin, and a long and bloody struggle began; they were so nearly matched in strength and advantage that neither dared unclench his hold for the sake of grasping the knife; the blood gushed from their mouths, and the combat would have probably ended in favor of the assassin, when steps and voices were heard advancing and they found themselves in the hands of a party of countrymen who were armed for the occasion and were scouring the banks of the river. They were forcibly torn apart, but so exhausted and breathless that neither could make any explanation, and they submitted quietly to the disposal of their captors.

The party of armed countrymen, though they had succeeded in their attempt and were sufficiently triumphant on the occasion, were sorely perplexed to determine how to dispose of their prisoners. After much discussion, one of them proposed to obtain the decision of the wisdom of the nearest magistrate. They accordingly proceeded with their prisoners to his mansion, about two miles distant, and called on him to rise and attend to business. A window was hastily thrown up, and the justice put forth his nightcapped head and, with more wrath than became his dignity, ordered them off and, in requital for their calling him out of bed in the cold, generously wished them to the warmest place which then occurred to his imagination. However, resistance was vain, he was compelled to rise, and, as soon as the prisoners were brought before him, he ordered them to be taken in irons to the city of Philadelphia. Lee improved the opportunity to take the old gentleman aside and told him who he was, and why he was thus disguised; the justice only interrupted him with the occasional inquiry: "Most done?" When he had finished, the magistrate told him that his story was very well made and told in a manner very creditable to his address and that he should give it all the weight it seemed to require. All Lee's remonstrances were unavailing.

As soon as they were fairly lodged in prison, Lee prevailed on the jailor to carry a note to Gen. Lincoln, informing him of his condition. The general received it as he was dressing in the morning and immediately sent one of his aids to the jail. That officer could not believe his eyes when he saw Captain Lee. His uniform, worn out when he assumed it, was now hanging in rags about him, and he had not been shaved for a fortnight, and he wished, very naturally, to improve his appearance before presenting himself before the Secretary of War, but the orders were peremptory to bring him as he was. The general loved a joke full well; his laughter was hardly exceeded by the report of his own cannon, and long and loud did he laugh that day.

When Captain Lee returned to Lancaster, he immediately attempted to retrace the ground, and so accurate, under all the unfavorable circumstances, had been his investigation, that he brought to justice fifteen persons who had aided the escape of British prisoners. It is scarcely necessary to say to those who know the fate of revolutionary officers that he received, for this hazardous and effectual service, no reward whatsoever.

DAVID CROCKETT'S FIGHT WITH A BEAR:
AS RELATED BY HIMSELF

I was compelled to move on slowly and was frequently falling over logs and into the cracks made by the earthquakes so that I was very much afraid I would break my gun. However, I went on about three miles when I came to a good, big creek, which I waded. It was very cold, and the creek was about knee-deep, but I felt no great inconvenience from it just then, as I was all over wet with sweat from running and I felt hot enough. After I got over this creek and out of the cane, which was very thick on all our creeks, I listened for my dogs. I found they had either treed or brought the bear to a stop, as they continued barking in the same place. I pushed on as near in the direction of the noise as I could, till I found the hill was too steep for me to climb, and so I backed and went down the creek some distance till I came to a hollow and then took up that, till I came to a place where I could climb up the hill. It was mighty dark, and it was difficult to see my way or anything else. When I got up the hill, I found I had passed the dogs and so I turned and went to them. I found, when I got there, they had treed the bear in a large, forked poplar and it was setting in the fork.

I could see the lump, but not plain enough to shoot with any certainty as there was no moonlight, and so I set in to hunting for some dry brush to make me a light, but I could find none, though I could find that the ground was torn mightily to pieces by the cracks.

At last I thought I could shoot by guess and kill him, so I pointed as near the lump as I could and fired away. But the bear didn't come; he only clumb up higher and got out on a limb which helped me to see him better. I now loaded up again and fired, but this time he didn't move at all. I commenced loading for a third fire, but the first thing I knowed, the bear was down among my dogs, and they were fighting all around me. I had my big butcher in my belt, and I had a pair of dressed buckskin breeches on. So, I took out my knife and stood determined, if he should get hold of me, to defend myself in the best way I could. I stood there for some time and could now and then see a white dog I had, but the rest of them and the bear, which were dark colored, I couldn't see at all; it was so miserable dark. They still fought around me and sometimes within three feet of me, but at last the bear got down into one of the cracks that the earthquakes had made in the ground, about four feet deep, and I could tell the biting end of him by the hollering of my dogs. So, I took my gun and pushed the muzzle of it about till I thought I had it against the main part of his body and fired, but it happened to be only the fleshy part of his foreleg. With this he jumped out of the crack, and he and the dogs had another hard fight around me as before. At last, however, they forced him back into the crack again as he was when I had shot.

I had laid down my gun in the dark, and I now began to hunt for it, and while hunting, I got hold of a pole and I concluded I would punch him awhile with that. I did so, and when I would punch him, the dogs would jump in on him and he would bite them badly and they would jump out again. I concluded, as he would take punching so patiently, it might be that he would lie still enough for me to get down in the crack and feel slowly along till I could find the right place to give him a dig with my butcher. So, I got down, and my dogs got in before him and kept his head towards them, till I got along easily up to him and, placing my hand on his rump, felt for his shoulder just behind which I intended to strike him. I made a lunge with my long knife and fortunately stuck him right through the heart, at which he just sank down, and I crawled out in a hurry. In a little time, my dogs all came out too and seemed satisfied, which was the way they always had of telling me that they had finished him.

I suffered very much that night with cold, as my leather breeches and everything else I had on was wet and frozen. But I managed to get my bear out of this crack after several hard trials, and so I butchered him and laid down to try to sleep. But my fire was very bad, and I couldn't find anything that would burn well to make it any better, and so I concluded I should freeze if I didn't warm myself in some way by exercise. So, I got up and hollered awhile, and then I would just jump up and down with all my might and throw myself into all sorts of motions. But all this wouldn't do, for my blood was now getting cold and the chills coming all over me. I was so tired, too, that I could hardly walk, but I thought I would do the best I could to save my life and then, if I died, nobody would be to blame. So, I went to a tree about two feet through, and not a limb on it for thirty feet, and I would climb up to the limbs and then lock my arms together around it and slide down to the bottom again. This would make the insides of my legs and arms feel mighty warm and good. I continued this till daylight in the morning, and how often I clumb up my tree and slid down I don't know, but I reckon at least a hundred times.

THE ROMANCE OF WAR:
SERGEANT JASPER AND SALLY ST. CLAIR

Sometime just before or about the beginning of the war, Sergeant Jasper, of Marion's Brigade, had the good fortune to save the life of a young, beautiful, and dark-eyed creole girl called Sally St. Clair. Her susceptible nature was overcome with gratitude to her preserver, and this soon ripened into a passion of love of the most deep and fervent kind. She lavished upon him the whole wealth of her affections and the whole depths of a passion nurtured by a Southern sun. When he was called upon to join the ranks of his country's defenders, the prospect of their separation almost maddened her. Their parting came, but scarcely was she left alone than her romantic nature prompted the means of a reunion. Once resolved, no consideration of danger could dampen her spirit, and no thought of consequences could move her purpose. She severed her long and jetty ringlets and provided herself with male attire. In these she robed herself and set forth to follow the fortunes of her lover.

A smooth-faced, beautiful, and delicate stripling appeared among the hardy, rough, and giant frames who composed the corps to which Jasper belonged. The contrast between the stripling and these men, in their uncouth garbs, their massive faces embrowned and discolored by sun and rain, was indeed striking. But none were more eager for the battle or so indifferent to fatigue as the fair-faced boy. It was found that his energy of character and resolution and courage amply supplied his lack of physique. None ever suspected him to be a woman. Not even Jasper himself, although she was often by his side, penetrated her disguise.

The romance of her situation increased the fervor of her

passion. It was her delight to reflect that, unknown to him, she was by his side, watching over him in the hour of danger. She fed her passion by gazing upon him in the hour of slumber, hovering near him when stealing through the swamp and thicket and being always ready to avert danger from his head.

But gradually there stole a melancholy presentiment over the poor girl's mind. She had been tortured with hopes deferred, the war was prolonged, and the prospect of being restored to him grew more and more uncertain. But now she felt that her dream of happiness could never be realized. She became convinced that death was about to snatch her away from his side, but she prayed that she might die and he never know to what length the violence of her passion had led her.

It was an eve before a battle. The camp had sunk into repose. The watchfires were burning low, and only the slow tread of sentinels fell upon the profound silence of the night air as they moved through the dark shadows of the forest. Stretched upon the ground, with no other couch than a blanket, reposed the warlike form of Jasper. Climbing vines trailed themselves into a canopy above his head, through which the stars shone down softly. The faint flicker from the expiring embers of a fire fell across his countenance and tinged the cheek of one who bent above his couch. It was the smooth-faced stripling. She bent low down as if to listen to his dreams or to breathe into his soul pleasant visions of love and happiness. But tears trace themselves down the fair one's cheek and fall silently but rapidly upon the brow of her lover. A mysterious voice has told her that the hour of parting has come, that tomorrow her destiny is consummated. There is one last, long, lingering look, and then the unhappy maid is seen to tear herself away from the spot to weep out her sorrows in privacy.

Fierce and terrible is the conflict that on the morrow rages on that spot. Foremost in the battle is the intrepid Jasper, and ever by his side fights the stripling warrior. Often during the heat and the smoke, gleams suddenly upon the eyes of Jasper the melancholy face of the maiden. In the thickest of the fight, surrounded by enemies, the lovers fight side by side. Suddenly, a lance is leveled at the breast of Jasper, but swifter than the lance is Sally St. Clair. There is a wild cry, and at the feet of Jasper sinks the maiden with the life blood gushing from the white bosom, which had been thrown as a shield before his breast. He hears not the din nor the danger of the conflict, but down by the side of the dying boy he kneels. Then for the first time does he learn that the stripling is his love, that often by the camp fire and in the swamp she had been by his side, that the dim visions in his slumber of an angel face hovering above him had indeed been true. In the midst of the battle, with her lover by her side and the barb still in her bosom, the heroic maiden dies!

Her name, her sex, and her noble devotion soon became known through the corps. There was a tearful group gathered around her grave: there was not one of those hardy warriors who did not bedew her grave with tears. They buried her near the river Santee "in a green shady nook that looked as if it had been stolen out of Paradise."

THE DESPERADOES' MISTAKE

During, the winter of 1836–7, I made a business tour of the Southern States. A great portion of the time was spent in the State of Mississippi. It was about this time that the astounding developments of Virgil A. Stewart had thrown all the country into an ebullition of excitement. An extensive organization of horse thieves, Negro thieves, and highwaymen under the name of the "Murrel Gang" had been formed and had cooperators and a rendezvous in every county and town of the Southwest. Its ramifications extended even to the new states and territories bordering on the shores of the western lakes. It was one of the most stupendous and cunningly contrived schemes of villainy ever concocted, and the originator and master spirit of this devilish organization evinced a tact and talent, which, if directed in an honorable channel, might have elevated him to an enviable distinction. The deep secrecy of his measures and his characteristic shrewdness, together with the extraordinary control he exercised over his followers who were found in all ranks of society—wealthy planters and professional men of apparent respectability, Mississippi boatmen and settlers of the backwoods, as well as the gamblers and loafers of the southern towns—would have done honor to a general of the order of Loyola.

Stewart's revelations of the plans and intentions of the gang implicated individuals whose characters and standing had before placed them above suspicion. The names of many occupying prominent political and professional positions in their respective communities were found recorded in the list of members of this infernal brotherhood, and so strong were the proofs of their complicity that their neighbors were forced to admit them. The consequence was that people became suspicious of each other, neighbor was distrustful of neighbor, and mutual confidence was entirely destroyed.

Such was the spirit of vengeance that Stewart had aroused against himself that the Governor of Mississippi found it necessary to furnish him with a strong and trusty body guard to protect him from assassination. Members of the gang, who had sworn to accomplish his death, were continually on the watch to waylay him, and whether on a journey or at home in the capital of the state, suspicious strangers were dogging his steps day and night. But with his watchful attendants ever about him, the fearless informer eluded certain death intended for him. But at length he began to wear of this continued vigilance, and by degrees, diminished the number of his guards till after a few months he even ventured almost alone on journeys through the state on his legitimate business. He, however, always took the precaution to go heavily armed and prepared for attack.

My business made it necessary to travel from Vicksburg to Columbus, in the northern part of the state, and my route lay along the "old Robinson Road" through the counties of Hinds, Madison, Leake, Winston, and Lowndes. I had started out on horseback and alone. But at a stopping place in Madison County, I chanced to make the acquaintance of a couple of traders returning to East Tennessee after a successful trip among the cotton planters of the Red River country. These men, who were acquainted with the country through which I was about to journey and who, in addition, were companionable sort of fellows, on hearing of my northern destination proposed that we should travel together. As a portion of the road led through the Choctaw and Chickasaw nations, and was but sparsely settled, I gladly availed myself of their friendly proposal, and after an early breakfast, we were on the road together.

My companions, as well as myself, were well armed, as was the custom of southern travelers in those days. At each stopping place or ferry, we were particular to examine our weapons to see that they were always in readiness for use. Robberies had been of frequent occurrence in the swamps through which we had to pass. After crossing the ferry of the Yukanukany, we stopped at the house of an old half-breed Choctaw named La Flore but more familiarly known among travelers as "Uncle Ben." Here our horses were fed and we ordered dinner.

After dinner, the old man informed us that Virgil A. Stewart, with two companions, had spent the previous night with him. They were also traveling up the Robinson Road bound to Huntsville, Alabama, "And," added Uncle Ben, speaking a language half-English, half-Choctaw, addressing himself to me, "I reckon, maybe so, you are Stewart's brudder?"

"No," I replied, "I have never seen the man."

"Well, den, stranger, you look same as Stewart. I reckon you better keep yer eye skinned."

"Why so, Uncle Ben?" I asked.

"Cause Murrel men pass by here dis morning on a hunt for Stewart, I reckon. I tell um he gone on—dey go on, too—no stop for dinner, nor nothin'—cheat me out of one dollar *mahoba*. Your blue coat and brass buttons same as him. He leetle man, same like you, and he ride nice black mare, same like you do. I tell you, stranger, keep your eye skinned and let them Murrel men keep a long trail 'tween you and dem. Dey'll shoot you same as Stewart, if dey see you 'fore dey do him."

Laughing heartily at the half-breed's earnest manner but thanking him for his friendly precautions, we settled our bills and, remounting our horses, were once more riding leisurely through the over-arching forest and occasionally discharging our pistols at the herds of deer which frequently crossed our path.

On reaching the ferry of the Little Black in Leake County, we again heard of Stewart and his friends who were some hours in advance of us, still followed by the two men our half-breed landlord had described to us. They were hard looking customers, the old ferryman said, and inquired particularly about the travelers preceding them, how many they were and how long before they had passed the river. The fellow, a very intelligent Negro, was satisfied, he said, that they were Murrel men in pursuit of the informer, for, when he had answered their hurried and eager questions, they leaped their horses from his flat and spurred off without paying their ferriage fees.

"Dey's bad, Murrel men, you may depend on it, marsters,"

exclaimed Cuffee as I handed him the money for our passage. "T'ank you, sir." And as he put the coin into his pocket, he looked up to repeat his thanks. But, the moment he caught my eye bent upon him, the old Negro went off into a spasmodic fit of genuine African guffaw: "*Yar he haw! Yar he haw*! Why, marster, you's cute, you is; *yar he haw*! Dat's neat done, but how in de world did you git 'cross de riber again, and I here all de time, and not know it?"

The Negro's manners and words were an enigma to me, and I good-naturedly demanded an explanation.

"Well, den, you's marster Stewart, what I ferried 'cross de stream here dis morning? Yes, I knows yer is."

"You never was more mistaken in your life, Sambo," I replied.

"No! Well, den, de Lord forgive me, marster, but I was just now ready to swar you was de same gen'l'man. I reckon your near kin to him, den, for you and him are as much alike as two persimmons."

I not only denied any relationship to Mr. Stewart but reiterated what I had asserted to Uncle Ben, that I had never even seen the man.

"Well, den, marster, take my advice, please." And the old ferryman placed his hand respectfully on my knee and looked earnestly in my eyes. "Don't let them bad-looking fellows, following the genewine Stewart, set their ugly eyes on you 'fore dey gits sight of him, for dey mean him harm and might shoot you for him by mistake. You look just like him and so does your nag." And, pointing up the bank of the river, the old Negro begged me to take the trail running northward through the swamp, which he informed us would lead to another well-traveled road, that by a much shorter route would again strike the Robinson Road in Winston County. This, he assured us, would, with ordinary travel, bring us to the crossing of the Noxubee several hours ahead of Stewart and his pursuers and thus avoid any possibility of a meeting with them or being seen by the suspicious-looking travelers.

Upon consultation we concluded that the ferryman was right and the best way to avoid all trouble and danger would be to follow his advice and strike off by way of the road he had pointed out. So, getting a more particular description of our new route and handing the man a new bright dollar for his interest in our safety, we took the path indicated.

After clearing the swamp, we found our trail leading through oak openings and over a gently undulating country covered with a tall crop of grass, the growth of the previous season. These pastures were the resort of thousands of deer, who leaped away from before our horses at every glade and hillside we approached. We were frequently tempted to try our pistols on them, but being desirous of gaining the advance, we hastened on. Toward nightfall we reached the traveled wagon-track the ferryman had directed us to and soon after, falling in with a settler's cabin, were permitted to spend the night there. Before daylight on the following morning, we were again on the road and by noon were scrambling through the swampy bottom of the Noxubee.

At the toll-gate beyond the swamp, we learned that Stewart, who was well known on all the traveled routes throughout the state, had but two hours proceeded us. His party was the last that passed the gate going north. The Murrel men were therefore yet in the rear, and we were now consequently between the two parties of horsemen. Spurring our horses, therefore, we pushed on, being determined if possible to overtake those ahead who were evidently traveling rapidly and either join them or leave them in our rear between us and the pursuing ruffians.

Stewart's party, doubtless aware that their enemies might be on their trail, had ridden late and early and for two days had thus eluded them. Their horses were comparatively fresh, while those of their pursuers were travel-worn. At the rate we now traveled we would, without doubt, have overtaken Stewart's party by the time they would have stopped for their mid-day feed. But unfortunately, the horse of one of my companions, falling through a rotten logway, so seriously injured himself that we were obliged to halt for some time, and when we again set forward were unable to travel faster than a walk on his account.

We had cleared the Noxubee swamp and had entered a densely wooded forest. On one side of our road a range of broken hills ran parallel to the path, and on the other a growth of thickets and canebrakes, upon the edge of a deep valley, broke off the prospect laterally. But along our path opened occasionally vistas, for many rods, where we could reconnoiter the road ahead and in our rear. We were riding along engaged in conversation, and regardless of the vicinity of strangers, when suddenly our attention was called to the sound of rapidly approaching horsemen. On checking our animals and looking behind us, we perceived a party of four men; they were well mounted and heavily armed. Each man had slung to the pommel of his saddle a short rifle, while pistols and bowie-knives stuck out all over their persons. If these were the men in pursuit of Stewart and his comrades, they had gained an important addition to their party on the road since passing the ferry of the Little Black.

We intended to let these suspicious-looking strangers pass us peacefully if they would, for to attempt to keep ahead of them, with our crippled horses, was altogether out of the question. They appeared to have discovered us at the same moment that we did them, and drawing rein while we still kept on, as if not aware of their approach, they fell back out of sight. If they really were Murrel men, their only object now, without doubt, was the assassination of the bold informer and not the molestation of peaceful travelers. The gang had ceased their operations as highwaymen since Stewart had turned state's evidence and were now endeavoring to disarm the suspicions of the public by suspending their acts of robbery. The death of their treacherous associate was what they were now most anxious to accomplish.

Scarcely had we ridden a mile after losing sight of the strangers when we were startled by the sharp report of a rifle from the ridge on our right. Simultaneous with the report, a bullet whistled in alarming proximity to my face. We had hardly time to turn in our saddles to the direction from whence came the leaden missile, when another shot was fired from the cover of the canebrake on our left. This also was evidently aimed at me but, missing its mark, took effect in the root of my mare's mane. Smarting with the wound and frightened by firing, she attempted to dash away with me down the road, but at that instant another shot, not ten yards from my left in the canebrake, struck my poor animal just above the eye. With a wild leap she threw herself forward and, rearing upon her hind feet, fell over backwards upon me. I found myself crushed to the ground beneath her weight and so entangled with the stirrup that I was unable to extricate myself from the dangerous position.

In the meantime, my two traveling companions had leaped from their saddles and, hastily leading their horses from the road, had thrown themselves behind the shelter of a huge cypress where they were watching the progress of the affair.

The ruffians, it appears, after discovering us ahead of them, had left the path and, dashing through the woods, had gained the advance where, on both sides of the road and screened by the thickets, they had awaited our approach.

I had no sooner fallen beneath my horse than I heard an exultant yell on the right of the road, and two men ran towards me with uplifted knives and pistols to make a finish of me. But disabled as I was, I could use one of my pistols; the other had fallen beyond my reach when I was thrown to the ground. Throwing myself upon my back as they approached, I leveled my pistol—a single-barreled, old-fashioned affair, for it was before the days of revolvers. Being ordinarily a good shot, I even under the present circumstances had confidence in my aim, and when the villains had come within three paces, I fired upon the foremost. The bullet tore an ugly gash through the ruffian's cheek, and furious with the wound, he leaped upon me.

At the same moment, the other two ruffians had jumped into the road and opened fire upon the traders, who, partially protected by the cypress, warmly returned shot for shot. I, however, had no time to observe what was going on beyond my own immediate vicinity. I was completely at the mercy of my assailants, and the wounded fellow had leveled an ugly-looking pistol at my head; I felt the cold iron pressed against my ear, and a chill of horror thrilled through my frame. With an unexpressed prayer to Heaven and a rapid farewell thought of home and home friends, I closed my eyes and braced my muscles for the murderous shot. I felt the cold metal pressed closer and closer to my head and was conscious of the pressure of the ruffian's finger upon the trigger; the next instant a stunning report, as of the bursting of a thunderbolt upon my head, rang in my ears. My face and hair seemed on fire, and I felt the crushing weight of some heavy body thrown upon my breast. Yet, strangely enough, with all this I felt a consciousness that yet I remained uninjured. As the weight was thrown upon my breast, I heard a fierce oath, accompanied with an exclamation of surprise and the words:

"Hold! Hold! Bill Parker, we're mistaken in our man! I tell you 'taint the chap we're after." And drawing the man from my breast, a tall, dark-complexioned, fierce-looking fellow returned his weapons to his belt, stood over me, and gazed inquiringly into my face. "I tell you, Bill," he continued, "we're on the wrong scent again; this is not the man we're after. Set him up, will you." And heaving at the body of my poor mare, the fellow released me from my confinement with no other injury than a slight bruise of my leg.

With a sullen look and a growl of disappointment, the wounded ruffian stood aside and, tearing his cravat from his neck, proceeded to bandage his bloody face, while his tall companion assisted me to my feet and calling to the other two men, still exchanging shots with the traders, ordered them to desist. Then turning to me:

"You've had a narrow escape, stranger," said he, with an oath. "We have followed you over a hundred miles, deceived by your resemblance to that arrant traitor, Virgil A. Stewart. Now, sir, that you have fortunately lost that fine black animal of yours, take my advice and at the next stopping place, exchange that blue cloth coat for a different garment, and while you are about it, it might be all the better, perhaps, to shave off those full whiskers of yours. I've known Stewart for years, but until I was close upon you, I would have sworn that you were the man, and while you resemble him, your life is not worth that dead nag, at least in the southern country. Good morning, sir." And, remounting their horses within the thickets, the four fellows soon disappeared on the back track towards the Noxubee.

Shortly after this singular adventure, I heard of the arrest of the leader of the Murrel Gang, and being in Nashville, Tennessee in the following spring, I was led by curiosity to visit the state prison there. Almost the first individual I encountered in the prison smithy was the tall, dark-eyed ruffian whose interference had saved my life near the Noxubee swamp. The man also recognized me with a stealthy nod of his head.

"Who is that prisoner?" I asked of the courteous and obliging turnkey that accompanied me.

"Him, sir, wielding the sledge hammer?"

"The same," I replied.

"That is the notorious John A. Murrel, till recently the terror of the south-western country."

AN OLD TRAPPER IN A TIGHT PLACE

"Well, youngsters," said Uncle Job, a veteran trapper, to a party of young fellows bound on an amateur trapping excursion to the Rocky Mountains, "when you have toted traps and peltries and fit Injuns as long as I have, you'll certainly have considerable more experience than you now have. Ha! Ha! Yer think, maybe, it's a mighty nice time ye'll have on't out on the trapping grounds, and I ain't going to say as how yer won't, but take my word for it, ye'll wish yourselves back in the settlements many a time afore ye'll get there, for what with fighting and hiding from Injuns and them pesky grizzlies and living like them spindle-shanked Diggers on the other side of the mountains, sometimes for weeks together, and nothing but pine cones and such trash as luck happens to throw in yer way to keep soul and body together, yer time 'll be anything but specially agreeable, till yer gets used to it, and then ye'll find it barely endurable. It's a mighty hard life, anyhow, boys!"

"Why, then, Uncle Job, do you go back again to the plains?" they asked.

"Well there, boys, yer have me, anyhow," answered the old man, "and to be right down honest with yer—*I likes it*! It's a fact, as sure as dry prairie grass 'll burn. I would not live a whole month in Saint Lewy for all the money there if I could not be allowed to spend the balance of the time out in the mountain country. I'm used to it, youngsters, and city air is rank pison to me; besides, I'd spoil for the want of a fight with some of the Red varmints of Blackfeet, Pawnees, and Poncas, for that's the best part of life on the plain, boys. And now," continued the old trapper as he lit his stone pipe, "as I'm in the humor on't, I'll tell yer about a fight—

and a long battle it was, too—I had with a party of them cowardly Blackfeet over on the Sweet-Water. It was something over twelve years ago and one fall, when I was trapping on the head waters of the Columbia.

"We had at the post about a dozen greenhorns, just like yourselves, only a few months from the settlements who hadn't yet got toughened to the kind of life we had to lead, and some of 'em was about dying with the ager and not a dose of medicine, or even a blessed drop of whiskey, to save them with. So, as I knew every part of the country from the Pacific to Saint Lewy, I was ordered, by the head trader of the post, to go to Fort Laramie and bring back a supply of calomel, Queen Anne, and suchlike, for our sick men.

"The distance was about six hundred miles over the mountains. We had come the spring before to the western side of the range by way of the Sweet-Water valley pass, and I concluded to take that route again toward Laramie.

"Well, after I had got over the main ridge, I kept along the south side of the Wind River mountains and stopped one day on the Green River to make me a new pair of moccasins, for the rough traveling of the hills had left me barefooted. While I was stitching away at my moccasins, I remembered a *cache* (that is, a lot of furs or provisions hidden or stowed away until it should be convenient to remove them) a party of us had made the spring before, about a day's travel out of my regular route. It was on the south branch of the Sweet-Water. We had started from the head of the Platte, on our way to the Columbia, with a small drove of pack mules loaded with provisions for the new post, and when on the South Branch one of the creturs give out, we had to cache his cargo. It was a package of jerked venison and a sack of flour with a small bag of rice for the sick, when we had 'em, and a five-gallon keg of whiskey—genuine Monongahela—none of yer common corn juice. It is a common practice with us trappers to cache our provisions where we know they will be safe for some future journey that way.

"Well, as I worked away at my moccasins, I all at once got to be mighty thirsty, and the thoughts of the whiskey popped right into my head. Says I to myself, says I, 'Job, wouldn't you like to have one good suck at that 'ere little red keg, specially when nobody at the post would be any wiser or poorer for it?' And I reckoned I would. So, I finished the buckskin, and the next morning started bright and early for the cache. Now, as I said, it was one day's journey from my route, and it would take another day to put me on the right course again; that, yer know, would use up two days that I certainly ought to give to my sick comrades at the post. But I argued in this way: 'Now I'm pesky dry for a drink of whiskey. I'm actually feeling bad for the want of it, and if I gratify my natural longing I'll certain better after it, and I can then tread so much faster that I shall more 'n make up for the lost time.' And that's the way I reconciled it to my conscience.

"Well. I reached the South Branch by the middle of the afternoon, and going down the stream a little ways from where I struck it, I found the cave where we had cached our provisions. It was a pretty large one I should reckon, about twice the length of this boat's cabin but 'twan't more'n half as high. I crawled into the narrow mouth of it and drew my rifle in after me, and as soon as my eyes got kinder used to the dim light, right up there in the corner I found everything all right. The jolly little red keg seemed actually to laugh all over at the sight of an old friend. And well it might, for it had been shut up there in the dark for more 'n six months, with nothing but the flour, and rice, and dried meat, to keep it company.

"I pulled out my sharp-pointed bowie and tapped the head of it in no time. But just as I raised the little fellow to get a taste of him, I heard a tramping of horses' feet outside and the howling of fifteen or twenty infernal Blackfeet. I had to drop the keg before a drop of the blessed stuff had wet my thirsty lips, and well it was I did, for at that moment the entrance to the place was darkened by a rascally Injun that had been fool enough to follow me. I raised my rifle and let him have it through his black head. His comrades dragged him out by the feet and gave another savage yell when they found he'd been wiped out. While they were tugging away at his stinking carcass, I busied myself in reloading my rifle to be ready for the next visitor. But though the darned cowards kept up a terrible hillabiloo, they didn't attempt to crawl into the cave anymore.

"Thinks I, *Now's your time, Job*, and raising little red to the top of the cavern, I took a good, long, glorious drink! I tell yer, boys, it's a fact that I have had many a good drink of the strong water in my day, but never in my life did I taste anything that was quite equal to that old Monongahela. It braced me right up, and I'd hardly had it down my throat than I felt that I was a host in myself, and enough, single-handed as I was, for all the Blackfeet west of the Mississippi.

"After a few minutes, three or four rifles were poked cautiously into the hole and fired at random into the cave toward me. But, standing on one side, I let them peg away. They were only using up their ammunition, and the sooner they got rid of that, the better for me.

"Next, they sent a shower of arrows through the opening but with no better effect than with their bullets. In the meantime, I had found a little hole through the rocks just large enough for the barrel of my gun, and watching a good chance, when the varmints were thick about the mouth, I took good aim and popped away at them, sending half an ounce of lead through the bodies of no less than three of them at once. At this the Injuns fell back, yelling vengeance, and I took another refreshing pull at little red. 'For,' says I, 'Job, now it's *your* treat, and here's to good luck for the next shot!' But they didn't try the shooting game anymore, as they found that was a game I could play at as well as themselves and I held all the trump cards. They kept losing, while I continued to hold my own.

"After they had been quiet for a considerable time, I poked my head out of the cave and peeped down the stream where I could see the cowardly wolves gathering armsful of dry sticks and grass, which I at once knew they intended to bring up to the cavern and smoke me out. I hadn't thought of this before, and, thinks I, the black rascals have got me now, sure. I can fight Injuns so long as my ammunition holds out, but when it comes to fire and smoke, I ain't a match nohow for them, shut up in the limestone rocks.

"Presently the savages came back agin to the mouth of the cave in such a direction that I couldn't bring old kill-deer to bear upon them and piling up their combustibles, set fire to it. The wind happened that evening to set directly into the place, and in a few minutes the nasty smudge began to suffocate me. I had to crawl farther and farther into the place as the smoke followed me, and I could hear the Injuns piling on the grass and wood all the time. They found they could get me out by no other means and were now trying to choke me to death with the horrid smoke. But fortunately, as I ran away from it, I saw a little streak of daylight ahead of me; it was a crevice in the rock through which the rays of the setting sun was streaming, as much as to say, 'Be of good heart, Job; they can't smoke you out so long as you choose to breathe through this nice little airhole.'

"I reached the place and laid down, breathing the pure air and laughing at the Red fools who were yelling and dancing for joy at the cute trick they thought they were playing me.

"It so happened that through the same crevice that admitted the light and air, I discovered a nice little pool of fresh water had formed on the floor of the cavern. Now, thought I, if I only had the little red fellow yonder, and the provisions, I could do first rate. So, holding my breath, I crawled back agin into the smoke, and catching the keg in one hand and the package of jerked meat in the other, I went back to my breathing-hole and made a comfortable supper while the black fiends outside were wasting their breath and fuel for nothing.

"After I had satisfied my appetite and taken another pull at the strong water, I laid down for a nap, for I knew the Injuns wouldn't trouble me while they kept up their smoke.

"Well, I had a pretty good night's rest, considering I had to keep one eye open. And in the morning, after the smoke had settled, I sat quietly at the side of the opening, expecting Mr. Injun to creep through after my scalp. They had no doubt I had given up the ghost and thought they were good for my carcass. But they reckoned without the host, for no sooner did a Blackfoot show his head that *pop!* A pill from kill-deer settled the job for him.

"Them Injuns, I reckon, thought they had holed the devil himself, for they war so surprised when they heard the bark of the old rifle and found another of them wiped out, that they even forgot to yell. They found that smoke couldn't kill the old man, and then they tried another plan. Their game now was to starve me out. And here again I had the trump cards in my own hands. The fact was, they hadn't the least idea that the cave had been used as a cache, and when they saw me take to it, they thought that I had discovered them and was hiding away from them there. They didn't count on the good things I had there, all to myself.

"I could understand enough of their gibberish to learn that they had determined to stand guard over me till I should be forced to yield to starvation, at least. But I had, you know, about two months' provision with me, and so long as that held out, and little red give down, I was all right. So I made up my mind to pass the time as agreeably as possible.

"I could hear that parties of Injuns rode away from the place every morning, and others come agin to take their place, standing guard over me by turns. At length, after four days, when they supposed I was about starved to such a degree as to be no longer dangerous to approach, a redskin poked his head into the opening and began to crawl cautiously into the cave. I was watching for him, and clutching him by the windpipe so that he could make no noise, I drew my bowie across his throat and dragged him into the darkness. Presently another followed, and him I served in precisely the same way. After some time, another Injun put his head down to the hole and called to his comrades. At this moment I leveled my rifle and let him have it. So that that morning I had wiped out three more of the rascals.

"They didn't trouble me anymore for some days; I think it must have been nigh a week, when making sure I had yielded to the fate they had decreed me, another attempt was made to enter the cavern. I kept at a distance till two of them had come in, when I sprang upon them and, with my rifle and knife, made a finish of them too.

"Now indeed it was that the Injuns were really sure that they had none but the very Evil One to deal with, and filling the air with their yells of disappointed vengeance, they mounted their mustangs and I could hear them riding away down the banks of the river.

"After a while, when I thought the coast was clear of the red fools, I ventured to the open air, and mounting upon the top of the river bank, I could see them spurring away over the prairie as if the Evil Spirit was behind them. I had been pent up in that dark hole for more than three weeks, as near as I could guess, and the strong light of the sun almost blinded me at first, but after a little while I got used to it, and I tell you what, boys, if this green earth and the blue skies ever looked beautiful to my eyes, they did on that blessed morning when I crept outen that living grave, for yer must remember it was half full of the stinking carcasses of them Blackfeet I had killed."

"But Uncle Job," asked one of the young men, "how did your sick men at the post get along without the medicine?"

"Poorly," was the reply. "Two of them had died. But they waited ten days for me to come back, and finding I didn't, they sent another man to Fort Laramie for the medicine and the others were saved.

"I reached the post again after an absence of about a month, and as I didn't like to acknowledge I had turned out of my way for the sake of the whiskey, while my comrades were suffering for the want of what I had been sent for, I said nothing about it more than that I had been a prisoner among the Injuns and managed to make my escape after a hard fight.

"Some months afterwards, when a party of us were trapping out on the Medicine Bow, we concluded to make a visit to our cache. The place was just as I had left it, only the bodies of the Blackfeet I had wiped out had been removed. The sack of flour and bag of rice were just as the spring party had cached them, but to the surprise of all of us, and to none more than myself, the whiskey keg was empty and the dried venison all gone.

"The fact was, boys," concluded Uncle Job, "although I had pretty considerable of a time of it with them cussed Blackfeet, upon the whole I felt too much ashamed of the affair to let on a single word about it."

THE WONDERFUL ESCAPE

In the autumn of 1779, a number of keel boats were ascending the Ohio under the command of Major Rodger and had advanced as far as the mouth of the Licking without accident. Here, however, they observed a few Indians standing upon the southern extremity of a sandbar, while a canoe, rowed by three others, was in the act of putting off from the Kentucky shore as if for the purpose of taking them aboard. Rodgers instantly ordered the boats to be made fast on the Kentucky shore while the crew, to the number of seventy men, well-armed, cautiously advanced in such a manner as to encircle the spot where the enemy had been seen to land. Only five or six Indians had been seen, and no one dreamed of encountering more than fifteen or twenty enemies.

When Rodgers, however, had as he supposed completely surrounded the enemy and was preparing to rush upon them from several quarters at once, he was thunderstruck at beholding several hundred savages suddenly spring up in front, rear, and upon both flanks. They instantly poured in a discharge of rifles and, then throwing down their guns, fell upon the survivors with the tomahawk. The panic was complete and the slaughter prodigious. Major Rodgers, together with forty-five of his men, were almost instantly destroyed. The survivors made an effort to regain their boats, but the five men who had been left in charge of them had immediately put off from the shore in the hindmost boat and the enemy had already gained possession of the others. Disappointed in the attempt, they turned furiously upon the enemy and, aided by the approach of darkness, forced their way through their lines, and with the loss of several severely wounded at length effected their escape to Harrodsburg.

Among the wounded was Captain Robert Benham. Shortly after breaking through the enemy's line, he was shot through both hips, and the bones being shattered, he instantly fell to the ground. Fortunately, a large tree had lately fallen near the spot where he lay, and with great pain, he dragged himself into the top and lay concealed among the branched. The Indians, eager in pursuit of the others, passed him without notice, and by midnight all was quiet. On the following day, the Indians returned to the battle-ground in order to strip the dead and take care of the boats. Benham, although in danger of famishing, permitted them to pass without making known his condition, very correctly supposing that his crippled legs would only induce them to tomahawk him upon the spot in order to avoid the trouble of carrying him to their town.

He lay close, therefore, until the evening of the second day, when perceiving a racoon descending a tree, he shot it hoping to devise some means of reaching it when he could kindle a fire and make a meal. Scarcely had his gun cracked, however, when he heard a human cry apparently not more than fifty yards off. Supposing it to be an Indian, he hastily reloaded his gun and remained silent, expecting the approach was an enemy. Presently the same voice was heard again, but much nearer. Still Benham made no reply, but cocked his gun and sat ready to fire as soon as an object appeared. A third halloo was quickly heard, followed by an exclamation of impatience and distress, which convinced Benham that the unknown must be a Kentuckian. As soon, therefore, as he heard the expression "whoever you are, for God's sake answer me!" he replied with readiness and the parties were soon together.

Benham, as we have already observed, was shot through both legs! The man who appeared had escaped from the same battle *with both arms broken*! Thus each was able to supply what the other wanted. Benham having the perfect use of his arms could load his gun and kill game with great readiness, while his friend having the use of his legs could kick the game to the spot where Benham sat, who was thus enabled to cook it. When no wood was near them, his companion would rake up brush with his feet and gradually roll it within reach of Benham's hands, who constantly fed his companion and dressed *his* wounds as well as his own—tearing up both of their shirts for that purpose. They found some difficulty in procuring water at first, but Benham at length took his own hat and, placing the rim between the teeth of his companion, directed him to wade into the Licking up to his neck and dip the hat into the water by sinking his own head. The man who could walk was thus enabled to bring water, by means of his teeth, which Benham could afterward dispose of as was necessary.

In a few days they had killed all the squirrels and birds within reach, and the man with the broken arms was sent out to drive game within gunshot of the spot to which Benham was confined. Fortunately, wild turkeys were abundant in those woods, and his companion would walk around and drive them towards Benham, who seldom failed to kill two or three of each flock. In this manner, they supported themselves for several weeks until their wounds had healed so as to enable them to travel. Then they shifted their quarters and put up a small shed at the mouth of the Licking, where they encamped until late in November anxiously expecting the arrival of some boat which should convey them to the falls of Ohio.

On the 27th of November, they observed a flat boat moving leisurely down the river. Benham instantly hoisted his hat upon a stick and hallooed loudly for help. The crew, however, supposing them to be Indians, at least suspecting them of an intention to decoy them ashore, paid no attention to their signals of distress but instantly put over to the opposite side of the river and, manning every oar, endeavored to pass them as rapidly as possible. Benham beheld them pass him with a sensation bordering on despair, for the place was much frequented by Indians and the approach of winter threatened them with destruction unless speedily relieved. At length, after the boat had passed him nearly half a mile, he saw a canoe put off from its stern and cautiously approach the Kentucky shore, evidently reconnoitering them with great suspicion. He called loudly upon them for assistance, mentioned his name, and made known his condition. After a long parley and many evidences of reluctance on the part of the crew, the canoe at length touched the shore and Benham and his friend were taken on board. Their appearance excited much suspicion. They were almost entirely naked and their faces were garnished with six weeks growth of beard. The one was barely able to hobble upon crutches, and the other could manage to feed himself with one of his hands. They were instantly taken to Louisville where their clothes, which had been carried off in the boat which deserted them, were restored to them, and after a few weeks' confinement, both were perfectly restored.

Benham afterwards served in the northwest throughout the whole of the Indian War, accompanied the expeditions of Harmer and Wilkinson, shared in the disaster of St. Clair, and afterward in the triumph of Wayne. Upon the return of peace, he bought the land upon which Rodgers had been defeated and ended his days in tranquility amid the scene which had witnessed his sufferings.

THE DESPERADO AND THE REGULATORS

An old man by the name of Yokum had been the terror of the part of Louisiana where he formerly resided, we believe upon Plaquemine Brulé or in that vicinity. It has often been told us by old settlers from that portion of the state that not one of Yokum's family or of the gang whom he kept around him had met with a natural death.

This patriarch in crime selected "Pine Island Prairie" in the lower part of Eastern Texas as a place where he would be but little troubled with inquisitive neighbors and where, from its location upon the road leading from Belew's Ferry upon the Sabine through Liberty and crossing the San Jacinto at the Attascaseta ford to Houston, he would be sure to *entertain*, that is, "keep" or "receive," almost every traveler that chose that route.

Knowing the advantages of a good character at home, he soon, by his liberality, apparent good humor, and obliging disposition, succeeded in ingratiating himself with the few settlers who were, with backwoods courtesy, called neighbors—anyone within fifteen miles being entitled to the benefit of the term.

The first thing that attracted general suspicion and inquiry was the appearance of his stud. Planters and stock-raisers in Texas keep many horses but they are usually of the small breed of Louisiana Creole ponies, or those of the Spanish kind. The larger breed of horses from the Northern or Western States are designated as "American horses," and seldom met with, unless perchance a physician, lawyer, or wealthy planter may keep one as his especial saddlehorse. Travelers, however, are generally mounted upon them.

No Texan can conceal his stock of cattle or his stud, as every acre of prairie and timber is thoroughly hunted over once and often twice a year by large parties of stock-raisers who join together and ride over the whole country within twenty and thirty miles of their residences, and very frequently much farther, gathering every four-footed beast into the nearest pen and selecting out their own for the purpose of branding them. Ignorant except of their own peculiar business, their knowledge of everything pertaining to cattle, their recollection of, and skill in managing them is wonderful. It is not surprising, then, that the large and increasing stock of American horses, which were found grazing in the prairie near Yokum's, excited their suspicion. Inquiries for missing travelers, and the non-appearance of some who were known to have stopped upon the road at houses east of Yokum's but who did not make their appearance again, furnished additional cause. At length, by a very singular train of events, things came to a crisis.

A man named Carey, an industrious, hard-working person, settled upon a prairie near Cedar Bayou in company with a Mr. Page. They owned a small tract and cultivated a small farm jointly.

Near them—in fact, the fences of their plantations joined— lived a Mr. Britton, a blustering, quarrelsome down-easter, who, in consideration of his Goliath-like proportions, determined upon ruling the prairie.

Britton, Page, and Carey occupied the same "league" of land, and ere long the former was embroiled with the two latter in a violent dispute, commencing with a difficulty in the division of the property and, aggravated by that fruitful subject, a quarrel about their dogs.

Page kept sheep but no dogs, and Briton dogs, but no sheep. Britton's favorite dog killed Page's sheep, and Page or Carey killed Britton's dog. Here, now, was a germ for a serious difficulty and in itself a very pretty quarrel as it stood. Soon after, Britton met Carey upon the prairie and horse-whipped him. Threats and recriminations followed, but nothing serious resulted from them for nearly a year.

At last, something again excited Britton's ire, and he sent word to Carey that he was braiding a lash for his especial benefit—a lash that would cut him to the bone.

Carey's business that afternoon caused him to visit a neighbor, a new settler who was living *pro tem.* in a small log pen or house. Here he found his antagonist—sitting in the door, and leaning his head back against the door-post—and also two or three other persons, who had called upon the newcomer.

Carey entered, placed a rifle which he was carrying upon the bed, and after remaining some half an hour, during which time nothing had passed between him and his enemy, rose to retire. His gun lay with its muzzle towards the door, and Carey stepped round the bed as if to raise the gun by the breech. As soon as he put his hands upon the piece, it was discharged and a ball passed through Britton's brain. He fell dead instantly, without word or groan. I am in error, however, in stating that he *fell* dead, for so quickly did death supervene the rifle's report that he remained sitting bolt upright and the spectators did not know, until Carey had left the room, that anything more serious than an accidental discharge of the rifle had taken place.

The perpetrator of this homicide—whether accidental or intentional, none but his Maker and himself can tell—immediately fled from the country and took refuge with old Yokum, probably judging that his late deed would be a fitting letter of introduction.

Yokum received him with open arms, promised to protect and defend him, and if necessary, to secure his retreat from the county in safety.

This, however, was very far from his real design, and he kept Carey housed for a long time, a prey to agonizing fears which were not allayed by the tales he was told of the threats that the county had made of taking him by force and lynching him

Thus, working upon his fears, Yokum prevented his prisoner—for such he really was—from carrying out the intention which he had expressed soon after his arrival of delivering himself up for trial as soon as the momentary excitement of the people had died away, and ultimately persuaded him of the absolute necessity that existed to dispose of his property in Texas as best he might and then to fly from the country. Yokum offered to purchase the "improvements," which were valuable, and to facilitate his exodus and that of Page's family, and placing full faith in his honesty of purpose, Carey gave him a letter to his friend directing him to make a deed of sale of the plantation to Yokum.

Yokum immediately rode over to the scene of the late disturbance and, finding Page ready to comply with his partner's wishes, left with him some of his fine American horses with which the family were to escape and which was to be the first payment, together with a sum of money which he promised them toward the purchase of the estate.

During Carey's residence in the backwoods of Alsatia, he had formed an acquaintance with one of the clan who seemed to have taken a fancy to him and to whom he probably was indebted for life. While Yokum was absent, this person opened Carey's eyes as to the whole plot which was now drawing to its close. The whole property was to be transferred to Yokum by Carey's agent, Page, for a nominal consideration, and Yokum promised to hold it till he could sell it to advantage and then to send the money to Carey or to pay it over to his agent. In the meanwhile, the horses were given, or lent, and a small sum of money.

This, however, was all pretense and Yokum's true design was to obtain a legal title to the plantation and then to dispose of Carey in such a manner that there would be no danger of his turning up again. There was another necessity for this course: Carey had learned too many and too dangerous secrets for Yokum to trust him out of his sight. Carey escaped and fled to the house of one of the most influential men in Liberty County, to whom he confided all his knowledge of Yokum and his doings and also stated his intention of delivering himself up immediately for trial.

The people were called together and determined to take the law in their own hands, to punish the guilty, and to drive the entire clan out of the country.

Upon their arrival at Yokum's house, they found that he had escaped and, setting themselves to work to make such investigation as they could, soon satisfied themselves of his undoubted crime.

A Negro informed them where the bones of a traveler could be found in an old well, and those of another were said to have been discovered bleaching upon the prairie. Yokum's family were ordered to leave the house, the furniture was removed, and the premises set on fire. The family, and all hangers-on, had a certain number of days allowed them to move their effects and leave the county, being threatened with death if they ever returned. This last measure was one of necessity as the safety of all those concerned in their removal depended upon it.

The Regulators set forth upon Yokum's trail and succeeded in finding him at a house near Spring Creek in the present county of Montgomery, and then known as Spring Creek County. The culprit was secured and carried some miles on the homeward route when his captors dismounted, informed him that his time had come, and, giving him one short half-hour to repent the villainies of a long lifetime, shot him through the heart.

The family of Yokum, and all connected with them, left the county and emigrated farther west, denouncing the lynching party and swearing that they would be revenged upon everyone who had a hand in the affair. There is no doubt but that some of these threats would have been fulfilled had not the citizens of Liberty County proved that they were terribly in earnest in their determination to take instant and fatal measures with anyone of the clan who should dare again to cross the county line.

The least objectionable of all Yokum's tribe, one of his sons, Christopher—perhaps the only one against whom some heinous crime could not have been established—had married a short time before the general breaking-up of the gang. His wife refused to accompany or to follow him but promised to live with him if he would return, and after waiting a year, he determined to do so. Whether this was a mere ruse to obtain a foot-hold again and to provide a house of refuge for others to carry out their threatened revenge, I know not, but it proved a fatal affair for him. As soon as the sheriff heard of his presence, he immediately put him in the jail at Beaumont in order to save his life and, if possible, to assist him to escape. But all precautions were useless. The people rose immediately upon learning of Yokum's arrival and, taking him out of jail, hung him on the first tree.

THE RANGER'S THRILLING INDIAN ADVENTURE

At nineteen years of age, Dr. Blank of Massachusetts joined the army of the provinces that in 1755 essayed to take Crown Point from the French. He marched to the lakes with Colonel Ephraim Williams, then whom a more gallant man never breathed the air of New England. The doctor fought under his command at Lake George, on the memorable 8th of September, saw (or imagined he saw) the fall of his brave leader, and is quite sure that he put a bullet into the French officer Mons. St. Pierre. The next year he joined the Rodgers' company of Rangers and was stationed with a party of them at Fort Ann, not far from where Whitehall now stands. But at that day it was a "dark and bloody ground," a frontier station in the forests which were filled with rival savages attached to France or England.

One day, in mid-winter, eight rangers with a sergeant were ordered out on some service; the doctor did not know what, but probably to seize some straggling Frenchman about Ticonderoga or Crown Point and bring him to the fort for the sake of obtaining intelligence. He was himself of the party. A narrow road, or rather path, led northward toward Canada, and they followed it for several hours. There had just been a heavy fall of snow, all the pines and hemlocks in the forest were loaded thick with it, and as the afternoon was still and clear, only occasional flakes or light masses dropped from the burdened boughs like feathers. These circumstances were stamped on the old man's mind, seeming like a constantly recurring dream. The rangers waded in Indian file through the snow, and as danger was apprehended, a man was placed some rods in advance, one on each flank, and another behind. This last was the doctor himself, "and this was the gun I carried," said he, taking a short heavy piece from the corner.

At length they descended into a hollow: the frozen sheet of Lake George lay not far on to the left, and a steep hill on the right. The ground, a short distance before them, was low and swampy, and a little brook had spread itself out on the path, making a frozen space free from trees, across which their advanced man was now slowly trampling, crushing his boots into the ice and water at every step. He paused suddenly, turned sharply round, and gave the low whistle appointed as the signal of alarm. He had seen the tracks of many moccasined feet in the fresh snow beyond. There was not time to think; the loud report of a gun broke the stillness. The Ranger gave a shrill scream, leaped four feet into the air, and fell flat. Instantly the Indian yell burst from the woods on our right and left, followed by the stunning rattle of more than fifty guns, and not a man of the rangers but one ever moved alive from the spot where he stood transfixed with surprise at the sudden death of his comrade.

That man was our hero, whose position, far behind the rest, saved him. He remembered the panic felt at the fierce burst of yells and musketry, and the sudden rush of the savage swarm from their ambush upon his fallen comrades, and in the next instant that his memory could recall, he was flying back to the fort. He heard sharp sudden yelps behind him, and glancing back, saw two Indians bounding on his track. He ran a mile, he should think, without turning or hearing a single sound, then, turning his head, saw an Indian leaping, silent as a specter, within a few rods of him. With admirable coolness, he turned quickly round and, raising his gun with a steady hand, fired with such good effect that the Abenaki pitched forward to the ground and his shaven head ploughed up the snow for yards by the impulse of his headlong pursuit. The young soldier turned and fled again, and as he did so, he heard the report of the other Indian's gun, followed by the loud humming of the ball. So alert and attentive were his faculties that he observed where the bullet struck upon a loaded bough in front of him, scattering the glittering particles of snow.

The path now led downward with a steep descent; at the bottom an ancient pine tree had fallen across it whose sharp broken branches rose up perpendicularly from the prostrate trunk four or five feet from the ground, blocking up the way like a bristling *chevaux-de-frise*. The rangers had previously turned aside to avoid it. There was no time to do so now. The doctor's limbs were small and light but as active as a deer's, and the Indian's tomahawk was close behind. Without hesitating, he ran down and sprang into the air. His foot caught so that he fell on the other side, but he snatched up his gun and ran again. In a moment he heard a wild and horrible cry, and turning as he ran up the opposite hill, he saw a sight that has murdered his sleep for many a night since. The daring savage had leaped like him, but not so well; he had tripped, and one of the broken branches had caught and impaled him on its upright point, passing upward into the cavity of his chest! He saw the starting eye-balls and the painted features hideously distorted, and paused to see no more.

About sunset the sentinels of Fort Ann saw him emerging from the woods, running as if the Indians were still behind him. A strong party sent out next morning found the bodies of the rangers stripped and frozen in the various positions in which they died, so that they appeared like marble statues. On a tree close by, the French officer who commanded the Abenakis had fastened a piece of birch bark inscribed with an insolent and triumphant message to the English. The bodies of the two Indians had been removed, although the white snow around the old pine tree retained ineffaceable marks of the tragedy that had been enacted there and was beaten hard by the moccasins of a crowd of savages who had gathered about that place.

This taste of war was enough for the doctor's martial zeal. He did not take to the field again till twenty years afterward, when he came to Washington's camp at Cambridge, armed with probe and balsam instead of musket and powder.

THE FIGHTING PARSON

New England, after the defeat of Burgoyne, seemed for a while to be left out of the war so far as any invasion of her territory was concerned, and in 1779 Yale College had recovered in a great measure from its troubles and was in a prosperous condition.

But in the midst of its tranquility a rumor reached New Haven that the British were about to make a decent upon it. The place was immediately thrown into a state of the greatest alarm, and a meeting was called to deliberate on what was to be done. Dr. Dagget was a professor of divinity in the college, but in the interim of regular presidents he had been elected president *pro tem*. The college of course would be again broken up by this invasion. The students, such as did not wish to unite in any plan of resistance, could easily scatter to the back country, but the great question was: what should be done with the inhabitants? Various plans and propositions were presented, and at length the president of Yale College was asked his opinion. It was well known that he had preached the duty of resistance as obedience to God and shown himself in every way an ardent patriot, but what he would advise when the overwhelming and insolent foe was at the door was quite another thing. The students, who had often been fired by his eloquent appeals, were not a little curious to know what their president and professor of divinity would counsel in this fearful emergency.

The character of the college they considered to be at stake, for if their president advised tame submission and abject attitude, on the ground that resistance would be of no avail, the institution at whose head he stood would be compromised. They hoped, therefore, he would take a manly course, even if he deemed it best to pursue a peaceable one. They were not long kept in suspense, for when their venerated teacher arose, the flashing eye and compressed lip told them at once that Yale need not fear for patriotic reputation. Instead of counseling moderation and weighing all the suggestions as to the various courses to be pursued, he took the ground of the soldier at once and said, no matter what else they might do, they must at all hazards *fight*; and then, to let them know that this was not the advice of one who by his profession and position was exempt from military duty, he coolly informed them if no other person was found to resist, he should fight alone.

It was finally resolved to raise a volunteer company of a hundred men who should march out in the morning and retard the enemy so as to give the inhabitants as much time as possible to remove their effects.

In the meantime, the exciting news came that Tyron, with a force 2,500 strong, had landed at West Haven, only five miles distant, and was about to march directly on the place. In an instant all was confusion and alarm, and the inhabitants, on foot and in carriages, alone and in groups, were seen pouring out of the city toward the open country. In the midst of the alarm, the volunteers, at the stirring notes of the fife and drum, hastily assembled and armed with such weapons as they could lay their hands on, took the road toward West Haven. It was a hot July morning, but they pressed cheerfully on, determined to retard if they could not arrest the heavy force advancing against them. Parson Trumbull, of North Haven, was there mounted on his horse that could stand fire as well as he, for both had been under it before. Dagget apparently had at the last moment backed out; the good professor of divinity could talk bravely, but when it came to smelling gunpowder, it made a difference.

But while they were marching along, a cloud of dust was seen to rise along the road toward New Haven, and soon a solitary horseman appeared in view, galloping fiercely forward. They at first thought it was a messenger sent to overtake them, but when the rider drew near, they beheld to their surprise President Dagget on his old black mare with a long fowling-piece in his hand. The faithful animal had often jogged around the streets of New Haven and along the country roads bearing her dignified master at a dignified rate of speed and was astonished to find herself tearing like a racer along the highway. The volunteers, supposing that he was going to join them and make good his word, received him with loud cheers. With Parson Trumbull and President Dagget to show them how to fight, they felt they could easily do their duty. To their surprise, however, he did not stop to join them, but turning neither to the right nor the left, pushed straight on toward the enemy. Concluding he was hastening forward to reconnoiter, they gave him a parting cheer and pressed on after him.

Dagget, after advancing some distance, turned from the main road and ascended an eminence crowned with a grove where he halted and took a survey of the surrounding country. The little band of volunteers, keeping more to the south, swept round the base of the hill and soon came upon the advance-guard of the enemy. Throwing themselves behind a fence, they poured in a destructive volley which brought it to a sudden halt. Following up their advantage, they broke cover and, leaping the fence, drove the astonished guard before them. Firing and shouting as they advanced, they chased it from fence to fence and across field after field, until they found themselves in front of the whole army. As far as the eye could reach on either side, the green fields were red with scarlet uniforms, the extending wings ready to enfold them and cut off every avenue of escape. Instantly halting and taking in the full extent of their danger, they did not wait for the word of command but turned and ran for their lives.

As they fled along the base of the hill, on the top of which Dr. Dagget had taken his station, they were surprised he did not join them. But the blood of the patriotic president was not thoroughly aroused, and he scorned the retreat. Casting a quiet glance upon the confusion and terror below him, he turned toward the enemy and, leveling his fowling-piece at those more advanced, blazed away. As the British pressed after the fugitives, they were surprised to hear every few moments the solitary report of a gun from the grove on the hill. At first, they paid but little attention to it, but the bullets finding their way steadily into the ranks, they were compelled to notice it and sent up a detachment to see what it meant. The president saw them coming but never moved from his position. His mare stood by him, and he could at any moment have mounted and fled, but this seemed never to have entered his head. He was thinking only of the enemy and loaded and fired as fast as he could.

When the detachment reached the grove, the officer commanding it saw, to his amazement, only a venerable old man in black quietly loading his fowling-piece to have another shot. Pausing a moment at the extraordinary spectacle of a single clergyman fighting the whole British army, he exclaimed, "What are you doing there, you old fool, firing on His Majesty's troops?" The professor of divinity looked up in the most unconcerned manner and replied, "Exercising the rights of war!" The whole affair seemed to strike the officer comically, and amused rather than offended at the audacity of the answer, he said, "If I let you go this time, you old rascal, will you ever again fire on the troops of His Majesty?" "Nothing more likely," was the imperturbable reply. This was too much for the good temper of the Briton, and he ordered his men to seize him. They did and dragged him roughly down the hill to the head of the column.

The volunteers in their retreat tore down the bridge over the river after crossing it, thus compelling the British to march two miles further up the stream before they could affect a passage. The latter immediately placed Dr. Dagget on foot at the head of the column and told him to lead the way. It was the 5th of July and one of the hottest days of the year, and as it was now near meridian, the heat was overpowering. The strongest man unaccustomed to exposure would sink under such a burning sun, and Dr. Dagget soon became exhausted from the heat as well as from the driving pace they kept him at. He, however, staggered on until, at last, feeling he could not take another step, he halted and endeavored to lean against the fence for support. But the enraged soldiers would not allow him a moment's rest and ruthlessly pricked him on with their bayonets, at the same time showering curses on his rebel head. With every indication of weariness, the point of the bayonet forced him to rally his sinking energies, while the blood flowed in streams down his dress.

As they entered the streets of the town, the soldiers commenced shooting the peaceable citizens whenever they cared to show themselves, and as one after another fell in his sight, Dr. Dagget expected his turn would come next. At length they reached the green and halted, when he sank exhausted and bleeding on the grass. A Tory coming out to welcome the British saw the pale, dusty, and bleeding president lying on the ground and, shocked at the sight, besought the commanding officer, in the name of humanity, to spare his life. He granted his request with an insulting epithet, and the wounded man was carried into a neighboring house more dead than alive. His utter exhaustion, combined with the brutal treatment he had received, brought on a fever that reduced him so low that his life was despaired of. Having a strong constitution, he rallied, however, and was able a part of the next year to preach in the chapel, but his system had received a shock from which it could not entirely recover, and in sixteen months he was borne to the grave, adding one more to the list of noble souls who considered no sacrifice too great for their country.

THE SEMINOLE CHIEFTAIN'S TOUCHING APPEAL

The "talk" of Coacoochee, or Wild Cat, to Col. Worth and to his own people, exceeds, in point of pathos and deep feeling, anything we have ever heard.

Wild Cat had repeatedly deceived the officers by "coming in," and after he had received supplies as an inducement to surrender, would make his escape and prosecute the war with renewed activity. He was finally captured by Major Childs and sent at once, with some fifteen others captured at the same time, to Arkansas. At New Orleans they were met by express orders from Col. Worth to return to Florida. He intended to use Coacoochee's influence and bring the war to a close.

A captive and in irons, he had been told by Worth that he had been brought back from Tampa Bay for the purpose of aiding in bringing the war to a close at once. He was told that he might select five of his companions who should be permitted to go to his band—then in the swamps—and induce them to come in. "Name the time," said Worth. "It shall be granted, but I tell you, as I wish you to tell your friends, that unless they fulfill your demands, yourself and these warriors now seated before us shall be hung to the yards of this vessel when the sun sets on the day appointed, with the irons on your hands and feet. I tell you this that we may understand each other: I do not wish to frighten you—you are too brave a man for that—but what I say I mean, and I'll do it. It is for the benefit of the White man and the Red man. This war must end, and you must end it."

Coacoochee rose and, running to Col. Worth, said in a subdued tone, "I was once a boy, then I saw the White man afar off. I hunted in these woods with a bow and arrow, then with a rifle. I saw the

White man and was told he was my enemy. I could not shoot him as I would a wolf or bear, yet like these he came upon me; horses, cattle, and fields he took from me. He said he was my friend; he abused our women and children and told us to go from the land. Still, he gave us his hand in friendship; we took it; whilst taking it, he had a snake in the other, his tongue was forked like the serpent, he lied and stung us. I asked but for a small piece of these lands, enough to plant and live upon, far south, a spot where I could place the ashes of my kindred, a spot only sufficient to lay my wife and child upon. This was not granted me. I was put in prison; I escaped; I have been again taken; you have brought me back; I am here; I feel the irons in my heart. I have listened to your talk; you and your officers have taken us by the hand in friendship. I thank you for bringing me back; I can now see my warriors, my women and children; the Great Spirit thanks you; the heart of the poor Indian thanks you. We know but little; we have no books which tell all things, but we have the Great Spirit, moon, and stars; these told me last night you would be our friend. I give you my word; it is the word of a warrior, a brave, a chief; it is the word of Coacoochee. It is true I have fought like a man; so have my warriors, but the White man was too strong for us. I wish now to have my band around me and go to Arkansas. You say I *must* end the war! Look at these irons! Can I go to my warriors? Coacoochee chained! No, do not ask me to see them. I never wish to tread upon my land unless I am free. If I can go to them *unchained*, they will follow me in, but I fear they will not obey me when I talk to them in irons. They will say my heart is weak. I am afraid. Could I go free, they will surrender and emigrate."

He was told in the most impressive manner that he could not be liberated until his entire band was collected at Fort Brooke; then he might go on shore and meet them unshackled. He saw that his fate was inevitable. The vessel was two miles from shore, sentinels were posted in every part of the ship, and escape by stealth or contrivance was impossible. As the reality forced itself upon his mind that there were but two alternatives, he became sad and dejected. He gathered his warriors about him and selected five who were to go to his band and inform them of the strait in which their chief and his fellow prisoners were placed.

"Has not Coacoochee," said he, "sat with you by the council fire when the wolf and the White man was around us? Have I not led the war dance and sung the song of the Seminole? Did not the spirits of our mothers, our wives, and our children stand around us? Has not my scalping knife been red with blood and the scalps of our enemy been drying in our camps? Have I not made the war path red with blood? And has not the Seminole always found a home in my camp? Then will the warriors of Coacoochee desert him? No! If your hearts are bad, let me see them now; take them in your hands, and let me see that they are dark with bad blood, but do not, like a dog, bite me so soon as you turn your backs. If Coacoochee is to die, he can die like a man. It is not my heart that shakes, no, it never trembles, but I feel for those now in the woods, pursued night and day by the soldiers, for those who fought with us until we were weak. The sun shines bright today; the day is clear; so let your hearts be; the Great Spirit will guide you. At night when you camp, take these pipes and tobacco, build a fire when the moon is up and bright, dance around it, then let the fire go out, and just before the break of day, when the deer sleeps and the moon whispers to the dead, you will hear the voices of those who have gone to the Great Spirit; they will give you strong hearts and heads to carry the talk of Coacoochee. Say to my band that my feet are chained. I cannot walk, yet I send them my word as true from my heart as if I was on the war path or in the deer hunt. I am not a boy; Coacoochee can die, not with a shivering hand, but as when grasping the rifle with my warriors around me.

"My feet are chained, but the head and heart of Coacoochee reaches you. The great White chief (Po-car-ger) will be kind to us. He says when my band comes in, I shall walk my land free, with my band around me. He has given you forty days to do this business in; if you want more, say so; I will ask for more; if not, be true to the time. Take these sticks: here are thirty-nine, one for each day; *this*, much longer than the rest, with the blood upon it, is the fortieth. When the others are thrown away and this only remains, say to my people that with the setting of the sun, Coacoochee hangs like a dog, with none but White men to hear his last words. Come then, come by the stars as I have led you to battle! Come, for the voice of Coacoochee speaks to you!

"Say this to my wife and child—" He could not continue. Sobs choked his utterances as he thought of those loved ones, and he turned away to hide the tears that coursed down his cheeks. Not a sound disturbed the silence which pervaded the assembly, and officers and men, women, and warriors testified by their tears their sympathy for the poor chieftain. In silence the chains were removed from the five messengers, and they prepared to depart. As the last one was going over the side, he removed from his person a handkerchief and breast-pin and, giving them to him, told him to hand them to his wife and child.

Forty days and nights were passed by the chieftain, as well as by the officers, in the most intense anxiety, and it was nearly as much to their relief as to that of Coacoochee and his fellow prisoners, when the sun rose on the fortieth day and found the entire number—seventy-eight warriors, sixty-four women, and forty-seven children—encamped within the bounds of Fort Brooke.

THE HORRORS OF A BOMBARDMENT:
NORFOLK IN 1776

The subjoined account of the burning of Norfolk, Virginia was some years ago received from the lips of a venerable old lady, since deceased.

I was only in my sixth year, when the cannonading and burning of Norfolk took place, by order of the Royal Governor Lord Dunmore, but young as I was, the impression of many things is as clear and vivid to me now as if they had happened yesterday. I was at the time residing with my uncle and aunt who had a very handsome residence on one of the principal streets running back from the river.

One day, toward the last of the year 1775, I remember my uncle coming home under great excitement, declaring the patriots had won the first battle at Great Bridge—that the old scoundrel Lord Dunmore had, with many of his followers and partisans, fled for their lives to a vessel in the stream—and thanking God that the patriot army under Col. Woodford would soon have possession of the town.

After this came a series of the most alarming rumors, which so affected my nervous and timid aunt that she was suddenly struck down with paralysis and was thus rendered incapable of assisting herself in the least.

At this time my uncle's household consisted of eleven persons: himself, his wife and two young children, my grandmother, myself, and five Negroes, two of whom were males. Fearing the male Negroes could not be trusted at such a time, they were sent away to a place of security and a strict watch was kept over the females, who could not be spared. I remember my grandmother carrying a silver-mounted dagger in her bosom and I was told to report the least suspicious conduct on account of the Blacks.

But the worst was yet to come. After several days of wild excitement, with the almost constant roll of the drum, the marching and countermarching of troops through the streets, the occasional thunder of cannon and the sharp rattle of musketry, news came that the governor was about to cannonade and burn the place. This intelligence was communicated to the authorities on the morning of January 1st, 1776, and six hours were allowed for the women, children, and non-combatants to leave the town.

My uncle came home in a state of great excitement and consulted with my grandmother as to what was best to be done. The doctor had been consulted previously and had given his opinion that my aunt could not be removed without a cost of life. And besides, where could she be taken, except into the open fields? For beyond the town there were but a few scattered houses and these would be over-crowded as hospitals for the sick and parties escaping from the doomed village. So, it was finally decided that we should remain and take the chances, and as our dwelling was pretty well back from the river, it was hoped we might escape the shots from the fleet and perhaps the general conflagration along the wharves.

For greater security, my horror-stricken and helpless aunt was placed in a room the farthest from the street and river, and into the same apartment we all crowded, Black and White, looking the dismay and terror we all felt at our hearts. I remember sitting down on a cricket at the feet of my grandmother and along with my elder cousin, burying my head in her lap while she held the younger child in her arms and spoke words of encouragement and hope to my poor aunt and the frightened Blacks—my uncle, meantime, with a sword at his side, pacing rapidly up and down the adjoining apartment and now and then stopping to listen to any sounds without.

As the time drew near for the opening of the awful work of destruction, we all became more and more agitated, and when at length the first heavy gun of the fleet broke the horrible suspense, we all simultaneously started up with a sort of mournful cry or wail, to which it seemed as if the whole town responded with a shriek of fear and execration. Then gun after gun thundered away in rapid succession, drums rolled, musketry rattled, and shout upon shout reached us with the stirring words:

"To arms! To arms! Turn out! Turn out! The foe is upon us!"

"Goodbye, my poor dear angel!" cried my uncle, hurrying to the side of my aunt and pressing his lips to lips that scarcely had the power to tremble, though the face showed deathly pallor and the eyes rained tears. "May God in his mercy preserve us!"

He turned, caught up each of his children, and kissed them with a trembling "God save you," treated me in the same fatherly manner, threw his arms around the neck of his weeping mother, grasped a hand of each of the trembling Blacks, and then rushed from the dwelling to the defense of his country, his home, and all he held dear on earth.

I am not able to follow up the events in consecutive detail. I can only recall such as made the deepest impression, without regard to the lapse of time between each. Soon after the departure of my uncle—I do not remember how long—I heard the wild shout of "Fire! Fire! The town is on fire! The town is on fire!" and there were sounds of galloping horses, whirling vehicles, and men running in bodies commingling with the almost constant booming of the heavy guns of the fleet, which were leveled against the place. We could see nothing in the room we were, and impulsively I started up and followed one of the Blacks upstairs against the warning of my grandmother. My fears had now become secondary to my desire to look upon the worst in all its horrors.

From a window in the second story, I saw smoke and flames rising up from several points along the river bank and could here and there catch a glimpse of excited crowds of men running to and fro, and once or twice, as the smoke was whirled aside by a strong breeze blowing toward me, I caught a momentary view of the tall spars and dark hull of a vessel that was belching forth its tongues of fire and missiles of destruction.

"De Lord of Heben, hab massy on us!" exclaimed the Black girl, who was standing at the window with me.

It was her last prayer. The next moment a ball crashed through the building, carrying her head with it, and her lifeless body sunk down at my feet, pouring upon me a stream of blood. I shrieked and fainted.

When I came to my senses, we were all down in the cellar, whither we had been removed for safety, and all were crying and wringing their hands. My aunt had been borne down upon her bed, upon one corner of which I had also been laid. I remember starting up and shrieking in terror, though for the time I had forgotten what had happened. Then there were a few minutes of wild confusion when my uncle suddenly appeared with a couple of other men, and, after commanding silence, said it was necessary that we should soon leave the house, for, beside the fact that the balls of the fleet could reach it, the fire was rapidly gaining ground and before morning, perhaps within an hour, so powerful was the breeze blowing toward us, we should be wrapped in flames and surrounded by fighting men.

He then went to his poor wife and began to speak some consoling words, but suddenly stopped and uttered a long, loud, piercing wail that seems yet to ring in my ears.

"What is it, my son?" cried my grandmother, starting up in alarm.

"She is dead! She is dead!" groaned my uncle.

So it was, in truth—my aunt was already dead and none could say when she died. It was no time to stand on ceremony, even with the most sacred things. A grave was dug in one corner of that very cellar, my poor aunt was buried forever from the living, and then we were all hurried into the street to make our escape.

It was now night, and the town lit up with the ghastly glare of the burning buildings, some of which had by this time caught so near my uncle's dwelling as to render it certain that it would soon go with the rest. The streets were crowded with people in the wildest state of excitement—citizens and soldiers, men, women, and children—some hurrying toward the river to give the enemy battle and some flying toward the open country loaded with a few of their most valuable articles which they were seeking to save from the general doom. In the whirl and confusion, I somehow got separated from my friends and while endeavoring to find my way back to them, a body of men came running directly over the place where I stood. I remember screaming in fear of being suddenly trampled to death and then being caught up by strong arms and borne rapidly forward to the steps of some great building which was on fire. Here I was dropped by the man who had saved me, but here, of course, I could not remain and, attempting to get away, I was knocked down by a party of armed men who were rushing to attack another party. I was not badly hurt and managed to crawl aside into the passageway of some building just as the firing began near me. There were shouts and yells, a discharge of firearms, and then a short hand-to-hand combat. One party was driven by the other, and on venturing to look out, I saw two British soldiers lying near, one dead and the other covered with blood, groaning and writhing and looking terribly ghastly in the lurid light. I turned away with a sickening feeling of horror and, perfectly bewildered, ran I knew not whither.

I next remember the falling of a building, some of the cinders and sparks of which reached me and set fire to my clothing, which a pale woman with a bandaged head assisted me to extinguish, saying, "God help you poor child! Who are you? And where do you belong?"

Before I could reply, there was a loud explosion near, followed by a wild cry, and instantly the woman turned and ran away.

After this, I scarcely know what happened to me or where I went, or how I escaped surrounding dangers. The whole lives confusedly in my memory, like the partial remembrance of some horrid dream. Pale, ghastly faces, bloody phantoms, burning and crashing buildings, the roar of cannon, the rattle of musketry, the clash of sabers, the heavy trampling of armed bodies, shouts, yells, shrieks, and groans—all these are mixed up in my recollection in wild and inextricable confusion.

By some means I was restored to my grandmother, but I never saw my uncle again. He was killed some time after in attempting to capture a British gunboat. They told me that the town was three days burning and was nearly all consumed and that everybody suffered terribly from the want of provisions, some actually dying of starvation. I heard this after I got back to my parents in Richmond and recovered from a slow fever. But this of course is known to history. My own recollections are what I have given, and I pray to God I may never witness the destruction of another town or city.

A TEXAN RANGER'S FEARFUL ADVENTURE
AMONG THE GUERILLAS

Many who took part in the Mexican campaign, with Taylor's command, will doubtless recollect among the quartermaster's men, stationed at Monterey, a somewhat noted Ranger of the name Jean Bruno.

They will the more readily call him to mind from the fact of his having lost one arm—I think it was the left one—and also from the dashing appearance he always made on horseback, being invariably mounted on the most spirited and unbroken nags in the quartermaster's stables. These noble animals he managed with the skillfulness of a ranchero, frequently using his teeth to assist his one hand in the control of them.

Jean was a Frenchman who had seen service in Algeria and had rendered himself quite famous on our line by numerous daring feats, such as conveying important dispatches where no other express riders could be induced to venture, cutting his way, single-handed and alone, through the enemy's pickets, charging in darkness through their camps and bivouacs, and by numerous consequent hairbreadth escapes, in one which he received the wound making necessary the amputation of the limb referred to.

Our little Frenchman was one of those constitutionally brave men who never experience the sensation of fear. In fact, he had little idea of the word. Yet, he was possessed of much prudence in dangerous positions, with a ready invention which carried him safely through them. He used to say, "Let me select my own horse and give me a brace of trusty revolvers and a dragoon saber, and I will guarantee to ride from Monterey to the city of Mexico and, if need be, pass every camp of the enemy on my way!"

As extravagant as was this boast of the Frenchman, I have no doubt he would cheerfully have undertaken it had he been so ordered.

At that anxious period, shortly previous to the decisive battle of Buena Vista, when the handful of volunteers left to garrison the city of Monterey were surrounded by more than ten times their own numbers, and when the dust of the enemy's columns was seen in every direction during the day, and through the night every hilltop and mountainside was illuminated by their signal fires, it became necessary to convey important intelligence to the small command of Colonel Morgan, still occupying Serralvo, the half-way depot between Monterey and Comargo.

But so vigilant was the enemy, and so closely had they beset the roads, that it was considered not only extremely hazardous, but almost impossible to open a communication with that post.

The rangers in the place were offered large rewards to induce some one or more of them to undertake the perilous journey, but there were none among them who would run the gauntlet. Had Jean Bruno been at hand, the application would not have been made in vain. But that courageous man was absent at Saltillo, whither he had been sent with dispatches to General Taylor.

The quartermaster now made a requisition upon the Fort Ohio Regiment, quartered in the plaza, and two young privates immediately volunteered to attempt the passage.

The services of these brave fellows were gladly accepted, and provided with excellent horses and well-armed, they set forth upon their perilous ride.

Scarcely, however, had the Ohioans left the plaza when the fearless and faithful Ranger Jearn Bruno himself, accompanied by a Mexican guide, galloped up to the commandant's quarters with return dispatches from headquarters.

As the officer had all confidence in the skill and experience of the Frenchman, he hardly gave him time to dismount from his panting steed when, ordering a fresh animal, he requested Jean to start forthwith, with a duplicate of the dispatch that had been given to the Ohioans. Ever ready to give a cheerful obedience to all orders, the Frenchman snatched a few mouthfuls of refreshment with his guide and was soon again dashing, with him in company, out of the city.

It was his intention, if possible, to overtake the young men who had proceeded him in order to ascertain what route they purposed to pursue, as he had determined to follow a different path in order that should one party fail, the other might possibly succeed in reaching their destination. Besides, the chances were that either would be more likely to pass the outposts of the enemy undiscovered than if they united their numbers.

Jean and his guide, however, had crossed the ford of Agua Frio without falling in with the Ohioans who, in obedience to instructions, had ridden rapidly, till past the first line of Mexican pickets.

Beyond the stream, coming upon hard, gravelly soil, Jean lost sight of their horses' tracks and, under the guidance of his trusty and experienced companion, left the main wagon road and struck out into a narrow and rarely-traveled mule trail, which leading directly across the mountains, would take them by a nearer route to Serralvo.

The distance was some seventy miles by the road and twenty less by the mountain path, and by this route, the guide assured Jean they would altogether avoid the pickets and scouts of the Mexicans.

The two men had ridden but a few miles on the trail when they came again upon the tracks of the Ohioans' horses. These were readily distinguished from the fact that Mexican horses were never shod. It seems that the young men, who had frequently passed between Monterey and Serralvo, had heard of this short cut and had not taken it.

For hours the Frenchman and guide rode along, now ascending some precipitous peak, then winding slowly along the verge of some overhanging cliff, and later galloping through some little, grassy valley watered by mountain streams where they would rest for a few moments to refresh their animals upon rich herbage.

At length night overtook the travelers still upon the mountain path, and Jose, the guide, proposed that they should draw rein at a sheep rancho not far ahead and await the return of day. Their route was dangerous in the obscurity, and Jean, unsuspicious of harm among the simple rancheros, consented.

As they reached the place, which with its range of substantial buildings surrounded by a high adobe wall, had more character of a hacienda of some wealthy proprietor than an ordinary sheep farm, they found the gates shut and all about the place apparently retired to sleep.

After calling several times and knocking loudly upon the gate, they heard voices within, and then a light appeared at one of the unglazed windows, soon after which they heard the removal of bars, and then the door being opened, they were invited in a very friendly manner to enter.

They found themselves in a sort of court, within which were several horses, two of which that appeared to have been freshly arrived and Jean had no doubt were American horses and belonged to his friends who had preceded him.

On the threshold of the house, the travelers were met by an old Mexican who, with a hospitable smile, bid them a happy evening and politely motioned them to enter.

Returning the salutation, Jean inquired if two Americans had not recently arrived.

"No," replied the Mexican, "we have seen no such persons, and they cannot have passed our place. Had they come, they would have been as welcome as yourselves, Señores."

The fellow's manners were courteous. There was an appearance of respectability and even gentleness to him. The night without was dark and threatening rain, and leaving his horse to the care of the faithful guide, Jean, wishing that the Ohioans might have been as fortunate as himself in obtaining shelter from the coming storm, entered the house with a feeling of much satisfaction.

In the large room where he seated himself, he found beside his host another Mexican whose countenance was not of a very prepossessing character, but not much more forbidding than the dark-skinned natives of his class usually are. Besides these persons, there was an old woman, who seemed to be the mistress of the house, and a rather pretty, young señorita, to whom the Frenchman immediately directed his compliments. But the girl received his advances with apparent indifference, and he observed that she frequently leaned her face upon her hands as though suffering from pain or anxiety, and he fancied she occasionally looked upon him with an expression of uneasiness.

As the express rider, like most of his countrymen in our army, had acquired a perfect knowledge of Spanish, the old Mexican remarked that for an American he spoke their language remarkably well—equal, in fact, to a Castilian.

"I am no American," said he.

"No American!" repeated the Mexican with an expression of surprise. "Then what countryman are you, may I ask?"

"I am a Frenchman," replied Jean.

"Oh, then," was the answer, "you are almost half Spaniard. But, if I am not much mistaken, you are here with those Americanos after all!"

There was a peculiar manner about his host and a certain tone, as he made this last remark that caused a feeling of uneasiness in the mind of the Frenchman, and for a few moments he made no reply, and when at length he spoke, asserting that he was now temporarily in the employ of the Americans, he heard a sound, like a half-suppressed sigh, from the young woman at his side.

At this moment Jose returned from the stable and, approaching Jean, whispered, "I hope, Señor, these people are friendly, but there is something about the place I don't like. The other buildings are full of suspicious looking fellows, who seem to me to be guerillas!"

Startling as was this report, which in his own mind was corroborated by the manners of the people in the house, and convinced the Frenchman that they had fallen into a trap, he preserved his presence of mind, and knowing it would be worse than folly to attempt to escape from the place by force, assumed a tranquil manner and inquired of the people if they would supply himself and his companion with supper.

While the women engaged themselves in preparation of the meal, Jean contrived to communicate with the guide and directed him to keep a good eye upon the men without, while he watched the two men in the house.

After a comfortable meal had been partaken of, the old woman and the two men withdrew, bidding our travelers a cheerful "good night" and calling upon them the guardianship of all the saints, while the girl remained behind for a moment, to direct them to their sleeping place.

She led them to an inner apartment—a sort of lumber room—from which a rickety ladder led to an upper loft.

"Up there, Señores," said she in an audible voice, evidently intended for other ears as well as those of the strangers, "you will find vacant cots. Take those upon the right, and do not, if you please, disturb the sleepers upon the other cots—they doubtless sleep soundly from fatigue. *Muy buenos noches!* (Very good night!)" And then approaching her face to the ear of the Frenchman, she added in a whisper: "For the love of God, Señor, fly from this place! Your life is in danger! Wait till all is quiet and escape from the window of the room."

Of course, Jean was now convinced that the suspicions of his guide were correct. The place, without doubt, was a rendezvous of guerillas, and his own life and that of the Mexican, his companion, was determined upon. However, without communicating his discovery to the man, he groped his way to the spot where the girl had directed him to find the cots and seated himself upon one, while Jose took possession of the other. Jean now looked about the place, and in the obscurity found himself in a large attic room devoted chiefly to the storage of maize, saddles, and such rubbish as would naturally accumulate about a Mexican farmhouse. At each end of the apartment was a small, open window, and by the dim light which struggled through them, he perceived two other cots, upon which two persons were lying, covered, face and all, with Mexican *serapes*.

There was something in the breathless repose of the sleepers that startled the Frenchman and, cautiously approaching one of the cots, he stooped his head to the face of the occupant and listened. Not a sound was heard—there was none of that heavy respiration peculiar the wearied sleeper. By degrees his vision became accustomed to the obscurity and, raising a corner of the *serape*, his eye fell upon the face of a corpse! He immediately recognized it as that of one of the Ohioans.

Horror-struck by the sight, he motioned Jose to his side and, stripping down the covering, exposed the bloody clothing of the murdered man. The Mexican would have uttered an exclamation of alarm had not the Frenchman placed his hand upon his mouth and enjoined the silence as their only chance of escape.

They now examined the other bed. It also contained a murdered man—the other unfortunate Ohioan. The two young men had apparently met death in sleep. They had been stabbed to the heart. After making this fearful discovery, our travelers held a hasty consultation. Jean repeated the warning of the young woman and directed Jose to examine one of the windows, while he inspected the other. That to which the Frenchman went looked upon the court, in which were their horses and where several persons were moving about and speaking in whispers to each other. Jose's window looked upon the rear of the house and upon the broken rocks of the mountain side. But the distance to the ground on this side was great, too great to leap, but at the expense of broken bones. By the way of the court the descent was easy enough, first up on the roof of a low outbuilding and then by the projecting corners of the stone building to the ground.

After a moment's hesitation, Jean determined to attempt this passage, even into the midst of the guerrillas, who were within the court. For this purpose, he examined his revolvers, loosened his saber, and directed Jose to see also to his arms. He was about to let himself from the window when a noise at the other window attracted his attention. Stepping lightly across the floor, he peered out of this last and perceived a pole leaning against the building, within reach of his hand. To this was attached a long lariat of rawhide. There was evidently some friendly assistance below, and drawing the rope through the window, they were provided with a sure and safe means of descent. It was the work of a moment only to tie one end of this to one end of the rafters and so drop cautiously to the ground.

As Jean, who was first to descend, let himself from the window, he heard hurried voices in the room below, and immediately several men made a rush for the attic; the next instant a carbine shot was heard, followed by a cry of terror, and the body of poor Jose, who was that moment stepping from the window, fell with a crushing weight upon him, causing the Frenchman to lose his hold upon the rope and fall to the ground.

Though considerably injured by the fall, he did not lose his presence of mind and, regaining his feet, looked about him for the most practicable mode of escape. While thus reconnoitering the place, a dark object approached from the shadow of the building and beckoned him to follow. It was the girl who had given him warning of his danger. He was about to join her when the gate of the court suddenly opened, and supplied with lighted torches, a score of Mexicans rushed out and surrounded the place. Jean found himself enclosed in the ring of eager ruffians, while the girl, pointing toward the side of the mountain, made good her own escape.

"Death to the *maldito Americano!*" shouted the fierce robber gang as they caught sight of the Frenchman and rattled shot after shot among the loose stones and rubbish where he was endeavoring to secrete himself. Finding it impossible thus to elude his enemies, Jean now determined to cut his way through them. He drew his saber, which he placed under his handless arm, and then with one of his revolvers charged upon the guerillas. They were well armed and fought with a ferocious bravery.

After discharging the six barrels of one revolver, each of which dispatched a Mexican, the fearless Frenchman had resort to his saber, and as his assailants gathered about him, he dealt his blows about him right and left, till to use his own words, he "build a barricade of dead greasers about him."

Finding the way now open to him, he made good his own escape to the rocks, toward which the girl had directed him. But though now out of the lair of the robbers, he was far from being out of danger. He knew his enemies would pursue him and, being familiar with the wild country, might easily track him out.

Many and various were the hairbreadth escapes through which the brave Ranger passed before he made good his escape from the mountains, for through that long night and until he came within sight of the white walls of Serralvo, the guerillas, infuriated by the loss of their comrades, continued to pursue him, and more than once they were almost within touching distance of him. At these times his fingers itched to press the trigger of his pistol upon them, but prudence dictated a better course, and finally, when the day was nearly spent, exhausted with fatigue, hunger, and excitement, he reached the camp of Colonel Morgan and placed in his hands the dispatch with which he had been entrusted.

THE GAMBLER'S DEN AT NATCHEZ

In the earlier days of steamboating in the west, the captains and pilots were men who had served their time and learned their trade upon broadhorns or keel boats, and a rough set they were. Almost born, and really educated upon the river, passing their days either in floating down stream, exposed to the various dangers of the voyage, or wearily working their boat up again in the face of the rapid current, liable at any time to be attacked by some of the many gangs of robbers that infested all the region through which they passed, exposed to heat and cold, to snow and rain, plying the oar by day and the whiskey bottle and fiddle bow by night, they formed a class strictly *sui generis*, and a devil-may-care, roistering, ready-handed, and open-hearted one at that.

Many tales are told of the exploits of these old river dogs, and among them one of a certain Captain Russel, familiarly known as Dick Russel, who commanded the old *Constellation* in the palmy days of boating.

Russel was a man of great strength—one of those minor Samsons that are occasionally encountered in the degenerate age—and his courage was in proportion to his muscular power. The boat which he commanded had stopped at Natchez, "under the hill," for the night, and many of his passengers had gone on shore to see the fun going on among the various drinking, gambling, and dancing houses that made up the town, such as it was. Now the said fun was never over decorous, seldom over safe, and one of the said passengers made both discoveries at his cost. He was robbed of his pocketbook, which contained the proceeds of the sale of his flat boat and cargo.

Early the next morning, Russel was informed of the robbery

and, sending for the loser, requested all the particulars.

Having satisfied himself that the money was really lost and that, too, in a notorious house immediately opposite the boat, on shore he went and, marching bold as a lion into the den of thieves, demanded the pocketbook and contents of the proprietor. Of course, the theft was denied and the denial accompanied with many a threat of vengeance upon Russel, whose prowess, however, they were too well acquainted with to make and overt demonstration.

"I'll give you," said Russel, "until I get my boat ready to go to hand over the money, and then if *that* don't come, the house shall." True to his word, just before the boat started, on shore he went again, accompanied by a gang of deck hands, bearing the largest cable the steamer possessed.

This was passed around the house and in and out of some of the windows, and when all was ready Russel again demanded the book.

No answer but curses being returned, he jumped on board the boat, sung out to the pilot to "go ahead" and to the engineer "to work her slow," and off the boat moved very moderately.

The rope began to tighten and the house to creak. Two minutes more would have done the business for building and people, when the latter signified their surrender and pitched pocketbook and money out the window.

PERILOUS ADVENTURE OF CAPTAIN BRADY

In the days when there were more Red men than White in western Pennsylvania, little parties, each under a favorable leader, were frequently sent into the woods as rangers to guard against surprise. One of these, commanded by Captain Samuel Brady, was sent into "French Creek country" in Butler County. On reaching the waters of Slippery Rock, a branch of the Beaver, he discovered an Indian trail and pursued it until dark. On the following morning, he recommenced the pursuit and came up with the Indians just as they were finishing their morning meal and preparing to renew their journey. Placing his men in such a manner as to intercept them, should any attempt be made to escape, at a given signal they delivered a close and well-directed volley and started up to rush upon the enemy with their tomahawks, when a band in their rear, who were on Brady's trail, fired upon them in turn, taking them completely by surprise, killing two of their number and throwing the remainder into confusion. Finding himself thus between two fires and vastly outnumbered, there was nothing left but flight, and Brady, directing his men to look out for themselves, started off at his topmost speed in the direction of the creek.

The Indians had a long and heavy account to settle with him and deemed this the opportunity to wipe it out with his blood. For this purpose, they desired to secure him alive, and fifty redskins, regardless of the others who had scattered in every direction, dropped their rifles and followed him. The Indians knew the ground—Brady did not—and they felt secure of their victim when they saw him run toward the creek, which was at this point a wide, deep, and rapid stream. A yell of triumph broke from them as he arrived at the bank and comprehended his desperate situation. There was apparently no escape, and for a moment the captain felt that his time had come. 'Twas but for an instant, however; he well knew the fate which awaited him, should he fall into the hands of his enemies, and this reflection nerved him to a deed which, perhaps in his calmer moments, he would have found himself incapable of performing.

Gathering all his force into one mighty effort as he approached the brink of the stream, and clinging with a death grip to his trusty rifle, he sprang across the chasm through which the stream ran and landed safely upon the other side, with his rifle in his hand. Quick as thought, his piece was primed, and he commenced to reload. His feet had barely made their imprint in the soft, yielding soil of the western bank before his place was filled by the brawny form of a warrior, who, having been foremost in the pursuit, now stood in wonder and amazement as he contemplated the gap over which the captain had passed. With a frankness which seemed not to undervalue the achievement of an enemy, the savage, in tolerable good English, exclaimed, "Blady make good jump! Blady make *very* good jump!" His conflicting emotions of regret at the escape of his intended victim and admiration of the deed by which that escape had been accomplished did not hinder the discovery that Brady was engaged in loading his piece, and he did not feel assured but that his compliment would be returned from the muzzle of the captain's rifle. He incontinently took to his heels as he discovered the latter ramming home the bullet, which might the next moment be searching out a vital part in his dusky form, and his erratic movements showed that he entertained no mean idea of his enemy's skill at sharp-shooting.

The outline of the most intricate field fortification would convey but a slight idea of the serpentine course he pursued, until satisfied that he was out of rifle shot. Sometimes leaping in the air, at others squatting suddenly on his haunches, and availing himself of every shelter, he evinced a lively fear, which doubtless had its origin in a previous knowledge of the fatal accuracy of the captain's aim. Brady had other views, however, and was not disposed to waste time and powder upon a single enemy, when surrounded by hundreds and when the next moment an empty barrel might cost him his life; and while the savage was still displaying his agility on the opposite bank, he darted into the woods and made his way to a rendezvous previously fixed upon, where he met the remainder of his party, and they took their way for home, not more than half defeated. It was not a great while before they were again on the war-path in search of further adventures.

Brady afterwards visited the spot, and out of curiosity, he measured the stream at the place where he jumped and found it to measure twenty-three feet from shore to shore, and the water he found to be twenty feet deep.

DARING EXPLOITS OF GENERAL PUTNAM

At one time, when General Putnam had command of the army in New York, he was visiting his outposts at West Greenwich when Gov. Tryon, with a corps of 1,500 men, was on a march against it. Putnam had with him only 150 men, with two pieces of artillery; with them he took his station on the brow of a steep declivity near the meeting house. The road turned to the north, just before it reached the edge of the steep; after proceeding in this direction for a considerable distance, it inclined to the south, rendering the descent gradual and tolerably safe.

As the British advanced, they were received with a sharp fire from the artillery, but perceiving the dragoons about to charge, Putnam ordered his men to retire to a swamp inaccessible to cavalry, while he himself dashed directly down the precipice, in a spot where one hundred stone steps had been cut out in the solid rock for the accommodation of foot passengers. His pursuers, who were close upon him, paused with astonishment as they reached the edge and saw him accomplish his perilous descent, and not one of them daring to follow, they discharged their pistols after him, one bullet of which passed through his hat. This wonderful feat has done more for the name of Putnam than almost any other one act. The declivity, from this circumstance, has since borne the name of "Putnam's Hill."

Somewhere near the time the above exploit took place, the following adventure was performed by General Putnam: The stronghold of Horse Neck was in the possession of the British, and Putnam, with a few followers, was lurking in its vicinity bent on driving them from the place. Tired of lying in ambush, the men became impatient and importuned the general with questions as to when they were going to have a bout with the foe. One morning he made a speech to the following effect, which convinced them that something was in the wind:

"Fellows! You've been idle too long, and so have I. I'm going to Bush's at Horse Neck in an hour with an ox-team and a load of corn. If I come back, I will let you know the particulars; if I should not, let them have it!"

Within an hour he was mounted in his ox-cart dressed as one of the commonest Yankee farmers and was soon at the Bush's Tavern, which was in possession of the British troops. No sooner did the officers spy him than they began to question him as to his whereabouts and, finding him a complete simpleton (as they thought), began to quiz him and threatened to seize his corn and fodder.

"How much do you ask for your whole concern?" asked they.

"In marcy sake, gentlemen," replied the mock clod-hopper, with the most deplorable look of entreaty, "only let me off, and you shall have my hull team and load for nothing, and if that won't dew, I'll give you my word, I'll return tomorrow and pay you heartily for your kindness and condescension."

"Well," said they, "we'll take you at your word; leave the team and provender with us, and we won't require any bail for your appearance."

Putnam gave up the team and sauntered about an hour or so, gaining all the information that he wished; he then returned to his men and told them of the foe and his plan of attack.

The morning came, and with it sallied out the gallant band. The British were handled with rough hands, and when they surrendered to General Putnam, the clod-hopper sarcastically remarked, "Gentlemen, I have only kept my word. I told you I would call and pay you for your kindness and condescension."

JOHN MINTER'S FEARFUL
ENCOUNTER WITH A BEAR

Some fifteen or twenty years ago, there lived in the state of Ohio a man by the name of John Minter. In his younger days, he had been a great hunter, spending most of his time in the woods in pursuit of game, and such was his proficiency with the rifle that he seldom failed in bringing down the swift-footed deer or the fleetest winged denizen of the air. He was celebrated for a terrible fight which he had on one occasion with a bear, in which he came so near losing his life that his passion for hunting was changed to disgust, and giving up the use of his rifle, he turned his attention to agriculture. The circumstances are as follows:

He had been out one day, as usual, with his rifle in pursuit of a flock of turkeys, but had been unsuccessful and was returning home in a surly mood, when he came, rather unexpectedly, upon a large black bear, who seemed disposed to dispute his passage. Quick as thought, his piece was at his shoulder and the bullet whizzed through the air, striking the bear full in the breast, and he fell to the ground as Minter supposed dead. Carefully reloading his rifle, not to throw away a chance, he approached the bear and poked his nose with the muzzle, to see if any spark of life remained. Bruin was only "playing 'possum," as it seems, for with far more agility than could be anticipated of a beast who had a rifle ball through his body, he reared upon his hind feet and made at the hunter. Minter fired again, but in his haste and trepidation, arising from the sudden and unexpected attack, he failed to hit a vital part, and a second wound only served to make the brute more savage and desperate. Drawing his tomahawk, he threw that, and as the bear dodged it and sprang upon him, he clubbed his rifle and struck him a violent blow across the head with the butt, which resulted in shivering the stock and, if possible, increasing his rage. Springing back to avoid the sweep of his terrible claws, Minter drew his long, keen hunting-knife and prepared for the fatal encounter which he knew must ensue.

For a moment the combatants stood gazing at each other, like two experienced duelists, measuring each the other's strength. Minter was a man of powerful frame and possessed of extraordinary muscular development, which, with his quick eye and ready hand, made him a very athletic and dangerous enemy. He stood six feet high and was beautifully proportioned. The bear, a male of the largest size and rendered desperate by his wounds, which were bleeding profusely, was a fearful adversary to encounter under any circumstances, more particularly so to Minter, who now had simply his knife to depend upon, to decide the contest between them.

As Bruin advanced to seize him, he made a powerful blow at his heart, which had it taken effect, would have settled the matter at once, but the other was too quick for him, and with a sweep of his tremendous paw, parried the blow and sent the weapon whirling through the air to a distance of twenty feet; the next instant the stalwart hunter was enfolded in the embrace of those fearful paws, and both were rolling on the ground in a death-like grapple.

The woods were open and free from underbrush to a considerable extent, and in their struggles, they rolled about in every direction. The object of the bear was, of course, to hug his adversary to death, which the other endeavored to avoid by presenting his body in such a position as would best resist the vice-like squeeze until he could loosen his grasp; to accomplish which, he seized the bear by the throat with both hands and exerted all his energy and muscular power to throttle him. This had the two-fold effect of preventing him from using his teeth and compelling him to release the hug to knock off the other's hands with his paws, thus affording Minter an opportunity to catch his breath and change his position.

Several times he thought he should be crushed under the immense pressure to which he was subject, but was buoyed up with the hope of reaching his knife, which lay within sight and toward which he endeavored to fall every time they came to the ground. With the hot breath of the ferocious brute steaming in his face and the blood from his own wounds mingling with that of the bear and running to his heels, his flesh terribly cut up and lacerated by his claws, he still continued to maintain the struggle against the fearful odds until he was enabled to reach the weapon, which he grasped with joy and clung to with the tenacity of a death grip. With his little remaining strength and at every opportunity between the tremendous hugs, he plied the knife until the bear showed evident signs of weakness and finally bled to death from the numerous wounds from whence flowed, in copious streams, his warm life's blood, staining the leaves and greensward of a crimson hue.

Releasing himself from the embrace of the now inanimate brute, Minter crawled to a decaying stump, against which he leaned and surveyed the scene. His heart sickened as he contemplated his own person. He had gone into the battle with a stout, heavy hunting shirt and underclothing with buck-skin leggings and moccasins and had come out of it with scarcely a rag upon him, except the belt around his waist, which still held a few strips of tattered cloth, and a moccasin on one foot. His body, from his neck to his heels, was covered with great gaping wounds, many of which penetrated to the bone, and the blood was flowing in torrents to the ground, covering him with gore from head to foot. For a space of more than half an acre, the ground was torn up and had the appearance of a butcher's shambles.

As soon as he had recovered his breath, he commenced to crawl toward his home, where he arrived after nightfall, looking more like a slaughtered beef than a human being. His wounds were dressed by his family and friends, and after being confined to his bed for many weeks, thanks to his healthy, rugged constitution, he entirely recovered; but he bore to his grave the marks of his terrible contest, in numerous scars and welts which covered his back, arms, and legs, where the bear's claws had left ineffaceable marks of his strength and ferocity.

THE MASSACRE AT FORT MIMMS:
AN INCIDENT OF THE CREEK WAR

Soon after the commencement of the War of 1812, that wonderful man, Tecumseh, the greatest warrior and orator ever produced in savage life, left his home in the North and suddenly appeared among the half-civilized tribes of the South, whom with that natural and fiery eloquence of which he was master, he upbraided for their effeminate pusillanimity, their degenerate civilization, counseling them to be warriors and men, and not women, to throw off the pale-face garments that disgraced them, resume their original costume, dig up the hatchet, declare eternal war against the Americans, and once more become sons worthy of their brave and noble sires.

The fiery eloquence of Tecumseh was not lost upon his Red brothers, and upon none was it more effective than the Creeks. It did not result in immediate hostility, but it was seed sown in productive soil, and though the wiser and more prudent rejected his fanatical counsel, a large portion received it as inspired language from the lips of a prophet. To this was soon added the tampering of British agents with the Creeks and Seminoles residing in the territory owned by Spain. At the town of Pensacola, firearms and various other presents were freely distributed among all the Indians who could be induced to assemble there to receive them, and they were urged to declare immediate war against the United States and get as many to assist them as possible. All this led the bolder and more warlike spirits to become dissatisfied with their hitherto peaceful mode of life, and in the end resulted in a terrible and bloody uprising.

Some fearful indications of this newly-awakened hostility soon became manifest along the borders; small parties of soldiers were attacked, houses were here and there burned, and men, women, and children butchered. In view of these fresh troubles, the governors of Georgia and Tennessee were required by the Federal Government to arm their militia, and General Jackson was ordered to march with two thousand men and put down the insurrection. He proceeded through the Choctaw and Chickasaw country as far as Natchez, when, finding all quiet, he returned with his array to the North.

But no sooner had General Jackson left the country than the same aggressive acts were resumed in a bolder manner. A few of the Indians, who remained friendly to the United States, were assailed by the furious war-party, and bloody contests resulted among themselves; Negroes were incited to rise against their masters and join the insurgents, the whole immediate country became a scene of the wildest alarm, and such of the settlers as could not escape to the northward, deserted their plantations, collected together, and immediately erected and established themselves in forts. Several of these were constructed on the Mobile and its different branches, but unfortunately too far apart to be of any assistance to each other in a time of peril.

To one of these, Fort Mimms, we will now direct attention and attempt to give some faint idea of the horrid scene which was there enacted. The story was told some years ago to a friend of ours, by one of the survivors, and we repeat it as nearly in the language of the narrator as we have been able to gather it.

Our fort was a rude affair, built after the manner of the wilderness and consisted of log cabins and stockades with a large area in the center. Within this enclosure—of families and volunteers, men, women, and children, Black and White—were collected something like three hundred souls. The garrison, about a hundred strong, was commanded by Major Beasly, a brave and noble officer, but an imprudent one, arising from an over-confidence in his own resources and a contempt for the foe.

Various rumors reached us from time to time that the Indians were preparing to attack the different stations throughout the country. This at first created no little excitement and alarm in our community, and the major went so far as to make a few repairs and double the guard at night, but as time passed on and no Indians appeared, even the timid and cautious began to grow more indifferent than was prudent for a people situated as we were.

One day, toward the latter part of August, a messenger arrived, saying the Creeks were abroad in great force, that they had fully declared war against the United States and were about to attempt the taking of all the stations in detail, beginning with Fort Mimms.

"We have heard just the same report more than once before," replied Major Beasly, "and yet not a savage has ventured to show himself in our vicinity."

"Their scouts have been here and reconnoitered the place when you little dreamed of it," rejoined the messenger, "and I tell you they are now on their way here to attack you."

"Have you seen them?"

"Not myself, but my information is nonetheless reliable."

"Very well, sir, we will see to it," was the closing answer of the Major.

The news of the messenger created fresh alarm among the women and children, and a few of the garrison, myself among the number, thought our commander made too light of even a possible danger, considering how many helpless beings there were under his charge, who might fall victims to the slightest neglect; but the majority of the men thought with Beasly, that if even the report of the Indians being abroad in great numbers was true, they would not attack a place where they would be so certain to be repulsed with great slaughter. Our post was considered impregnable to any mere savage assault, and our overweening confidence in our fancied strength became the weakness by which we fell.

The fatal 30th of August, 1813—ah! Never shall I forget it! It was about the hour of noon, of a hot sultry day, and I was sitting in the shade of the houses, playing with a little curly-haired boy, my musket leaning against the palisades a few yards distant, when suddenly the sentinel fired his piece and shouted, "To arms! To arms! The Indians are upon us!"

Groups of men who were lounging about instantly sprang to their feet, grasped their weapons, and made a rush to the gate, which had carelessly been left wide open for the purpose of allowing persons to pass in and out at their convenience. At the same moment a large body of Indians bounded forward, with the most appalling yells, and poured in a destructive volley. Several fell dead and many others were severely wounded. We returned the fire—those of us who had been able to seize our muskets and get first to the defense—and numbers of the dusky foe were sent howling to the dust. Then began a most terrible fight and slaughter on both sides. The Indians, in a large compact body, were crowding forward to force their way in through the open gate, and we were striving to drive them back and shut them out. It was a hand-to-hand encounter, in which every sort of weapon was used. We stabbed them with bayonets, cut them with knives, knocked them down with muskets and bludgeons, and split open their skulls with axes. They fought in the same manner, with a tiger-like ferocity and with about equal success. Our yells and theirs mingled, as we grappled in the work of death, and White friend and dusky foe soon strewed the earth around, locked in a last bloody embrace.

At length a body rushed past us and took possession of one of the blockhouses, and as this somewhat thinned the immediate crowd at the gate, we were enabled, by redoubled exertions, to close and secure it. This gave us a momentary respite, and one we greatly needed, for our terrible exertions had nearly overcome us. For a minute I stood leaning against one of the palisades, panting and scarcely able to stand. I had received no serious injury, but I was much cut and bruised and covered with blood from head to foot. Before me was a horrible and sickening sight. Not less than ten of my comrades and some fifteen savages lay dead within a space of twenty feet square, with cloven skulls, glaring, death-glazed eyes, and bloody, distorted visages, while all around were wounded and dying men, whose deep groans and maddening shrieks were awful to hear. Among these was Major Beasly, who, in gallantly attempting to repair his error, had fallen mortally wounded and would command us no more. A large number of women, with the wildest cries of distress and woe, now came rushing forth from the cabins in search of fathers, sons, husbands, and brothers, and as fast as they could, they bore away their friends, the wounded, dying, and dead, with lamentations that pierced the heart and rent the air. It was an awful scene, but there was one more awful yet to come.

The Indians without the fort now rushed forward in a body and poured a murderous fire through the loopholes, by which a number of both sexes were killed and wounded. We now charged upon the loopholes, forced back the enemy, and gave him a galling fire in return. As soon as the savages could reload their weapons, they rallied and again charged upon the fort, and we in turn were obliged to give way. This species of warfare was continued for more than an hour, numbers falling on both sides. Meantime, from one of the blockhouses, a destructive fire was being poured upon the assailants, and in the other a most fearful struggle was taking place. The Indians who had rushed past us at the gate had taken possession of this, and it was necessary to dislodge them. This could only be accomplished by a close and deadly encounter, during which so many fell on both sides that the place literally ran with blood like a slaughterhouse. At length it was carried over the dead bodies of every Indian in it, and the guns turned upon the foe without, who now for the first time fell back in dismay. This again gave us a little respite, which we employed in putting to death every savage within the walls.

We now began to indulge the hope that the Indians, being so signally repulsed, would withdraw altogether, but in this we were terribly disappointed. Their bold and sanguinary chief, one Weatherford by name, collected, harangued, and urged them to a renewal of the contest, promising them success. He told them they had come to the assault numbering two to one of all the fort contained, counting men, women, and children, and if they did not carry it and avenge the death of their companions by an utter extermination of the Whites, they would be forever disgraced and be pointed at by even squaws as cowards unfit to live. His words roused in them the most vindictive fury, and procuring axes, they returned to the attack with all the ferocity of demons.

Our first knowledge of this fresh assault filled us with the most heart-sickening dismay. With the most appalling yells, a large body rushed to the gate and began to hew it down, the immediate assailants being covered by another large body of sharpshooters, who concealing themselves behind every available breastwork, kept up a steady fire upon the loopholes. We now, indeed, felt that our doom was sealed, but being determined to sell our lives dearly, we ordered the women into the cabins and returned boldly to the defense, doing all those men in our situation could do.

Alas! Of what avail? One by one our ranks were thinned, till at length the gate gave way with a crash and with the wildest yells of triumph, the dusky horde came pouring into the area. Our only alternative was now to rush into the cabins, make a last stand, and die with the women and children, for no one had any hope of escape.

The doors were thrown open by the terrified watchers of the strife, and most of the then living garrison succeeded in passing in and closing them, but several were overtaken and either toma-hawked or shot at the very thresholds. Two companions entered the same apartment with myself, and in there was a sight that at any less fearful time would have made our hearts ache. A wife lay in a swoon by the dead body of her husband; a prattling child had a hand of the bloody corpse and was trying to make it speak; a trembling old man, with white hair, was kneeling on the ground and sobbing with bowed head; there were women flying to and fro in a distracted state, wringing their hands, crying, and shrieking; and there were two or three wounded men, groaning and dying.

But to all these we gave little heed. Our work was still to fight to the last and die with the rest, and we began to load and fire through the windows upon the savages, who with yells of exultation, were now busy killing the wounded and tearing the reeking scalps from all.

I know not how long it was after this before the appalling cry of fire arose. Our foes had succeeded in setting the roofs in a blaze and now began to beat in the doors. Then such a shriek of horror as rent the air from the lips of women and children! Oh, merciful God! It was terrible beyond description! Even imagination sinks before it. It was paralyzing.

How I got to the burning roof I scarcely know, but I remember the flames of fire playing about me, of bursting through them, of leaping to the ground, of running to the wood, of stopping my ears against the shrieks behind! I escaped, but God only knows how. Sixteen others miraculously escaped also. All the rest perished, either in the flames or by the hands of their savage butchers. It was a massacre almost without a parallel. The blackened ruins of Fort Mimms held the bones of nearly three hundred victims of savage ferocity!

MOODY, THE JERSEY REFUGEE

In about the central part of Sussex County, New Jersey, two miles south of the village of Newton, the county seat, are two ponds or bodies of water which go by the name of the Big and Little Muckshaw. The lower or Little Muckshaw loses itself at its western extremity in a marsh or swamp, which is almost impassable, except after a long drought. This vicinity possesses some considerable interest from having been the haunt of one of those fiends in human shape, who preyed upon the substance of the patriotic citizens of the neighborhood during that dark and gloomy period in our Revolutionary contest, when even the Father of his country was wrapped in despondency at the gloomy prospect for the future.

Bonnel Moody was a ruffian of the deepest dye and possessed of all those qualities which constitute an accomplished freebooter and highwayman. He was shrewd, cunning, and artful as a fox, energetic and determined in the pursuit of an object, void of all pity or remorse, avaricious as a miser, and with a brute courage that made him formidable in combat; he was a dangerous enemy in the midst of the inhabitants of Sussex County, as they learned to their cost during the war.

His place of retreat, or rather his lair—for it was more like the haunt of some wild beast than the abode of human beings—was on the west side of the swamp above mentioned, where nature seemed to have provided him with a retreat more impregnable than art could possibly have furnished him without her aid. A point of land projects into the western side of the marsh, affording only a very narrow and difficult foothold for one man to pass between its base, and an inlet of the pond which washes the foot of the rocks. The ledge then recedes in the shape of a crescent, forming a little cove, with water in front and rocks behind and above. About forty-five yards from this point is a huge rock, sheltered and screened by overhanging trees and shrubs, in which is a cavern, where Moody and his gang of marauders found shelter and retreat when their deeds of rapine and murder had roused the inhabitants of the vicinity to rid themselves of the dangerous foe. This cavern is eighteen feet high in front, gradually receding until it meets the foundation at a distance of fifteen feet, and about fifty feet in length from north to south.

Beyond this cavern the ledge again approaches the marsh, into which it projects, forming an elbow almost impossible to pass around, and on the opposite side it again recedes, presenting a bold and rugged aspect, heightened by the gloom of perpetual shade, numerous cavern-like fissures, and masses of rock which have fallen from time to time from the overhanging ledge. One of these is a large, flat slab, about ten feet long, six high, and between three and four feet thick, which has fallen in such a position as to leave a passage behind it of about a yard in width. The rocks above project over this slab, so as to shield it effectually from that quarter, and a half dozen men might defend themselves behind this natural buckler against the attack of an army.

Such was the haunt of Moody and his congenial band of Tory cutthroats and murderers, and from here like a flock of ravenous wolves would they issue, when opportunity offered, and lay waste and destroy all within their reach until danger threatened, when they would retreat to this natural fastness with their ill-gotten plunder, here to divide and secrete it. From the brow of the ledge, which rises nearly a hundred feet from the water, they had a fair view of every avenue to their hiding place, and no one ever approached it alive except Moody and his associates, or perhaps some friend of theirs with provision or information. There were those so lost to principle as to furnish this crew of land-pirates with the necessities of life and with accurate intelligence of every movement on the part of the Americans which occurred in their vicinity. Several attempts to capture the wretch were frustrated by these loyal friends.

At one time, when a party, having tracked him for some

distance, were about to spring upon him, he was alarmed by a Negro in time to make his escape; and on another occasion a young woman mounted a horse and rode some twelve or fourteen miles of a dark night to warn him of a projected attack by a party of Whigs who had determined to capture him at all hazards. One cold winter night he broke into the house of a Mr. Ogden, and after robbing it of everything of any value, he took the old man out in the yard and made him take an oath not to make known his visit until a sufficient time had elapsed for himself and his party to make their escape. Two or three men who were working for Mr. Ogden, and who slept in a loft upstairs, not feeling bound by the old man's oath, alarmed the neighborhood and commenced a pursuit. Their track was easily followed in the snow, and in the morning, they came upon a camp where the marauders had slept overnight and where their fires were still burning. The chase was kept up until they reached Goshen, in the state of New York, where they recovered part of the plunder, but the rascals escaped. These expeditions in pursuit of the Tory wretch were called "Moody-hunting" and were followed up frequently with great determination and energy.

One night, about twelve o'clock, he made his appearance at the bedside of the jailor and demanded the key of the jail. The poor, frightened official readily gave it up, although he had often declared that he would not surrender it to him, and with it Moody opened the doors and set all the prisoners free. Two of them were condemned to death—one, who was condemned to die for robbery, being unacquainted with the neighborhood, wandered about all night and next day in the woods and was discovered in a hollow tree the next evening by a party of "coon hunters," who brought him back, and he was subsequently hung in front of the jail, protesting his innocence to the last. He was subsequently proved to be guiltless of the crime for which he suffered, and the wretch who actually committed the deed confessed on his deathbed that he it was who did the act for which another had suffered. On this occasion, Moody was more just than the law, and the prisoner's cause better than his fortune.

While the American army was encamped at Morristown, a man very shabbily dressed and mounted on a broken-down nag, all of whose "points" were exhibited to the fullest extent, was seen one day to enter the camp and pass leisurely through it, scrutinizing everything as he went, and although he assumed a perfect nonchalance and was to all appearance a simple-hearted and rather soft-headed country farmer, yet there was something in his manner which attracted the attention of an officer who was drilling a squad of recruits in the open air. One of these thought there was something about the face which he recognized and told his officer so. One of the squad was mounted and ordered to bring him back. Moody—for it was he who had thus boldly entered the American lines and reconnoitered their ranks—shot him dead as he came up and secreted the body by the side of the road. Another being sent to assist the first, Moody secreted himself in the woods and escaped.

Having been driven from his former haunts by the untiring activity of the Whigs, and being too well known to venture much abroad, he determined to join the British army in New York. While attempting to cross to the city with a companion in an open boat, they were captured, brought back to Morristown, and hung as traitors and spies. Moody was said to have come from Kingwood township, Hunterdon County, and was employed by the British to obtain recruits in New Jersey among the Tory inhabitants, act as a spy upon the Americans, and by his maraudings to keep the inhabitants so busy at home as to prevent their joining or aiding the American army.

THE WHITE HORSEMAN

The bell of the meetinghouse at Lexington rang out loud and shrill on that clear, frosty morning in April, 1775, startling from his slumbers the hardy yeoman, who as he leaped from his pallet and endeavored to rouse his dormant faculties, was not long in conjecturing the meaning of those untimely sounds. *Ding, dong, ding, dong*; how they thrilled along the nerves of the half-awakened sleeper as he tried to peer from his window into the gloom of the incipient day. And as those soul-stirring sounds echoed and reverberated through the chilling atmosphere, one and another household was awakened, and soon glowworm tapers might be seen flitting to and fro, until every house within reach of those reverberations gave token of wakefulness and activity.

Soon, as the first gray of the coming morning stole over the picture, groups and squads of armed and unarmed men appeared, all hurrying toward the point whence came the warning voice of the old bell as it continued its call *to arms*. There was no hesitation, no halting in the step of those who gathered around the person of Capt. Parker to learn the import of those thrilling clarion notes. Every man capable of bearing arms had been enrolled in the bands of the "minute men," and the presence of one hundred men about the doors of that old church gave token how well they deserved the title. "What's the matter, Cap'n? What's the matter?" was the query of each as he arrived on the ground, and all were answered alike: "The British are on the way to Concord to capture the stores, and we must let 'em know that they ain't going to have 'em without a brush."

There was, to the Americans, something cruel in the idea of being deprived, by force, of the very humble means of defense which they had been able after great exertions to collect, and although the determination to fight had not as yet been fully formed, every man saw at once but two alternatives: the loss of their stores, or bloodshed. The first they were not prepared to put up with, and the only course was to defend them. Still, they, one and all, determined not to take the initiative but let the haughty Britons bear the responsibility of firing the first shot.

They had not long to wait. The tramp of the British soldiers was soon heard on the road, and in a few moments the head of the column appeared in sight. The officer at the head, ordering two companies from column into line, rode forward, flourished his sword, and ordered the rebels to disperse. But they, notwithstanding the immensely superior force, did not at once obey, and the troops were ordered to fire. The first volley, which killed four Americans, was returned, and then Capt. Parker ordered every man to "take care of himself and fight on his own hook." Having sworn that he "never would run from the British," the captain continued to load and fire his piece until he was wounded. Dropping on his knees, he still continued his warfare until he was bayoneted in his tracks.

The whole of the scene described took place in full view of an old man named Hezekiah Wyman, a window in whose house overlooked the ground. Hezekiah was nearly eighty and had been deemed too old to be enrolled in the bands of the minute men, but he soon gave evidence of a spirit which led him to perform deeds of valor unequaled by any during the day.

"Wife," said he, turning to his aged partner, who had turned from the window horror-struck when the first volley was fired and it became evident there was to be a contest. "Wife, isn't there an old gun barrel somewhere up garret?"

"I believe there was, but what on earth, husband, do you want of a gun; you ain't going to fight the British, are you? Massy souls," continued she, seeing her husband moving toward the stairs. "What can you do with a gun, an old man like you, eighty last November; I should think you had seen enough of fighting already. There lies Capt. Parker and his men bleeding on the ground before your eyes."

The old man made no reply, but proceeded upstairs and soon

returned with an old rusty gun barrel in his hands, and in spite of his wife's incessant din, he went to the shop, and, having stocked it, put it in complete order for use. He then saddled his horse, a tall, raw-boned animal, white as the snow, and mounted him. Telling his wife to take good care of the house, he gave his horse the whip and took his way toward Concord. He soon met the British on the retreat and was not long in perceiving that there was a wasp's nest about their ears. Determined to do his part, he dashed forward and delivered the contents of his gun full in the face of the soldiers on the extreme left, and reining back his steed to reload, he dealt a second death with his never-failing bullet.

The tall, gaunt form of the assailant, his gray hairs floating in the breeze, and, above all, the color of his horse made him conspicuous among the crowds of Americans which now hovered on the British flanks, and the regulars gave him the cognomen of "Death on the pale horse." Innumerable bullets flew about his head as he made his first assault, but undismayed, the old patriot continued to appear and disappear first on one flank, then on the other, and again in the rear, dealing death among the Redcoats, until a vigorous charge of bayonets drove him and others back. He had by this time, however, run short of ammunition and was obliged to pick up some along the road from the boxes of those who had fallen.

He soon appeared again, and an officer yielded his life to the summons of that old rusty home-made firelock, before he was again driven off. But occasionally the old horse and his rider could be seen through the smoke, and the report of that old gun was the death knell to one of his enemies. Thus did he continue his work until Earl Percy arrived with reinforcements for the British, and with the aid of artillery drove the Americans back and held them in check while the harassed corps of Col. Smith could rest and refresh. No sooner were they on their way again, however, than the old Yankee was seen cantering at full speed over the hills, gun in hand, ready for another shot.

"Here comes 'Death on the pale horse' again," exclaimed the regulars. "Look out for yourselves, for one of us has got to die in spite of fate!" And one of them did die, for Hezekiah did not believe in wasting powder and ball when such large game was afoot.

Throughout that long and bloody march from Lexington to Charlestown, the appearance of the White Horseman was dreaded by the trained troops of Britain, for every wound made by Hezekiah was fatal. Even after they had entered Charlestown, his white steed would make its appearance from behind a barn, house, or other convenient shelter, and every crack of his piece sent a British soldier to his long account. Even to their tents on Bunker's Hill, Hezekiah followed them, and then finding no more opportunities, he reluctantly turned his horse's head homeward and reached his house unharmed and took his seat at his accustomed evening meal, which had awaited his coming, as though nothing unusual had happened.

"For goodness sake, husband," was his wife's first salutation, "where *have* you been! What have you been doing?"

"*Picking cherries*," replied he, "picking cherries."

BLACK DICK AND THE LYNCHERS:
A FEARFUL MISSISSIPPI TRAGEDY

The small city of Grand Gulf, in Mississippi, was on a certain Saturday night in May, 1848, a scene of the greatest alarm and excitement. A most brutal, and, as it was supposed at the time, a double murder had been committed by a notorious Negro named Dick. He was a man of great muscular power, activity, and resolution, and but for his uncontrollable temper and savage disposition, would have been of great value to any master. A gentleman named Taylor originally owned him, and although a person of great strength and courage, found much difficulty in keeping the refractory slave in subjection. At times he would run away and remain for days in the bush, and no one save his master cared to seek him. Mr. Taylor informed me that upon one occasion, when he came upon Dick unperceived by him, the fellow had a long knife in his hand with which he was butchering, in imagination, all of those who had incurred his displeasure, and his recollection of causes of offense must have been very accurate and the list of offenders a long one, to judge of the number of those over whose ideal slaughter he was gloating. It is said that when the idea of committing murder once fairly enters a man's brain, it never again abandons possession, but haunts him like a demon, urging him on, like the air-drawn dagger of the Thane. And so it proved with Dick.

A man named Greene, who owned a small "force," was engaged in the brick-making business, and envying Taylor the possession of so valuable a man as Dick, endeavored to purchase him. For a long time, Taylor refused, telling Greene honestly that Dick was a very troublesome Negro, one that could be kept in order only by an owner that he feared, and that he (Greene) had neither the physical ability nor the resolution to conquer him.

At length, wearied with Greene's pertinacity, Taylor set a price upon his man, so exorbitant indeed that he had no idea of its being paid, but Greene quickly closed the bargain, purchasing at the same time a tyrannical master and his own death-warrant.

As soon as Dick was released from Taylor's control, he gave free vent to his natural disposition, and in a very short time inspired his master, his overseer, and in fact everyone upon the plantation with such fear that he became virtually the master of the place. His owner did not dare to punish him, nor did he think it at all safe to hint of selling him, and things went from bad to worse until finally a tragedy was enacted, sufficiently bloody to gratify even the morbid tastes of the readers of Reynolds' school of novels.

Greene, returning to the house very early on the above-mentioned Saturday and feeling quite unwell, ordered Dick's wife, a house servant, to make him a cup of tea. He then threw himself upon the bed and had nearly fallen asleep when a loud noise in the kitchen, shrieks, and cries of murder aroused him. A Negro boy rushed into the room and begged him to come into the kitchen and prevent Dick from murdering his wife.

Greene sprang from the bed, and without stopping to dress, ran into the kitchen where he found that Dick had knocked down the woman Maria with a flat-iron, for no other reason than because he had ordered her to iron a vest for him immediately, as he wanted to go to a ball, and she replied that she would do so as soon as she had prepared a cup of tea for her master, but could not before.

Before Greene could interpose either remonstrance or force, Dick—whose blood was up—seized him by the throat. Greene endeavored to retreat and succeeded in making his way to his bed-room, Dick still clinging to him. In this room two loaded guns leaned against the wall, but before Greene could possess himself of either, Dick, who yet held him by the throat, fired two pistols at his head—strange to say, without any other effect than breaking the glass of a window behind them.

Releasing his clasp of Greene's throat, Dick now seized him by the hair, drew him out of the room, across the piazza, and into the grass plot in front of the cottage, and in less time than the description of the deed occupies, cut him literally to pieces, inflicting seven wounds that would either of them have been mortal and hacking and scarring the body all over.

The plantation Negroes were all present, but offered no assistance to their master. As soon as they recovered from their paralysis of fear, they ran and hid themselves in the woods.

When Dick had satisfied himself that his master was done for, with his bloody knife in his bloody hand, he rushed out of the enclosure and down the hill, to finish the punishment of his wife. She, with one other kitchen servant, was concealed in the foot of the hill, but when Dick called her, beside herself with fright, she left her hiding place and went to him. Without a word, the Negro cut her through and through, and then leaving her for dead, started down Bluff Road, which led around the town to the mouth of the Big Black River and would doubtless have made his escape but for the shrewdness of the same young Negro who had at first given Greene the alarm.

Without stopping to see the result of the affray, the lad immediately ran down to the town, went first to a tavern upon the main road, and then to another some distance up the river and near Bluff Road. The boarders at either place were just awaiting the tea bell and mustered pretty strongly. Fifty men, at least, immediately started for the scene of the murder, a part by the direct road and a part through the lad's advice—by the circuitous one.

The latter party captured the murderer, knife in hand, and brought him directly to the sheriff's office, when they were met by the other and stronger company, headed by a brother of the murdered man. They also had made a capture, and one that caused more alarm, for a time, than the tragedy itself.

Halfway between the bluff and the town, a Negro heading for the latter, at full speed, with a butcher knife in one hand and hatchet in the other, ran right among them and was seized and pinioned. The affair began to look like an insurrection among the Negroes. The first party kept on to Greene's house and, searching it, found concealed in and under Dick's bed twenty-one dangerous weapons of several kinds.

The two parties, as I have before said, met at the sheriff's office. The first, much the stronger of the two, declared their intention of taking the prisoner and burning him alive that very night and were only prevented from so doing by the representations of the sheriff, that if they did, all chance of discovering those who were implicated with Dick would be thrown away, and besides, that the next day being Sunday, the execution of Dick would be witnessed by many plantation Negroes and might produce a salutary effect upon them.

Having procured a temporary reprieve, the sheriff endeavored to obtain assistance enough to seize the Negro, but was unsuccessful, and on the next day the murderer was hung and his body burned. Had it not been for the active interference of a Mr. Smith, the then-editor of the Grand Gulf paper, the prisoner would have been burned at the stake; but the latter begged that a jury might be selected and the prisoner receive at least the form of a trial. The question was put to a vote, and all but five or six of the hundreds assembled voted in favor of a jury.

There was no real necessity for anticipating thus the slow, but in this case, sure action of the law, and the only excuse that it will admit of is the fact that sixteen Negroes had been arrested the previous night who proved to have been implicated with Dick—at least so far as furnishing him with weapons. This created a very general fear of an intended insurrection, which perhaps the immediate execution of the ringleader might quell.

BIG JOE LOGSTON'S DESPERATE
ENCOUNTER WITH TWO INDIANS

Joe Logston was one of that class of half horse, half alligator Kentuckians who could, to use his own words, "out-run, out-hop, out-jump, throw down, drag out, and whip any man in the country." Joe was a powerful fellow, of six feet three in his stockings and proportionally stout and muscular, with a handsome, good-natured face and a fist like a sledge-hammer. Fear was a word he knew not the meaning of, and to fight was his pastime, particularly if his scalp was the prize he fought for.

On one occasion he was mounted on his own favorite pony—Joe owned two or three others which he had "run" from the Indians—which was leisurely picking its way along the trail, with his head down and half asleep, when he came to a fine vine of grapes. Joe laid his gun across the pommel of his saddle, set his hat on it, and filled it with grapes. He turned into the path and rode carelessly along, eating his grapes, and the first intimation he had of danger was the crack of two rifles, one from each side of the road. One of the balls passed through the paps of his breast, which for a male were remarkably prominent, almost as much as those of many nurses. The ball just grazed the skin between the paps but did not injure the breast bone. The other ball struck the horse behind the saddle, and he sunk in his tracks.

Thus was Joe eased off his horse in a manner more rare than welcome. Still, he was on his feet in an instant, with his rifle in his hands, and might have taken to his heels, and we will venture the opinion that no Indian could have caught him. That, he said, was not his sort. He had never left a battleground without leaving his mark, and he was resolved that that should not be the first. The moment the guns fired, one very athletic Indian sprang toward him with tomahawk in hand. His eye was on him, and his gun to his eye, ready, as soon as he approached near enough to make a sure shot, to let him have it. As soon as the Indian discovered this, he jumped behind two pretty large saplings, some small distance apart, neither of which were large enough to cover his body, and to save himself as well as he could, he kept springing from one to the other.

Joe, knowing that he had two enemies on the ground, kept a look out for the other by a quick glance of the eye. He presently discovered him behind a tree loading his gun. The tree was not quite large enough to hide him. When in the act of pushing down his bullet, he exposed pretty fairly his hips. Joe, in the twinkling of an eye, wheeled and let him have his load in the part exposed. The big Indian then, with a mighty "Ugh!" rushed toward him with his raised tomahawk.

Here were two warriors met, each determined to conquer or die, each the Goliath of his nation. The Indian had rather the advantage in size and frame, but Joe in weight and muscular strength. The Indian made a halt at the distance of fifteen or twenty feet and threw his tomahawk with all his force, but Joe had his eye on him and dodged it. It flew quite out of the reach of either of them. Joe then clubbed his gun and made at the Indian, thinking to knock him down. The Indian sprang into some brush or saplings to avoid his blows. The Indian depended entirely on dodging, with the help of the saplings.

At length, Joe, thinking he had a pretty fair chance, made a side blow with such force that missing the dodging Indian, the gun, now reduced to a naked barrel, was drawn quite out of his hands, and flew entirely out of reach. The Indian now gave another exulting "Ugh" and sprang at him with all the savage fury he was master of. Neither of them had a weapon in his hands, and the Indian seeing Logston bleeding freely, thought he could throw him down and dispatch him. In this he was mistaken. They seized each other, and a desperate scuffle ensued. Joe could throw him down, but could not hold him there. The Indian being naked, with his hide oiled, had greatly the advantage in a ground scuffle and would still slip out of Joe's grasp and rise.

After throwing him five or six times, Joe found that between loss of blood and violent exertions, his wind was leaving him and that he must change the mode of warfare or lose his scalp, which he was not yet willing to spare. He threw the Indian again and, without attempting to hold him, jumped from him and, as he rose, aimed a fist blow at his head which caused him to fall back, and as he would rise, Joe gave him several blows in succession, the Indian rising slower each time. He at last succeeded in giving him a pretty fair blow in the burr of the ear, with all his force, and he fell, as Joe thought, pretty near dead. Joe jumped on him and, thinking he could dispatch him by choking, grasped his neck with his left hand, keeping his right one free for contingencies.

Joe soon found the Indian was not so dead as he thought and that he was making some use of his right arm, which lay across his body, and on casting his eye down, discovered the Indian was making an effort to unsheathe a knife that was hanging at his belt. The knife was so short and so sunk in the sheath that it was necessary to force it up by pressing against the point. This the Indian was trying to effect, and with good success. Joe kept his eye on it and let the Indian work the handle out, when he suddenly grabbed it, jerked it out of the sheath, and sunk it up to the handle in the Indian's breast, who gave a death groan and expired.

Joe now thought of the other Indian, and not knowing how far he had succeeded in killing or crippling him, sprang to his feet. He found the crippled Indian had crawled some distance toward them and had propped his broken back against a log and was trying to raise his gun to shoot him, but in attempting to do which he would fall forward and had to push against his gun to raise himself again. Joe, seeing that he was safe, concluded that he had fought long enough for healthy exercise that day, and not liking to be killed by a crippled Indian, he made for the fort. He got in about nightfall, and a hard-looking case he was—blood and dirt from the crown of his head to the sole of his feet, no horse, no hat, no gun—with an account of the battle that some of his comrades could scarce believe to be much else than one of his big stories, in which he would sometimes indulge. He told them they must go and judge for themselves.

Next morning a company was made up to go to Joe's battle-ground. When they approached it, Joe's accusers became more confirmed, as there was no appearance of dead Indians and nothing Joe had talked of but the dead horse. They, however, found a trail as if something had been dragged away. On pursuing it they found the big Indian at a little distance, beside a log, covered up with leaves. Still pursuing the trail, though not so plain, some hundred yards farther they found the broken-backed Indian lying on his back with his own knife sticking up to the hilt in his body, just below the breast-bone, evidently to show that he had killed himself and that he had not come to his end by the hand of an enemy. They had a long search before they found the knife with which Joe killed the big Indian. They at last found it forced down into the ground below the surface, apparently with the weight of a person's heel. This had been done by the crippled Indian. The great efforts he must have made alone, in that condition, show among thousands of other instances what Indians are capable of under the greatest extremities.

Some years after the above took place, peace with the Indians was restored. That frontier, like many others, became infested with a gang of outlaws who commenced stealing horses and committing various depredations. To counteract which, a company of regulators, as they were called, was raised. In a contest between these and the depredators, Big Joe Logston lost his life.

THE PATRIOTIC QUAKERESS

When the British army held possession of Philadelphia, General Harris' headquarters were in Second Street, the fourth door below Spruce, in a house which was before occupied by General Cadwalader. Directly opposite resided William and Lydia Darrah, members of the Society of Friends. A superior officer of the British army, believed to be the adjutant general, fixed upon one of their chambers a back room for private conference, and two of them frequently met there with fire and candles in close consultation.

About the 2nd of December, the adjutant general told Lydia that they would be in the room at seven o'clock and remain late and that they wished the family to retire early to bed, adding, that when they were going away, they would call her to let them out and extinguish their fire and candles. She accordingly sent all the family to bed, but, as the officer had been so particular, her curiosity was excited. She took off her shoes and put her ear to the key-hole of the conclave. She overheard an order read for all the British troops to march out, late in the evening of the 4th, and attack General Washington's army, then encamped at White Marsh. On hearing this, she returned to her chamber and laid herself down. Soon after, the officers knocked at her door, but she rose only at the third summons, having feigned to be asleep.

Her mind was so much agitated that, from this moment, she could neither eat nor sleep, supposing it to be in her power to save the lives of thousands of her countrymen, but not knowing how she was to convey the necessary information to General Washington, not daring to confide it even to her husband. The time left was, however, short; she quickly determined to make her

138

way, as soon as possible, to the American outposts. She informed her family that, as they were in want of flour, she would go to Frankford for some; her husband insisted that she should take with her the servant maid, but to his surprise she positively refused.

She got access to General Howe and solicited, which he readily granted, a pass through the British troops on the lines. Leaving her bag at the mill, she hastened toward the American lines and encountered on her way an American, Lieutenant Colonel Craig of the light horse, who with some of his men, was on the look-out for information. He knew her and inquired whither she was going. She answered, in quest of her son, an officer in the American army, and prayed the colonel to alight and walk with her. He did so, ordering his troops to keep in sight.

To him she disclosed her momentous secret, after having obtained from him the most solemn promise never to betray her individually since her life might be at stake with the British. He conducted her to a house near at hand, directed a female in it to give her something to eat, and then speeded for headquarters where he brought General Washington acquainted with what he had heard. Washington made, of course, all preparation for baffling the meditated surprise. Lydia returned home with her flour, sat up alone to watch the movement of the British troops, and heard their footsteps, but when they returned in a few days after, she did not dare to ask a question, though solicitous to learn the event.

The next evening, the adjutant general came in and requested her to walk up to his room, as he wished to put some questions. She followed him in terror, and when he locked the door and begged her with an air of mystery to be seated, she was sure that she was either suspected or had been betrayed. He inquired earnestly whether any of her family were up the last night he and the other officer met; she told him that they all retired at eight o'clock. He observed: "I know *you* were asleep, for I knocked at your chamber door three times before you heard me; I am entirely at a loss to imagine who gave Washington information of our intended attack, unless the walls of the house could speak. When we arrived near White Marsh, we found all their cannons mounted and the troops prepared to receive us, and we have marched back like a parcel of fools."

CROCKETT'S FIGHT WITH A COUGAR:
AS RELATED BY HIMSELF

Night was fast closing in, and as I began to think that I had just about sport enough for one day, I might as well look around for a place of shelter for the night and take a fresh start in the morning, by which time I was in hopes my horse would be recruited. Near the margin of the river, a large tree had been blown down, and I thought of making my lair in its top and approached it for that purpose. While beating among the branches, I heard a low growl, as much as to say, "Stranger, the apartments are already taken."

Looking about to see what sort of a bed-fellow I was likely to have, I discovered, not more than five or six paces from me, an enormous Mexican Cougar, eyeing me as an epicure surveys the table before he selects his dish, for I have no doubt the cougar looked upon me as the subject of a future supper. Rays of light darted from his large eyes, he showed his teeth like a Negro in hysterics, and he was crouching on his haunches ready for a spring, all of which convinced me that unless I was pretty quick upon the trigger, posterity would know little of the termination of my eventful career, and it would be far less glorious and useful than I intended to make it.

One glance satisfied me that there was no time to be lost, as Pat thought when falling from a church steeple and exclaimed, "This would be mighty pleasant, now, if it would only last," but there was no retreat either for me or the cougar, so I leveled my Betsey and blazed away. The report was followed by a furious growl, which is sometimes the case in Congress, and the next moment, when I expected to find the tarnal critter struggling with death, I beheld him shaking his head as if nothing more than a bee had stung him.

The ball had struck him on the forehead and glanced off, doing no other injury than stunning him for an instant and tearing off the skin, which tended to infuriate him the more. The cougar wasn't long in making up his mind what to do, nor was I neither, but he would have it all his own way and vetoed my motion to back out.

I had not retreated three steps before he sprang at me like a steamboat; I stepped aside, and as he lit upon the ground, I struck him with the barrel of my rifle, but he didn't mind that, but wheeled around and made at me again. The gun was now of no use, so I threw it away and drew my hunting knife, for I knew we should come to close quarters before the fight would be over. This time, he succeeded in fastening on my left arm and was just beginning to amuse himself by tearing the flesh off with his fangs, when I ripped my knife into his side and he let go his hold, much to my satisfaction.

He wheeled about and came at me with increased fury, occasioned by the smarting of his wounds. I now tried to blind him, knowing that if I succeeded, he would become an easy prey, so as he approached me, I watched my opportunity and aimed a blow at his eyes with my knife, but unfortunately it struck him on the nose and he paid no other attention to it than by a shake of the head and a low growl. He pressed me close, and as I was stepping backward, my foot tripped in a vine and I fell to the ground.

He was down upon me like a nighthawk upon a June bug. He seized hold of the outer part of my right thigh, which afforded him considerable amusement; the hinder part of his body was towards my face. I grasped his tail with my left hand and tickled his ribs with my hunting knife, which I held in my right. Still the critter wouldn't let go his hold, and as I found that he would lacerate my leg dreadfully unless he was speedily shaken off, I tried to hurl him down the bank into the river, for our scuffle had already brought us to the edge of the bank. I stuck my knife into his side and summoned all my strength to throw him over. He resisted, was desperate heavy, but at last I got him so far down the declivity that he lost his balance and rolled over and over till he landed on the margin of the river, but in his fall, he dragged me along with him.

Fortunately, I fell uppermost and his neck presented a fair mark for my hunting knife. Without allowing myself time even to draw breath, I aimed one desperate blow at his neck and the knife entered his gullet up to the handle and reached his heart. He struggled for a few moments and died. I have had many fights with bears, but they were mere child's play; this was the first fight ever I had with a cougar, and I hope it may be the last.

ADVENTURES OF SIMON KENTON

In the summer of 1778, Colonel Bowman ordered Simon Kenton, the celebrated Indian fighter of Kentucky, to take his friend Montgomery and another young man named Clarke and go on a secret expedition to an Indian town on the Little Miami, against which the colonel meditated an expedition and of the exact condition of which he wished to have certain information. They instantly set out in obedience to their orders and reached the neighborhood of the town without being discovered. They examined it attentively and walked around the houses during the night with perfect impunity. Thus far all had gone well, and had they been contented to return after the due execution of their orders, they would have avoided the heavy calamity which awaited them.

But, unfortunately, during their nightly promenade, they stumbled upon a pound in which were a number of Indian horses. The temptation was not to be resisted. They each mounted a horse, but not satisfied with that, they could not find it in their hearts to leave a single animal behind them, and as some of the horses seemed indisposed to change masters, the affair was attended with so much fracas that at last they were discovered. The cry ran through the village at once that the Long Knives were stealing their horses right before the doors of their wigwams, and old and young, squaws, boys, and warriors, all sallied out with loud screams to save their property from these greedy spoilers. Kenton and his friends quickly discovered that they had overshot the mark and that they must ride for their lives, and while two of them rode in front and led, the other brought up the rear and, plying his whip from right to left, did not permit a single animal to lag behind.

In this manner they dashed through the woods at a furious rate with the hue and cry after them, until their course was suddenly stopped by an impenetrable swamp. Here, from necessity, they paused for a few moments and listened attentively. Hearing no sounds of pursuit, they resumed their course, and skirting the swamp for some distance, in the vain hope of crossing it, they bent their course in a straight direction toward the Ohio. They rode during the whole night without resting a moment, and halting for a few minutes at daylight, they continued their journey throughout the day and the whole of the following night, and by this uncommon expedition, on the morning of the second day they reached the northern bank of the Ohio.

Crossing the river would now ensure their safety, but this was likely to prove a difficult undertaking, and the close pursuit, which they had reason to expect, rendered it necessary to lose as little time as possible. The wind was high and the river rough and boisterous. It was determined that Kenton should cross with the horses, while Clark and Montgomery should construct a raft in order to transport their guns, baggage, and ammunition to the opposite shore. The necessary preparations were soon made, and Kenton, after forcing his horses into the river, plunged in himself and swam by their side. In a very few minutes the high waves completely overwhelmed him and forced him considerably below the horses that stemmed the current much more vigorously than himself.

The horses being thus left to themselves, turned about and swam again to the Ohio shore, where Kenton was compelled to follow them. Again he forced them into the water, and again they returned to the same spot, until Kenton became so exhausted by repeated efforts as to be unable to swim. A council was then held and the question proposed: "what was to be done?" That the Indians would pursue them was certain; that the horses would not and could not be made to cross the river in its present state was equally certain. Should they abandon their horses and cross on the raft or remain and take such fortune as heaven should send them? The latter alternative was unanimously adopted. Death or captivity might be tolerated, but the loss of so beautiful a lot of horses, after having worked so hard for them, was not to be thought of for a moment.

As soon as it was determined that themselves and the horses were to share the same fate, it again became necessary to fix upon some probable plan of saving them. Should they move up or down the river or remain where they were? The latter course was adopted. It was supposed that the wind would fall at sunset and the river become sufficiently calm to admit of their passage, and as it was supposed probable that the Indians might be upon them before night, it was determined to conceal the horses in a neighboring ravine while they should take their stations in an adjoining wood. A more miserable plan could not have been adopted. If they could not consent to sacrifice their horses in order to save their own lives, they should have moved either up or down the river and thus have preserved the distance from the Indians which their rapidity of movement had gained.

The Indians would have followed their trail and, being twenty-four hours march behind, could never have overtaken them. But neglecting this obvious consideration, they stupidly sat down until sunset, expecting that the river would become more calm. The day passed away in tranquility, but at night the wind blew harder than ever, and the water became so rough, that even their raft would have been scarcely able to cross. Not an instant more should have been lost in moving from so dangerous a post, but as if totally infatuated, they remained where they were until morning, thus wasting twenty-four hours of most precious time in total idleness. In the morning the wind abated and the river became calm, but it was now too late. Their horses, recollecting the difficulty of the passage on the preceding day, had become as obstinate and heedless as their masters and positively and repeatedly refused to take the water.

Finding every effort to compel them entirely unavailing, their masters at length determined to do what ought to have been done at first. Each resolved to mount a horse and make the best of his way down the river to Louisville. Had even this resolution, however tardily adopted, been executed with decision, the party would probably have been saved, but after they were mounted, instead of leaving the ground instantly, they went back upon their own trail in the vain effort to regain possession of the rest of their horses, which had broken from them in the last effort to drive them into the water. They wearied out their good genius and literally fell victims to their love for horse-flesh.

They had scarcely ridden one hundred yards—Kenton in the center, the others upon the flanks, with an interval of two hundred yards between them—when Kenton heard a loud halloo, apparently coming from the spot which they had just left. Instead of getting out of the way as fast as possible and trusting to the speed of his horse and the thickness of the wood for safety, he put the last capping stone to his imprudence and, dismounting, walked leisurely back to meet his pursuers and thus give them as little trouble as possible. He quickly beheld three Indians and one White man, all well mounted. Wishing to give the alarm to his companions, he raised his rifle to his shoulder, took a steady aim at the breast of the foremost Indian, and drew the trigger. His gun had become wet on the raft and flashed.

The enemy was instantly alarmed and dashed at him. Now, at last, where flight could be of no service, Kenton betook himself to his heels and was pursued by four horsemen at full speed. He instantly directed his steps to the thickest part of the wood, where there was much fallen timber and a rank growth of underwood, and had succeeded, as he thought, in baffling his pursuers, when, just as he was leaving the fallen timber and entering the open wood, an Indian on horseback galloped round the corner of the wood and approached him so rapidly as to render flight useless. The horseman rode up, holding out his hand and calling out "Brother! Brother!" in a tone of great affection. Kenton observes that if his gun would have made fire, he would have "brothered" him to his heart's content, but being totally unarmed, he called out that he would surrender if they would give him quarter and good treatment.

Promises were cheap with the Indian, and he showered them out by the dozen, continuing all the while to advance with extended hands and a writhing grin upon his countenance, which was intended for a smile of courtesy. Seizing Kenton's hand, he grasped it with violence. Kenton, not liking the manner of his captor, raised his gun to knock him down, when an Indian who had followed him closely through the brushwood instantly sprung upon his back and pinioned his arms to his side. The one who had just approached him then seized him by the hair and shook him until his teeth rattled, while the rest of the party coming up all fell upon Kenton with their tongues and ramrods, until he thought they would scold or beat him to death. They were the owners of the horses which he had carried off and now took ample revenge for the loss of their property. At every stroke of their ramrods over his head—and they were neither few nor far between—they would repeat in a tone of strong indignation, "Steal Indian hoss!! Hey!!"

Their attention, however, was soon directed to Montgomery, who, having heard the noise attending Kenton's capture, very gallantly hastened up to his assistance, while Clark very prudently consulted his own safety in betaking himself to his heels, leaving his unfortunate companions to shift for themselves. Montgomery halted within gunshot and appeared busy with the pan of his gun, as if preparing to fire. Two Indians instantly sprung off in pursuit of him, while the rest attended to Kenton. In a few minutes Kenton heard the crack of two rifles in quick succession, followed by a halloo, which announced the fate of his friend. The Indians quickly returned, waving the bloody scalp of Montgomery, and with countenances and gestures which menaced him with a similar fate.

They then proceeded to secure their prisoner. They first compelled him to lie upon his back and stretch out his arms to their full length. They then passed a stout stick at right angles across his breast, to each extremity of which his wrists were fastened by thongs made of buffalo hide. Stakes were then driven into the earth near his feet, to which they were fastened in a similar manner. A halter was then tied around his neck and fastened to a sapling which grew near, and finally a strong rope was passed under his belly, lashed strongly to the pole which lay transversely upon his breast, and finally wrapped around his arms at the elbows, in such a manner as to pinion them to the pole with a painful violence and render him literally incapable of moving hand, foot, or head in the slightest manner.

During the whole of this severe operation, neither their tongues nor hands were by any means idle. They cuffed him from time to time with great heartiness, until his ears rung again, and abused him for a "Tief! A hoss steal! A rascal!" and finally, for a "Cussed White man!" I may here observe, that all the western Indians had picked up a good many English words, particularly our oaths, which from the frequency with which they were used by our hunters and traders, they probably looked upon as the very root and foundation of the English language. Kenton remained in this painful attitude throughout the night, looking forward to certain death and most probably torture as soon as he should reach their towns. Their rage against him seemed to increase rather than abate from indulgence, and in the morning, it displayed itself in a form at once ludicrous and cruel.

Among the horses which Kenton had taken, and which their original owners had now recovered, was a fine but wild young colt, totally unbroken and with all his honors of mane and tail undocked. Upon him Kenton was mounted, without saddle or bridle, with his hands tied behind him and his feet fastened under the horse's belly. The country was rough and bushy, and Kenton had no means of protecting his face from the brambles, through which it was expected that the colt would dash. As soon as the rider was firmly fastened to his back, the colt was turned loose with a sudden lash, but after exerting a few curvettes and caprioles, to the great distress of his rider but to the infinite amusement of the Indians, he appeared to take compassion on his rider and, falling into a line with the other horses, avoided the brambles entirely and went on very well. In this manner he rode through the day. At night he was taken from the horse and confined as before.

On the third day they came within a few miles of Chillicothe. Here the party halted and dispatched a messenger to inform the village of their arrival in order to give them time to prepare for his reception. In a short time, Blackfish, one of their chiefs, arrived and, regarding Kenton with a stern countenance, thundered out in very good English, "You have been stealing horses?"

"Yes sir."

"Did Captain Boone tell you to steal our horses?"

"No sir, I did it of my own accord." This frank confession was too irritating to be borne. Blackfish made no reply, but brandishing a hickory switch which he held in his hand, he applied it so briskly to Kenton's naked back and shoulders as to bring the blood freely and occasion acute pain.

Thus, alternately beaten and scolded, he marched on to the village. At the distance of a mile from Chillicothe, he saw every inhabitant of the town, men, women, and children, running out to feast their eyes with a view of the prisoner. Every individual, down to the smallest child, appeared in a paroxysm of rage. They whooped, they yelled, they hooted, they clapped their hands, and poured upon him a flood of abuse to which all that he had yet received was gentleness and civility. With loud cries, they demanded that their prisoner should be tied to the stake. The hint was instantly complied with.

A stake was quickly fastened into the ground. The remnant of Kenton's shirt and breeches was torn from his person—the squaws officiating with great dexterity in both operations—and his hands being tied together and raised above his head were fastened to the top of the stake. The whole party then danced around him until midnight, yelling and screaming in their usual frantic manner, striking him with switches and slapping him with the palms of their hands. He expected every moment to undergo the torture of fire, but that was reserved for another time. They wished to prolong the pleasure of tormenting him as much as possible, and after having caused him to anticipate the bitterness of death until a late hour of the night, they released him from the stake and conveyed him to the village.

Early in the morning he beheld the scalp of Montgomery stretched upon a hoop and drying in the air before the door of one of their principal houses. He was quickly led out and ordered to run the gauntlet. A row of boys, women, and men extended to the distance of a quarter of a mile. At the starting place stood two grim-looking warriors with butcher knives in their hands, at the extremity of the line was an Indian beating a drum, and a few paces beyond the drum was the door of the council house. Clubs, switches, hoe-handles, and tomahawks were brandished along the whole line, causing the sweat involuntarily to stream from his pores at the idea of the discipline which his naked skin was to receive during the race.

The moment for starting arrived, the great drum at the door of the council house was struck, and Kenton sprung forward in the race. Kenton avoided the row of his enemies and, turning to the east, drew the whole party in pursuit of him. He doubled several times with great activity, and at length observing an opening, darted through it, and pressed forward to the council house with a rapidity which left his pursuers far behind. One or two of the Indians succeeded in throwing themselves between him and the goal, and from these alone he received a few blows, but was much less injured than he could at first have supposed possible.

As soon as the race was over, a council was held in order to determine whether he should be burnt to death on the spot or carried round to the other villages and exhibited to every tribe. The latter course was determined on, and Kenton passed through many difficulties and underwent much suffering. For three weeks he was vibrating between life and death, where no wisdom, or foresight, or exertion of his own could save him. He was eight times exposed to the gauntlet and three times tied to the stake, at each of which he expected nothing but death. Finally, however, he was sent to Detroit.

Here he remained in a state of easy restraint from October 1778 until June 1779, when he made his escape and arrived safely at Louisville after a march of thirty days.

A SHE-DEVIL AMONG THE TORIES

Nancy Hart and her husband settled before the Revolutionary War a few miles above the ford on Broad River in Elbert County, Georgia. An apple orchard still remains to point out the spot. In altitude, Mrs. Hart was a Patagonian and remarkably well-limbed and muscular. In a word, she was "lofty and sour." Marked by nature with prominent features, circumstances and accident added, perhaps, not a little to her peculiarities. She was horribly cross-eyed, as well as *cross-grained*, but nevertheless, she was a sharp-shooter. Nothing was more common than to see her in full pursuit of the bounding stag. The huge antlers that hung round her cabin, or upheld her trusty gun, gave proof of her skill in gunnery, and the white comb, drained of its honey and hung up for ornament, testified to her powers in bee-finding.

The clouds of war gathered and burst with a dreadful explosion in this state. Nancy's spirit rose with the tempest. She declared and proved herself a friend to her country, ready "to do or die."

On the occasion of an excursion from the British camp at Augusta, a party of Tories penetrated into the interior and, having savagely murdered Colonel Dooly in bed, in his own house, they proceeded up the country for the purpose of perpetrating further atrocities. On their way, a detachment of five of the party diverged to the east and crossed Broad River to make discoveries about the neighborhood and pay a visit to their old acquaintance, Nancy Hart. On reaching her cabin, they entered it unceremoniously, receiving from her no welcome but a scowl, and informed her they had come to know the truth of a story circulating about her that she had secreted a noted rebel from a company of King's men, who were pursuing him and who, but for her aid, would have caught and hung him. Nancy undauntedly avowed her agency in the fugitive's escape.

She told them she had at first heard the tramp of a horse rapidly approaching and had then seen a horseman coming towards her cabin. As he came nearer, she knew him to be a Whig and flying from pursuit. She let down the bars a few steps from her cabin and motioned him to enter, to pass through both doors, front and rear, of her single-roomed house, to take the swamp and secure himself as well as he could. She then put up the bars, entered her cabin, closed the doors, and went about her business. Presently some Tories rode up to the bars and called out boisterously to her. She muffled her head and face and, opening the door, inquired why they disturbed a sick, lone woman. They said they had traced a man they wanted to catch near her house and asked if anyone on horseback had passed that way. She answered no, but said she saw somebody on a sorrel horse turn out of the path into the woods, some two or three hundred yards back. "That must be the fellow," said the Tories, and asking her direction as to the way he took, they turned about and went off "Well fooled," said Nancy, "in an opposite course to that of my Whig boy; when, if they had not been so lofty minded, but had looked on the ground inside the bars, they would have seen his horse's tracks up to that door, as plain as you can see the tracks on this here floor, and out of t'other door down the path to the swamp."

This bold story did not much please the Tory party, but they could not wreak their revenge upon the woman, who thus unscrupulously avowed her daring aid to a rebel and the cheat she had put upon his pursuers, otherwise than by ordering her to aid and comfort them by giving them something to eat. She replied, "I never feed King's men, if I can help it. The villains have put it out of my power to feed even my own family and friends by stealing and killing all my poultry and pigs, except that one old gobbler you see in the yard."

"Well, and that you shall cook for us," said one, who appeared the head of the party, and raising his musket, he shot down the turkey, which another of the men brought into the house and handed to Mrs. Hart, to clean and cook without delay. She stormed and swore awhile—for Nancy occasionally swore—but seeming, at last, resolved to make a merit of necessity, began with alacrity the arrangements for cooking, assisted by her daughter, a little girl some ten or twelve years old, and sometimes by one of the soldiers, with whom she seemed in a tolerably good humor, exchanging rude jests with him. The Tories, pleased with her freedom, invited her to partake of the liquor they had brought with them, an invitation which was accepted with witty thanks.

The spring, of which every settlement has one near at hand, was just at the edge of the swamp, and a short distance within it was a high snag-topped stump, on which was placed a conch shell. This rude trumpet was used by the family to give information by means of a variation of notes to Mr. Hart or his neighbors, who might be at work in the field or clearing just beyond the swamp, that the "Britishers" or Tories were about, that the master was wanted at the cabin, or that he was to "keep close" or "make tracks" for another swamp. Pending the operations of cooking, Mrs. Hart had sent her daughter, Sukey, to the spring for water, with directions to blow the conch in such a way as would inform him that there were Tories in the cabin and that he should "keep close" with his three neighbors who were with him till he heard the conch again.

The party had become merry over their jug and sat down to feast upon the slaughtered gobbler. They had cautiously stacked their arms where they were in view and within reach, and Mrs. Hart, assiduous in her attentions upon the table and to her guests, occasionally passed between them and their muskets. Water was called for, and as there was none in the cabin—Mrs. Hart having so contrived that—Sukey was again sent to the spring, instructed by her mother to blow the conch so as to call up Mr. Hart and his neighbors immediately. Meanwhile, Mrs. Hart had slipped out one of the pieces of pine which constitutes a "chinking" between the logs of the cabin and had dexterously put out of the house, through that space, two of the five guns.

She was detected in the act of putting out the third. The party sprang to their feet. Quick as thought, Mrs. Hart brought the piece she held to her shoulder and declared she would kill the first man who approached her. All were terror-struck, for Nancy's obliquity caused each one to imagine her aim was at him. At length one of them made a motion to advance upon her. True to her threat, she fired. He fell dead upon the floor. Instantly seizing another musket, she brought it to the position in readiness to fire again. By this time Sukey had returned from the spring and, taking up the remaining gun, carried it out of the house, saying to her mother, "Daddy and them will soon be here."

This information increased the alarm of the Tories, who understood the necessity of recovering their arms immediately. But each hesitated, in the confident belief that Mrs. Hart had one eye, at least, upon him for a mark. They proposed a general rush. No time was to be lost by the bold woman; she fired again and brought down another Tory. Sukey had another musket in readiness, which her mother took and, posting herself in the doorway, called upon the party to "surrender their Tory carcasses to a Whig woman." They agreed to surrender and proposed to "shake hands upon the strength of it," but the conqueror kept them in their places for a few moments till her husband and his neighbors came up to the door.

They were about to shoot down the Tories, but Mrs. Hart stopped them, saying they had surrendered to *her*, and her spirit being up to boiling heat, she swore that "shooting was too good for them." This hint was enough. The dead man was dragged out of the house; the wounded Tory and the others were bound, taken out beyond the bars, and hung. The tree upon which they were hung was pointed out, in 1838, by one who lived in those bloody times and who also showed the spot once occupied by Mrs. Hart's cabin, accompanying the designation with the emphatic remark: "Poor Nancy—she was a honey of a patriot, but the devil of a wife."

THE ROSE OF GUADALOUPE:
A TEXAN RANGER'S STORY

I don't know much about story-telling, boys," said the oldest Ranger of our party as he cleared his throat and replenished his pipe, "but I can tell you of a thing that once happened in my settlement, which, if it is not altogether new to most of you, at least has the plain truth to recommend it.

"Some of you recollect old Andrew Lockhart, who used to live down in the big bend of the Warloupe (Guadaloupe), just below the Quero settlement. At the time I speak of, he had a daughter just seventeen and as beautiful and delicate as a prairie flower. Many a youngster's head was turned by her beauty, and many a brave lad's heart burned to win and wear the 'Rose of the Warloupe.' Old Andrew was mighty proud of his gal and loved her as deeply as any father could love a child. One summer evening, she strolled out in the prairie to gather flowers, when suddenly a war party of the Comanches dashed out of the timber bottom and rushed upon her. She shrieked and turned to fly, but it was no use; a delicate gal could hardly escape such fleet pursuers as were on her trail, and before she had run twenty yards, the chief dashed by and, stooping from the saddle as he passed, seized her around the waist and raised her by his strong arm to a seat before him. Without halting his horse for a moment was this feat accomplished, and before the poor gal could scarcely cry aloud for aid, she was borne rapidly towards the mountains.

"Her old father was frantic with grief and rage. Hastily collecting his neighbors and friends, he pursued the savages who had thus forcibly stolen his child and, with the sagacity and skill of an old frontiersman, tracked them to their mountain haunts. Late one evening, we came in sight of the Comanche encampment and, finding that we had not been discovered by the Indians, concluded to defer the attack until daybreak on the next morning. Secreting ourselves as well as we could, we waited with impatience for the hour of the coming fight. As soon as the first streak of light was seen in the sky, the Texan war-shout was raised, and we rushed down upon the village.

"The Comanches turned out in numbers, and a fierce battle began. I cannot describe to you the perils we went through that day. There were only about forty of us, while the Comanches were two hundred strong. Notwithstanding the great odds against us, we fought them desperately from daylight until dark, and many of their greatest warriors fell before our steady fire. But it wouldn't do—it wouldn't do—the odds were too great; they overpowered us, and we were compelled to fall back.

"Old Andrew fought like a devil that day. On every part of the field his voice was heard cheering his friends on, and you could see his white hairs waving in the wind as he headed a charge or sometimes fought single-handed with some big warrior of the tribe. Several times he was within a few feet of the tent where his daughter was confined and could hear her voice calling on him for aid. But it wouldn't do; he was driven back with the rest of us, and we dragged him away when we retreated. He was the last man to quit the fight and seemed to have been the mark for every bullet and arrow that was shot at us, yet, strange to say, he escaped unhurt. We were not strong enough to whip them," said the old Texan, as his voice grew husky with emotion, "and we were compelled to leave the poor gal in the hands of her savage enemies."

"Well, what became of her?" said a young Ranger, drawing his hand across his eyes.

"She was delivered up sometime afterwards, when we made a treaty with the Comanches at San Antonio. She returned to her father's house, but she never recovered from the hardships and cruelties she endured at the hands of the Indians. She was always melancholy and downcast. Her health was injured, her spirits gone, and her heart broken. She lived only a few months, then drooped and died. Curses on them Comanche dogs!" said the old Texan, grinding his teeth in the excitement of his feelings. "I have never sent a bullet through one of their infernal hearts from that day to this without remembering, as I pulled the trigger, the fate of that poor gal."

THE SWAMP ROBBERS OF LOUISIANA

Kidnapping and horse-stealing had become the order of the day—or rather, of the night—for scarcely one passed that some planter had not to deprecate the loss of one or more of his chattels. Faithful and esteemed family servants were spirited away in the most mysterious manner. Choice stock disappeared from the stables, though secured never so strongly under lock and bolt, and watched over by trusty and vigilant sentinels—sometimes ward and warden would disappear together. Dwellings were liable on any occasion to nocturnal visitations and, unless the occupants slept with one eye open and were prepared to defend their premises, some valuable article—a fine rifle, or double-barreled shot gun, or perchance a saddle and bridle—would in the morning be reckoned among the things that were stolen. When a saddle was thus taken, it was usually accompanied by some favorite blooded colt of the planter's, or perhaps his nearest neighbor's span of matched carriage horses. In short, no one was secure from plunder. For some months this state of things had continued, and of late the scoundrels, whoever they were, had become bold by success, and the highways were not only becoming unsafe, but absolutely dangerous to travel. Several prominent planters had been murdered, shot down from behind trees for the valuables about their persons, while passing from their places to the neighboring villages. Some even had been attacked within sight and sound of their very homes, and indeed, several had been shot while riding through their own fields, their persons rifled and their horses ridden off to the swamps.

These extraordinary occurrences opened the eyes of the community to the alarming fact that a large and skillfully organized gang of shrewd villains were running off their property. But who were they? And where did they rendezvous? These were the questions that each asked of his neighbor, but without any satisfactory answer. That they were not far off was very evident from the celerity of their movements, and all their operations showed the most consummate management and system. Were they strangers, who under the cover of night only, stole from their hiding-places upon the settlements, or were they old residents, with whom they were in daily and hourly contact—their neighbors and associates and the employees on their estates? These were perplexing queries which the planters asked of themselves but hardly dared to breathe aloud, lest they might arouse unjust suspicions and implicate innocent persons.

A number of planters forthwith resolved themselves into a Vigilance Committee and called a meeting of good citizens to take into consideration this alarming state of affairs and institute measures for ridding the country of the obnoxious characters, whose immediate neighborhood no one doubted. Patrols were appointed, and a regular system of guard and watch was determined upon, besides which a numerous party, made up of the most responsible citizens and trustworthy servants, were directed to keep continually on the hunt through swamps and canebrakes, in search of the haunts of the robbers.

So cunningly devised, however, were the plans of the rogues, and so secret their movements, that even their footsteps could be traced but a little distance from the scenes of their depredations. With the most consummate skill they managed to obliterate every sign as they penetrated the surrounding forests, so that it became impossible to follow them.

Thus, matters remained for several weeks, no one having yet obtained a trace of either their stolen property or of the thieves. The country was scoured in every direction where it was thought possible for a hidden rendezvous to exist. But in the wide swamps and among the sluggish lagoons that covered a good portion of the country between the Red River and Caddo Lake were many wild and apparently unapproachable spots yet unexplored by the foot of man. There were dark and gloomy recesses, impenetrable to horseman or pedestrian, where the rank growth of cypresses and other gigantic products of the festering sloughs were festooned with masses of the luxuriant *tillandsia* (Spanish Moss) and clustering vines and where the light of day had never penetrated. Within these frightful shadows, breathing only of poisonous vapors and malaria, nothing save the musky alligator and his congenial associates, noisome lizards and water-moccasins, could long exist. Many of these wild spots, surrounded by waveless and discolored lagoons, could be approached only with great labor and by means of "dug-outs," winding among partially submerged roots of climbing vines and cypresses. But once within the intricate labyrinth, whose unbroken mass of fetid vegetation, reeking with moisture and slime, sent a chill through the trembling frame, there was no escape but to those familiar with their winding passages. Within these sunless jungles the hapless captive was as completely shut out from the sympathies of the world, and for the time as hopelessly imprisoned, as if the bolts and bars of a Bastille had been turned against him.

For the first three weeks after the organization of the Vigilance Committee, the incursions of the thieves were almost suspended; only at times some atrocious robbery, more bold and daring than ever before perpetrated, would astonish the community, and again throw it into an ebullition of excitement. Again, every individual would sally out in the vain endeavor to trace the footsteps of the adroit rogues.

Among those most active in carrying out the measures of the committee were two extensive cotton planters on Soda Lake, who settled in the country but a few years, had rapidly added to the number of their hands and were considered the most successful cultivators of the staple in the parish. They were also among the most influential citizens, and their position and wealth had already pointed them out as leaders in the crusade against the robbers. These men were *Colonel* Betts and *General* Hawley, for be it remembered, it then was, as it is still, the custom in the southwestern states to attach a military handle to every respectable citizen's name.

Besides these worthy men, there was a very popular middle-aged lawyer named Benson, or Colonel Benson as he was called, in contradistinction to a captain of that ilk. This individual had been a resident of the parish for years and, being a person of a free and easy address and also gifted with a peculiar talent for stump oratory, had represented the parish in the state legislature and was now canvassing his congressional district as a candidate for the honor of serving the dear people at Washington.

There was also a certain Parson Redfield, a very pious preacher, who warmly advocated the propriety of prefacing the deliberations of the committee with an address to the "Throne of Divine grace" and who, on all occasions, evinced the greatest zeal in ferreting out the supposed hiding-places of the obnoxious gang, himself often leading the van into the most suspicious-looking coverts of the swamps. These men were extremely officious and managed, in a great measure, the proceedings against the marauders.

But there were a few quiet but shrewd observers among the citizens, who were of the opinion that those who were so loud in their cries of "Stop, thief!" would bear to be watched a little themselves, and apparently approving of the recommendations of those active and zealous advocates of good order and justice, they determined to follow their own judgments. To impeach the intentions or integrity of persons of their high standing in the community would have been like putting their necks into the hangman's noose, and they therefore continued to keep an eye upon their movements, while they acquiesced in their plans. Colonel Devoll, a wealthy planter, being the heaviest loser, was expected to take an active part in the premises, but to the surprise of all, he continued apparently indifferent to a matter so absorbingly interesting to his neighbors. With all this apparent unconcern, however, he ultimately proved himself the most efficient and valuable member of the organization.

Shreveport, the capital of Caddo Parish, from its peculiar situation at the foot of the Great Red River Raft, and being on the frontier of the States of Louisiana, Arkansas, and the then Republic of Texas, was the resort and stopping-place of many strangers, and its streets were often filled with a variety of characters. Like all Southern river towns, it was frequently honored by the professional visits of gamblers of every degree, from thimble riggers to the wealthy monte and faro dealers from the dens of New Orleans. These last were regarded, in the cotton and sugar growing state, with much more approbation than anywhere else and were even sometimes admitted to the society of the most respectable.

At this period there were a good number of these gentry in the place. But so accustomed had the citizens become to their presence that they were not thought of as having any connection with the existing state of things in the parish. Colonel Devoll, however, set himself quietly to watch their motions.

There was one of these "professional sporting gentlemen," as the fraternity pompously style themselves, who had excited his suspicion. One day, at the fashionable hotel, he had seen this blackleg introduce one of his comrades to Colonel Benson, the congressional candidate. The lawyer acknowledged the honor with due courtesy and, extending his hand, received the introduced as one he had never met before. But Devoll, whose eyes were following their motions, detected by a covert sign the two men exchanged with each other, that there was a mutual understanding between them. Without mentioning this circumstance to anyone, the planter continued his quiet observations, and it was not long before he discovered that Betts and Hawley, as well as the pious and zealous parson, were on terms of disguised intimacy with Captain Curtis, as the gambler was called.

Very slight circumstances are received by some minds as conclusive evidence, and when they are coupled one with another, they present a chain of testimony that forces an involuntary conviction. So it was with Colonel Devoll, as he passed in review all the various facts he had collected of the gambler and his covert intercourse with the other individuals he had been led to suspect. On one occasion, after a shower had laid the dust of the road, the Colonel chanced to meet Curtis riding in the direction of Hawley's plantation, where he had become a frequent visitor. After passing the gentlemanly horseman, the colonel's attention was called to the peculiar footprints of the gambler's horse. He observed on the left hind shoe an uncommon arrangement of the nails and an extraordinary notched appearance of the toe-cock. On the inner side of the left foot there were five nails, while on the outer there were only three. Whether this arrangement was the result of carelessness or design on the part of the smith was not clear, but such was the fact, and the observant Colonel made a note of it.

That same evening, he encountered his neighbor Betts on his way from town to his plantation and, by a singular coincidence, and to his surprise, discovered that the tracks of his blooded saddle nag were precisely like those of the captain's animal, only in his case the right shoe bore the odd arrangement of nails instead of the left, and the toe-cock was marked in the same manner.

A few days after making this discovery, Colonel Devoll's suspicions were further strengthened by the fact that Parson Redfield's favorite riding nag made similar tracks in the dust. Knowing the shop where the suspected persons were in the habit of having their horseshoeing done, the colonel called upon the proprietor and by adroit questioning ascertained that this peculiar manner of putting on the shoes were by special direction of his patrons. He also ascertained the fact that only those persons he had previously suspected had ever ordered their horses' shoes put on in that manner. The smith assured him that he could immediately recognize the tracks made by those shoes, for though each one had a peculiar mark, they were all after the same general character. He was not aware of any other gentlemen in the parish having their horses shod in that manner. The usual mode was four nails in each side of the shoe, with smooth toe-cocks.

The theory that immediately suggested itself to the mind of the colonel, after revolving these facts, was that these peculiar shoe tracks were adopted as a kind of freemasonry, by which the members of the gang might know that their leaders were abroad; or, in case of a sudden journey or flight being necessary, their comrades might be able to follow them if need be; and this theory of subsequent events proved correct.

Living in the vicinity of Alexandria, Rapides Parish, was an eccentric half-breed Indian named Delaware Dave. This man was noted, far and near, for a peculiar faculty he possessed of following a scent, even after it was weeks old. In some instances, he had been known to pursue, as if by instinct or clairvoyance, the obliterated footsteps of the chase for three or four weeks and finally come upon the flying camp of the hapless fugitive. If a horse was long astray or a vicious plantation mule had hidden itself away in the intricacies of the canebrakes, Delaware Dave was forthwith sent on the track and the animal captured. In short, Dave was an invaluable fellow when he could be kept sober, for, like almost all half-breed Indians—neither Red nor White—he was an incorrigible drunkard.

After consulting with his judicious neighbors, Colonel Devoll determined to send a trusty messenger to a friend in Alexandria to obtain the services of the half-breed in ferreting out the whereabouts of the gang that was infesting the parish.

Accordingly, in a few days, Dave arrived at the colonel's plantation, and after a three days' glorious drunk, which was a part of his contract, he announced that he was ready for business and demanded to know what was required of him. Now among Dave's eccentricities was the remarkable fact of his honesty, for when once entrusted with a secret, it was inviolable, and he devoted all his energies to the accomplishment of what he was set about. In fact, his peculiar vocation—the only one he was fit for—had become a passion with him, and he hunted his game, whatever it might be for the time, with the avidity of an animal of the feline species.

He was taken out upon the road near Shreveport and shown one of the odd horse-shoe marks I have described and directed to follow it wherever it went and report the result of his observations to Colonel Devoll within three days.

At the end of that time, Dave returned, but all the discovery he had made was that the animal that made the tracks had passed between the town and the plantations of Betts and Hawley, sometimes alone and at others accompanied with similar tracks; more frequently, however, there were two horsemen together. These, from the half-breed's description, were Benson and the parson.

So far, then, nothing new had been elicited but a confirmation of the fact that there was daily intercourse between the suspected parties. And Dave was directed to continue his hunt.

At the expiration of another three days, the cunning half-breed again returned, and this time his report was still more important. He had followed the priest and the lawyer by an unfrequented route, deep into the swamp, to the shore of Soda Lake, where they evidently had embarked, horses and all, on a flat in the direction of a large island. The horsemen were accompanied by two Negroes whom they had driven before them. In corroboration of Dave's second report, it was well known that two valuable house servants were missing from the two in the past two days. The colonel also learned that the two men Dave described were absent. So far, then, so good. Things were progressing promisingly.

Again, the half-breed was ordered to the swamp and, being told where he could find a dug-out, was directed to follow up the scent nor return till he had found the depot of the rogues. And in twenty-four hours he again made his appearance and in the most excited manner announced the entire success of his hunt. He had come upon an extensive camp of White men and Negroes on the upper end of the island, where the two men he had been following were engaged in superintending the loading of a covered flat boat, evidently intended to be dispatched down the Red River into the Mississippi.

It was not many hours before, acting upon this important information, a small party of neighboring planters were in the saddle, on their way towards Shreveport, in quest of the accomplished Captain Curtis and to arouse the citizens. Nor was it long after their arrival there that similar parties halted at the gates of the two suspected planters, who were immediately arrested and conducted to the presence of that stern administrator of justice, Judge Lynch, and committed till further developments might be made. Chartering a steamboat that lay in front of the town, a large force of armed citizens embarked upon the lake and steamed up toward the island under the pilotage of Delaware Dave.

The lake being navigated for the greater part of the year, and the steamer belonging to that particular trade, no great attention was paid to her by the occupants of the hidden camp till her bows were run into the swampy shore and the armed citizens, rushing into the thickets, surrounded the spot. Then followed a desperate and sanguinary fight, which continued for several hours, for the villains were prepared for any emergency, and resulted in many wounds and deaths on both sides; the besieged, however, suffering greatest.

Many of the ruffians were taken and, being strongly bound,

were conveyed to the boat under the guard of their recent captives. Many others escaped—some by secreting themselves in the deep jungles of the swampy island, and others by swimming from island to island to the opposite shore.

Among those taken were the two leaders, the congressional candidate and the canting parson.

A few days after the fight at the island, the incorruptible Judge Lynch was called upon to mete out final justice to the robbers. With all due form, the jury of the assembled people investigated the facts and rendered their verdict, in compliance with which the culprits were suspended from the trees of the swamp, like so many scarecrows hanging in cornfields to frighten away the plundering birds.

As might be supposed, after the breaking up of this band of desperadoes, Delaware Dave became a noted character. But the poor fellow did not long after live to enjoy his deserved renown. One morning his body was found in the river, riddled with bullets, and his throat cut from ear to ear—the work, no doubt, of some of the survivors of the gang.

LEWIS AND THE RATTLESNAKE

The family of John Lewis were the first settlers of Augusta, in the state of Virginia, and consisted of himself, his wife, and four sons: Thomas, William, Andrew, and Charles. Of these, the first three were born in Ireland, from whence the family came, and the last was a native of Virginia.

Lewis was a man of wealth and station in the old country, and the cause of his immigration to America was an attempt, on the part of a man of whom he hired some property, to eject him therefrom, which led to an affray in which the noble landlord lost his life. Fearing, from the high standing of his antagonist, the desperate character of his surviving assailants and the want of evidence to substantiate his case, that his life would be in danger if he stayed, Lewis fled the country, accompanied by a party of his tenantry, and settled in the then western wilds of Virginia.

The father appears to have been a man of remarkable force and energy, and all four of his sons rendered themselves conspicuous for deeds of daring and determined bravery during the early history of Western Virginia and that of her infant sisters, Ohio and Kentucky, which would require volumes to relate.

Charles Lewis was, even in early youth, distinguished for those qualifications which have rendered the class to which he belonged –the Indian fighters—so remarkable among men. He was a young man when the Indians commenced their attacks upon the settlement of Western Virginia, but entered the contest with a zeal and courage which outstripped many of his older and more boastful compeers. His astonishing self-possession and presence of mind carried him safely through many a gallant exploit, which has rendered his name as familiar and his fame as dear to the memories of the descendants of the early settlers as household words. Cool, calm, and collected in the face of danger, and quick-witted where others would be apt to be excited and tremulous, he was able to grasp on the instant the propitious moment for action and render subservient to his own advantage the most trifling incident.

He was so unfortunate, on one occasion, as to be taken prisoner by a party of Indians while on a hunting excursion. Separated from his companions, he was surprised and surrounded before he was aware of his danger, and when he did become aware of his critical situation, he saw how futile it was to contend and how reckless and fatal it must be to himself, should he kill one of his antagonists. He knew full well that the blood of his enemy would be washed out in his own, and that, too, at the stake; whereas, if he surrendered peaceably, he stood a chance of being adopted by the Indians as one of themselves. Revolving these things in his mind, he quietly delivered up his rifle to his enemies and was led away by his captors, who rejoiced exceedingly over their prisoner. Bare-headed, with his arms bound tightly behind him, without a coat, and barefooted, he was driven forward some two hundred miles toward the Indian towns, his inhuman captors urging him on when he lagged with their knives and tauntingly reminding him of the trials which awaited him at the end of the journey. Nothing daunted, however, by their threats and menaces, he marched on in the weary path which led him farther and farther from his friends, perfectly tractable, so far as his body was concerned, but constantly busy in his mind with schemes of escape. He bided his time, and at length, the wished-for moment came.

As the distance from the White settlements increased, the vigilance of the Indians relaxed and his hopes increased. As the party passed along the edge of a precipice, some twenty feet high, at the foot of which ran a mountain torrent, he, by a powerful effort, broke the cords which bound his arms and made the leap. The Indians, whose aim it was to take him alive, followed him and then commenced a race for life and liberty, which was rendered the more exciting by the fact that his pursuers were close upon him and could at any moment have dispatched him. But such was not their desire, and on and on he sped, now buoyed up by hope as his recent captors were lost to sight, and soon despairing of success as he crossed an open space which showed them almost at his heels.

At length, taking advantage of a thicket through which he passed and which hid him from their sight for a moment, he darted aside and essayed to leap a fallen tree which lay across his path. The tangled underbrush and leaves, which grew thickly around and almost covered the decaying trunk, tripped him as he leaped, and he fell with considerable force on the opposite side. For an instant he was so stunned by the fall as to lose his consciousness, but soon recovered it to find that the Indians were actively searching every nook in his immediate vicinity and that he had fallen almost directly upon a large rattlesnake which had thrown itself into the deadly coil so near his face that its fangs were within a few inches of his nose. Is it possible for the most vivid imagination to conceive of a more horrible and terrifying situation?

The pursuit of his now highly exasperated and savage enemies, who thirsted for his recapture that they might wreak upon him a fearful revenge, which of itself was a fearful danger calculated to thrill the nerves of the stoutest system, had now become a secondary fear, for death in one of its most terrifying and soul-sickening forms was vibrating on the tongue and darting from the eye of the fearful reptile before him, so near, too, that the vibratory motion of his rattle, as it waved to and fro, caused it to strike his ear. The slightest movement of a muscle—a convulsive shudder, almost the winking of an eyelid—would have been the signal for his death. Yet in the midst of this terrible danger, his presence of mind did not leave him, but like a faithful friend did him good service in his hour of trial.

Knowing the awful nature of his impending fate, and conscious that the slightest quivering of a nerve would precipitate it, he scarcely breathed, and the blood flowed feebly through his veins as he lay looking death in the eye. Surrounded thus by the most appalling danger, he was conscious that three of the Indians had passed over the log behind which he lay without observing him and disappeared in the dark recesses of the forest. Several minutes—which to him were as many hours—passed in this truly terrifying situation, until the snake, apparently satisfied that he was dead, loosed his deadly coil and, passing *directly over his body*, was lost to sight in the luxuriant growth of weeds which grew up around the fallen tree. Oh! what a thrill, what a revulsion of feeling shook his frame as he was relieved from this awful situation. Tears, tears of joyous gratitude coursed down his cheeks as he poured out his heart to God in thankfulness for his escape.

"I had eaten nothing," said he to his companions after his return, "for many days. I had no firearms, and I ran the risk of dying with hunger before I could reach the settlements, but rather would I have died than have made a meal of that generous beast." He was still in imminent danger from the Indians, who knew that he had hidden in some secluded spot and were searching with the utmost zeal every nook and corner to find him. He was fortunate enough, however, to escape them, and after a weary march through the wilderness, during which he suffered intensely from hunger, he reached the settlements.

DARING EXPLOITS OF COLONEL
JACK HAYS, THE TEXAN RANGER

Were an account of the Indian fights, skirmishes, and adventures of Colonel Hays to be given to the world, it would fill a volume, and the work would be looked upon rather as the effusion of a fertile imagination, consisting of legendary tales and the adventures of some fictitious knight-errant, than to be the faithful account of the achievements of a man, living and moving among us. But that "truth is stranger than fiction" is exemplified daily, and we are almost inclined to believe that there are but few things which exist in the imagination of man that could not, with the proper spirit, perseverance, and determination, be reduced to living reality.

It was some time in the month of July, 1844, that he was engaged in one of the most remarkable Indian fights perhaps on record. Remarkable, not for the numbers engaged, nor the duration of the conflict, but from the fearful odds against the rangers. At the time we speak of, Hays was surrounded by as gallant a little band of noble and brave men, numbering only fourteen, as ever fought for the liberty of any land. Among this Spartan band were the names of a Gillespie, a Walker, and a Chevalier, whose noble deeds have since made them known to the world. On this occasion, Hays had gone out with his men some eighty miles from San Antonio, toward the river Pierdenales, for the purpose of ascertaining the position of the Indians and to watch their movements. On arriving near the river, they discovered some ten or fifteen Comanche warriors, well mounted, who immediately made demonstrations of fight. As the Rangers advanced upon them, however, they would retreat, and thus endeavored to lead the Texans toward a ridge of thick undergrowth. But Hays was too well acquainted with the Indian character to be caught by their snares, and he immediately judged by their maneuvering that an ambush had been laid for him and with difficulty restrained the impetuosity of his "boys" from advancing to the attack.

He then marched around the thicket, where he supposed the Indians to be concealed, and drew up on another ridge separated from their position by a deep ravine. He had occupied this situation but a short time, when the Indians discovered who he was and, knowing their man, gave up the hope of catching him by stratagem. The Indians then showed themselves to the number of seventy-five and challenged him to the contest. Hays accepted the challenge and signified to them that he would meet them and immediately started down the hill with his men toward the Indians, moving at the same time in the slowest possible pace until reaching the bottom of the ravine, where he was hid from the view of the Indians by the brow of the hill upon which they were formed. Then turning at full speed down the ravine, followed by his little troop, he turned the point of the ridge, came up in the rear of the enemy, and charged their column, when every eye of the Indian phalanx was looking in momentary expectation of seeing him rise the hill in their front! His first fire upon them with short rifles, being deadly, threw them into utter confusion. The yells, imprecations, and war-whoops that filled the air after the report of the rifles would have blanched many a cheek as it echoed wildly over the plain. But there stood Hays and his gallant men as firm and undaunted as the rock.

The Indians, seeing their great superiority in numbers, soon rallied when the Ranger ordered his men to throw down their rifles and prepare with their five-shooters to receive the charge of the enemy. In order to resist attack on all sides, as the Indians were surrounding them, Hays formed his men in a circle, fronting outwards, being still mounted on their horses, and for fifteen or twenty minutes maintained that position, never firing a shot until the Indians came within the length of their lances of them. Their aim was sure, and every fire brought down a warrior. Some twenty-one of the Red men were killed on that spot, before they desisted, and then the rangers, changing their ground, charged them in turn. The fight lasted for nearly an hour, the two parties alternately charging each other. By this time the Texans had exhausted the loads in their five-shooting pistols and the chief was again rallying his warriors for one more desperate struggle.

Hays' numbers were now reduced, and the crisis was an awful one. He saw that their only salvation was to kill the Indian chief and demanded of his men if anyone had a charge left. The lamented Capt. Gillespie replied that he had reserved his rifle.

"Dismount, then," said Hays, "and make sure work of that chief."

Although speared through the body, the gallant Gillespie dismounted, and at the crack of his rifle, the chief fell headlong from his horse. Panic-struck, the Indians fled in dismay, pursued by the Texans who gained a complete victory. On the battlefield of Pierdenales lay some thirty-odd of their dead; how many were wounded was not known. On the part of the Rangers, two were killed and some four or five wounded, among whom were Gillespie and Walker, since celebrated in American history, who were both speared through the body.

At another time, Hays went out with a party of some fifteen or twenty men upon the frontier of Texas, then many miles west of the White settlements, for the purpose of surveying and locating lands in the vicinity of a place well known as the "Enchanted Rock." We are unable to give to the reader the traditionary cause why this place was so named, but nevertheless, the Indians had a great awe, amounting almost to reverence for it, and would tell many legendary tales connected with it and the fate of a few brave warriors, the last of a tribe now extinct, who defended themselves there for many years as in a strong castle, against the attacks of their hostile brethren. But they were finally overcome and totally annihilated, and ever since, the "Enchanted Rock" has been looked upon as the exclusive property of these phantom warriors. This is one of the many tales which the Indians tell concerning it. The rock forms the apex of a high, round hill, very rugged and difficult of ascent. In the center there is a hollow in the shape of a bowl and sufficiently large to allow a small party of men to lie in it, thus forming a small fort, the projecting and elevated sides serving as a protection.

Not far from the base of this hill, Hays and his men, at the time of the expedition spoken of, which occurred in the year 1841 or '42, were attacked by a large force of Indians. When the fight commenced, Hays, being some distance from his party, was cut off from them, and being closely pressed by the Indians, made good his retreat to the top of the hill. Reaching the "Enchanted Rock," he there entrenched himself and determined to sell his life dearly, for he had scarcely a gleam of hope left to escape. The Indians who were in pursuit, upon arriving near the summit, set up a most hideous howl and, after surrounding the spot, prepared for the charge, being bent upon taking this "Devil Jack," as they called him, at all hazards, for they knew who was the commander.

As they would approach, Hays would rise and level his rifle; knowing his unerring aim, they would drop back. In this way he kept them at bay for nearly an hour, the Indians howling around him all the while, like so many wolves. But finally becoming emboldened, as he had not yet fired his rifle, they approached so near that it became necessary for him to go to work in earnest. So, as they continued to advance, he discharged his rifle, and then seizing his five-shooter, he felled them on all sides, thus keeping them off until he could reload. In this manner he defended himself for three long hours, when the Indians becoming furiously exasperated, rushed in mass, and gained the top on one side of the hill; his men, who had heard the crack of his rifle and had been fighting most desperately to reach their leader, now succeeded in breaking through the file of Indians on the other side and arrived just in time to save him.

"This," said the Texan who told us the story, "was one of *Jack's* most narrow escapes, and he considers it one of the *tightest little places* that he ever was in. The Indians, who had believed for a long time that he bore a charmed life, were then, more than ever, convinced of the fact."

THRILLING ESCAPE FROM A PRISON-SHIP

In the year 1813, an American privateer, the *Mary Ann*, was captured by a British man-of-war and the whole crew, some forty in number, carried into Plymouth and placed on board a loathsome prison-ship where they were subjected to all the indignities and cruelties which the English government, through its unfeeling officers, then knew so well how to inflict upon their unfortunate prisoners of war. They presented a most forlorn and wretched appearance. They were robbed of nearly all their valuables and clothing, fed with rations barely sufficient to sustain life, and literally packed and jammed into such close quarters that the foul air infused a pestilential poison through their systems. They were ragged and dirty, gaunt and ghastly, with pale, pinched faces, hollow cheeks, and sunken, restless eyes. Many were sick, several were dying, numbers had died, and the least afflicted could make no calculations of life. It was a scene of wretchedness and misery to sicken the heart of any being possessing the common feelings of humanity.

Probably the most restless people in the world are the Americans, and for this reason, they make the most troublesome prisoners. They will not settle down to inactivity under any wrong or oppression; they will not bear any burden meekly or tamely; nurtured in the lap of freedom, they chafe fearfully under any restraint; their liberty they will seek at any hazard—they pant for it as for the air they breathe; show them the remotest possibility of accomplishing their purpose, and no danger, no thousand dangers, will deter them from the attempt; destroyed they may be, but not subdued.

This was especially the case with the American prisoners in

England during the War of 1812. The French, as a general thing, yielded a quiet submission to the oppressive laws which held them in bondage, but the Americans were continually plotting escape, even when escape seemed impossible. No prison—no matter how strong its bolts and bars, how broad and high its walls, how deep and dangerous its moat, or how numerous and vigilant its guard —could shut out all hope from the heart of the native-born freeman of yet regaining his liberty by some personal and desperate hazard.

Among the daring crew of the *Mary Ann* was a young man, twenty-two years of age, a native of New London, Connecticut, by the name of Isaac Wheeler. He was rather small in person, with light hair and blue eyes, and his features in repose had a mild, inoffensive, almost sleepy expression. Unless you were a remarkable judge of physiognomy, he would probably be the last person you would select for a bold and desperate enterprise, and yet the man had a perfect love of danger, and such a feeling as actual fear was unknown to him. He made his boast, when taken, that it was not in the power of the English government to keep him long a prisoner, and for this insolence, as it was termed by his captors, he received some very harsh treatment, though all affected to believe it was mere Yankee braggadocio.

But no sooner was Wheeler fairly on board the prison-ship at Plymouth than he secretly began to plan and plot and execute. With a precaution for just such an emergency, he had, previous to his capture, prepared a saw from the main spring of a watch and sewed it up in a seam of his under-shirt where it had been overlooked by the men who searched and robbed him. With this, having taken into his confidence three other desperate fellows, he now began to work at the grates of one of the portholes of the seventy-four, and in less than a week, in spite of the vigilance of the guards, the bars were in a condition to be removed by a strong and sudden wrench. Waiting only for a dark and stormy night, which shortly after came, the fastenings were removed, and Wheeler was the first to crawl through.

Unfortunately for the quiet success of his scheme, he slipped and plunged into the water below and was heard by the sentry on duty above him, who instantly gave the alarm. In a minute, lights were dancing to and fro, and men were tumbling over the sides of the vessel into boats. So quickly were the boats manned and in pursuit of the fugitive that only one of his companions ventured to follow him, and he was riddled with balls within twenty feet of where he touched the water. This would have been the fate of Wheeler had he struck out for the shore, but being a remarkable swimmer, he dove and went under the vessel and came quietly up to breathe at the stern. By this time half-a-dozen boats were circling round the ship on an eager search, the excited crews cursing and grumbling and firing at everything which their fancy conjured into the appearance of a struggling man.

One boat shortly approached so near to the fugitive with its flashing lights that he felt discovery to be certain if he remained longer where he was, and accordingly he dove again and swam underwater the whole length of the keel, coming up under the bow. But another boat was here, and he had scarcely time to catch his breath when his head was perceived. This was announced by a yell of exultation, and in the same instant, five or six shots were fired at him. Only one ball hit him, and this passed through the fleshy part of his shoulder, barely missing the bone, which would have disabled him and rendered his recapture or death certain. He dove again and, being much out of breath, was obliged to come quickly to the surface, which he did within fifty feet of the bow on one side of the vessel and directly under one of the searching boats, to which he clung for a minute in a dangerous proximity to his foes, swimming with it as it was rowed forward and hearing the crew boast that, if not already dead, they would soon have his heart's blood.

Another boat soon approached this, and as the lights of the second craft began to flash upon him, Wheeler saw that he could remain no longer concealed where he was and once more dove and went under the seventy-four, coming up on the other side. Here again, he was not safe, for another boat was rowing from stern to bow, and determined now to be free or die in the attempt, he silently but swiftly struck out toward a schooner at some distance, whose light was faintly gleaming over the rough waves.

This last attempt at life and liberty fortune seemed disposed to favor, and to his great joy, the poor fugitive soon heard the gruff voices of his pursuers growing fainter and fainter behind him. Onward he pressed, buffeting the rough waves and thanking God for the driving storm that in a measure was shielding his flight. He now for the first time felt some pain in his shoulder, and he knew that his blood was mingling with the briny waters, but the hope of freedom made him buoyant, and he pressed forward to new perils with a comparatively light heart.

At length he reached the schooner and, finding a small boat alongside, noiselessly crawled into it and stretched himself out to rest. He had not lain long when he became conscious that his shoulder and arm were swelling and growing stiff, and as it was necessary for his safety that he should reach the shore during the night, and believing that every moment's delay would render the attempt more difficult, he resolved to re-commit himself to the waters immediately and swim while he could.

Half an hour later, more dead than alive, he crawled up the side of a pier and again laid himself down to rest. As soon as he felt he had recovered sufficient strength for the further task, he got upon his feet and hurried forward toward the lights of the town, hoping to find some friendly shelter where he might remain concealed till all search for him should be over, when it was his design to ship on board some foreign trader and thus get clear of the country.

While animated with this hope, and just as he had begun to hasten along one of the darker streets of the city, a man suddenly sprung out from the corner of a building, clapped one hand roughly on his shoulder, flashed a light in his face with the other, and in a gruff tone demanded his name and business, where he came from and whither he was going. All this was so sudden and unexpected and took the fugitive so completely off his guard, that he began to stammer, he knew not what, and quickly broke down in confusion.

"Unless I'm greatly mistaken," said the watchman, for such he was, "you're one of the Yankee prisoners just escaped from the prison-ship, and I'll just lock you up till morning and see."

"Oh, if that's all, I've not the least objection to your satisfying yourself on that score," replied Wheeler, who had now recovered his presence of mind and got all his wits to work.

"Wounded, too—all bloody here—shot, as I live!" pursued the

other, holding up his lantern. "Thought I heard firing a while ago. Yes, you're the man I want."

"And there's another you want just behind you," said Wheeler.

The watchman turned to see who was alluded to and at the same instant received a trip and a blow from Wheeler that sent him sprawling into the gutter. Almost the next moment he was upon his feet, in pursuit of the now flying fugitive, giving the signal of alarm, and shouting "Stop, thief! Stop, thief!" at the top of his lungs.

Fortunately for our hero, there was a dark, narrow street or lane close at hand, and into this he turned and bounded forward with the speed of a deer, the enraged watchman shouting and following and every moment losing ground in the chase. This street, not a long one, was completely deserted, and with no obstruction before him, the young man felt certain of escaping the enemy behind, but the shouts of his pursuer were now beginning to be answered from different quarters, and to his chagrin he perceived that his only safety would be in sudden concealment. This was fearfully apparent when, shortly after, a party of men entered the street at the other end and came hurrying down to meet him. He could not hope to pass them if he continued forward, and if he turned back, it would be to encounter the watchman and several others who were joining him. His only alternative seemed to be to draw himself up in the jut of some doorway and take the chances of the nearest party hurrying past without discovering him, and instantly adopting this plan, he bounded up to a door and, to his joyful surprise, found it slightly ajar. Pressed by the danger without, he did not stop to consider the perils within but pushed at once into a dark passage, softly closing the door behind him. Then hurrying along the passage till he came to a flight of stairs, he went bounding up these, two at a time, but scarcely had he reached the second story, when the door was burst open with a shout, and he heard the steps of several men entering the building in hot pursuit.

His situation was now critical in the extreme, and for the first time he experienced a feeling of despair take possession of his soul, but mentally repeating the old proverb, "While there is life, there is hope," he hurried around through a dark entry to another flight of stairs and was soon at the top of these. Another similar effort landed him in the fourth story, and then he bethought him of the roof. Luckily, he had not to grope long before his hand rested upon a ladder that led up to a trapdoor, and in less than a minute he was hurrying over the roof, hearing his pursuers clamoring below him, both in the street and in the building.

Over the roofs of several buildings the daring fellow now hastened, till he came to one considerably below the others, when, without a moment's hesitation, he lowered himself by his hands and dropped quietly down upon it. So remarkable had been his escapes thus far, that hope now revived, and this was greatly increased when, on taking hold of a trapdoor at his feet, he found it unfastened. Without a thought as to where his present descent might lead, he swung himself down into a kind of cockloft and secured the trap by hooks on the underside. This done, he breathed freer and sat down to think and rest. A voice now reached him, and after listening to it a short time, he became satisfied it was that of a woman praying. This gave him fresh hope, for to a true Christian woman he believed a distressed fugitive would not have to appeal in vain, and he at once resolved to see her and tell her all.

It was so dark where he was that nothing whatever could be seen, and so he began to grope about for the second trapdoor through which to descend from the loft to the upper story. In attempting to find this, he slipped from the joists over which he was crawling and, falling upon some weak laths, went through them with a crash and, with a large body of plastering, came down upon a bed in the room below. The female, whose voice he had heard, was kneeling beside the bed and was so frightened at the appearance of a bloody man in such a strange manner that, clasping her hands and uttering a sort of suppressed shriek, she swooned away.

Here was a new adventure and new danger, but Isaac Wheeler was equal to the occasion. Perceiving a closet full of female clothing, he at once resolved upon an effective disguise, and in ten minutes he was leaving the still unconscious woman, dressed in her own apparel and carrying his own sailor garments in a bundle. He went boldly down two flights of stairs, passed several rooms occupied by lodgers, and reached the street without molestation, where he beheld quite a crowd collected in front of the building in which he sought refuge. Taking a contrary direction, he moved off without suspicion, and in the course of an hour was far from the scene of danger. A sum of money which he found in the woman's dress enabled him to pay his way and escape too close a scrutiny, and traveling on foot to another seaport, he took passage for one of the German States and thus secured the liberty for which he had risked his life.

After the declaration of peace, Isaac Wheeler returned to his native land and astonished his friends with an account of his adventures. He subsequently became master of a vessel and acquired a competency. After a lapse of years, he sought out the woman he had so strangely robbed and made her ample restitution for her loss. In the year 1845, he fell victim to the yellow fever at Havana, leaving a handsome property to his relatives.

THE RIFLEMAN OF CHIPPEWA

At the time of the French and Indian Wars, the American army was encamped on the Plains of Chippewa near the headwaters of the Mississippi. Colonel St. Clair, the commander, was a brave and meritorious officer, but his bravery sometimes amounted to rashness, and his enemies have accused him of indiscretion. In the present instance perhaps he may have merited the accusation, for the plain on which he had encamped was bordered by a dense forest, from which the Indian scouts could easily pick off his sentinels without in the least exposing themselves to danger.

Five nights had passed, and every night the sentinel who stood at a lonely outpost in the vicinity of the forest had been shot, and these repeated disasters struck such dread among the remaining soldiers that no one would come forward to offer to take the post, and the commander, knowing it was only throwing away men's lives, let it stand for a few nights unoccupied.

At length, a rifleman of the Virginia corps volunteered his services for this dangerous duty; he laughed at the fears of his companions and told them he meant to return safe and drink his commander's health in the morning. The guard marched up soon after, and he shouldered his rifle and fell in. He arrived at the place which had been so fatal to his comrades and, bidding his fellow soldiers "goodnight," assumed the duties of his post. The night was dark, thick clouds overspread the firmament, and hardly a star could be seen by the sentinel as he paced his lonely walk. All was silent except the gradually retreating footsteps of the guard; he marched onward, then stopped and listened till he thought he heard the joyful sound of "All's well"—then all was still, and he sat down on a fallen tree and began to muse. Presently a low rustling among the bushes caught his ear; he gazed intently toward the spot whence the sound seemed to proceed, but he could see nothing save the impenetrable gloom of the forest. The sound drew nearer, and a well-known grunt informed him of the approach of a bear. The animal passed the soldier slowly and then quietly sought the thicket to the left.

At this moment the moon shone out bright through the parting clouds, and the wary soldier perceived the ornamented moccasin of a savage on what an instant before he believed to be a bear! He could have shot him in a moment, but he knew not how many other such animals might be at hand; he therefore refrained and, having perfect knowledge of Indian subtilty, he quickly took off his hat and coat, hung them on a branch of the fallen tree, grasped his rifle, and silently crept toward the thicket. He had barely reached it when an arrow, whizzing past his head, told him of the danger he had so narrowly escaped.

He looked carefully around him, and on a little spot of cleared land he counted twelve Indians, some sitting, some lying full length on the thickly strewn leaves of the forest. Believing that they had already shot the sentinel, and little thinking there was anyone within hearing, they were quite off their guard and conversed aloud about their plans for the morrow.

It appeared that a council of twelve chiefs was now held, in which they gravely deliberated on the most effectual means of annoying the enemy. It was decided that the next evening, forty of their warriors should be in readiness at the hour when the sentinel should be left by his comrades and that when they had retired a few paces, an arrow should silence him forever and they would then rush on and massacre the guard.

This being concluded, they rose, and drawing the numerous folds of their ample robes closer round them, they marched off in Indian file through the gloomy forest, seeking some more distant spot where the smoke of their nightly fire would not be observed by the White men.

The sentinel rose from his hiding place, returned to his post, and taking down his hat, found that an arrow had passed clean through it. He then wrapped himself in his watch-coat and returned immediately to the camp and without any delay demanded to speak to the commander, saying that he had something important to communicate.

He was admitted, and when he had told all that he had seen and heard, the colonel bestowed on him the commission of lieutenant of the Virginia corps, which had been vacant by the death of one of his unfortunate comrades a few nights back, and ordered him to be ready with a picket guard to march an hour earlier than usual to the fatal outpost, there to place a hat and coat on the branches and then lie in ambush for the intruders.

The following evening, according to the orders given by Colonel St. Clair, a detachment of forty riflemen, with Lieutenant Morgan at their head, marched from the camp at half-past seven in the evening toward the appointed spot, and having arranged the hat and coat so as to have the appearance of a soldier standing on guard, they stole silently away and bid themselves among the bushes.

Here they lay for almost an hour before any signs of approaching Indians were heard. The night was cold and still, and the rising moon shone forth in all her beauty. The men were becoming impatient of their uncomfortable situation, for their clothes were not so well adapted to a bed of snow as the deer-skin robes of the hardy Chippewas.

"Silence!" whispered Lieutenant Morgan. "I hear the rustling of the leaves."

Presently, a bear of the same description as had been seen the night before passed near the ambush; it crept to the edge of the plain, reconnoitered, saw the sentinel at his post, retired toward the forest a few paces, and then suddenly rising on his feet let fly an arrow which brought the sham sentinel to the ground. So impatient were the Virginians to avenge the death of their comrades that they could scarcely wait till the lieutenant gave the word of command to fire; then they rose in a body, and before the Chippewas had time to draw their arrows or seize their tomahawks, more than half their number lay dead upon the plain. The rest fled to the forest, but the riflemen fired again and killed or wounded several more of the enemy. They then returned in triumph to relate their exploits in the camp. Ten chiefs fell that night, and their fall was, undoubtedly, one principal cause of the

French and Indian wars with the English.

Lieutenant Morgan rose to be a captain and at the termination of the war returned home and lived on his own farm till the breaking out of the American Revolution. And then, at the head of a corps of Virginia riflemen, appeared our brave and gallant Colonel Morgan, better known by the title of General, which he soon acquired by his courage and ability.

THE HORSE STEALERS OF ILLINOIS:
A LAWYER'S STORY

About three or four years ago, more or less, while I was practicing law in Illinois on a pretty large circuit, I was called on one day in my office by a very pretty woman, who, not without tears, told me that her husband had been arrested for horse stealing. She wished to retain me on the defense. I asked her why she did not go to Judge R., ex-Senator of the United States, whose office was in that town. I told her that I was a *young* man at the bar. She mournfully said that he had asked a retaining fee beyond her means; besides, he did not want to touch the case, for her husband was suspected of belonging to an extensive band of thieves and counterfeiters, whose headquarters were on Moore's prairie.

I asked her to tell me the whole truth of the matter, and if it was true that her husband did belong to such a band.

"Ah, sir," said she, "a better man at heart than my George never lived, but he liked cards and drink, and I am afraid they made him do what he never would have done if he had not drank. I fear it can be proved that he had the horse; he didn't steal it, but another stole it and passed it to him."

I didn't like the case. I knew there was a great dislike to the gang located where she named, and I feared to risk the case before a jury. She seemed to observe my intention to refuse the case and burst into tears.

I never could see a woman weep without feeling like a weak fool myself. If it hadn't been eyes brightened by "pearly tears," (blast the poet that made them come into fashion by praising 'em!) I'd never have been caught in the lasso of matrimony. My would-be client was pretty. The handkerchief that hid her streaming eyes didn't hide her ripe lips, and her snowy bosom rose and fell like a white gull in a gale of wind at sea. I took the case, and she gave me the particulars.

The gang, of which he was not a member, had persuaded him to take the horse. He knew that it was stolen, and like a fool acknowledged it when he was arrested. Worse still, he had trimmed the horse's tail and mane to alter his appearance, and the opposition could prove it.

The trial came up. I worked hard to get a jury of ignorant men, who had more heart than brains, who if they could not fathom the depths of argument or follow the labyrinthine mazes of law, could feel for a young fellow in a bad fix, a weeping pretty wife, nearly heart-broken and quite distracted.

Knowing the use of "effect," I told her to dress in deep mourning and bring her little cherub of a boy, only three years old, into court and sit as near the husband as the officers would let her. I tried the game in a murder case, and a weeping wife and sister made a jury render a verdict against law, evidence, and the judge's charge and saved a fellow that ought to be hung as high as Haman.

The prosecution opened very bitterly and inveighed against thieves and counterfeiters who had made the land a terror to strangers and travelers and who had robbed every farmer in the region of his finest horses. It produced witnesses and proved all and more than I feared it would. The time came for me to rise for the defense. Witness, I had none. But I determined to make an effort, only hoping so to interest the jury as to secure a recommendation to gubernatorial clemency and light sentence.

So, I painted his picture. A young man entering into life wedded to an angel, beautiful in person, possessing every noble and gentle attribute. Temptation lay before and all around him. He kept a tavern. Guests, there were many. It was not for him to inquire their business; they dressed well, made large bills, and paid promptly. At an unguarded hour, when he was insane with liquor, they urged upon him. He deviated from the path of rectitude. The demon alcohol reigned in his brain, and it was his first offense. Mercy pleaded for another chance to save him from ruin; justice did not require that his young wife should go down sorrowing to the grave and that the shadow and taunt of a felon father should cross the path of that sweet child. O, how earnestly did I plead for them! The woman wept; the husband did the same; the jury looked melting. If I could have had the closing speech, he would have been cleared, but the prosecution had the close and threw ice on the fire I had kindled. But they did not quite put it out.

The judge charged according to law and evidence, but evidently leaned on the side of mercy. The jury found a verdict of guilty, but recommended the prisoner to the mercy of the court. My client was sentenced to the shortest imprisonment the court was empowered to give, and both jury and court signed a petition to the governor for an unconditional pardon, which has since been granted, but not before the following incident occurred.

Some three months after this, I received an account for collection from a wholesale house in New York. The parties to collect from were hard ones, but they had property, and before they had an idea of the trap laid, I had the property, which they were about to assign before they broke, under attachment. Finding I was a neck ahead and bound to win, they "caved in" and forked over $3,794.18 (per memorandum book) in good money. They lived in Shawneetown about thirty-five or forty miles southeast of Moore's prairie. I received the funds just after the bank opening, but other business detained me till after dinner. I then started for C. intending to go as far as the village of Mount Vernon that night.

I had gone along ten or twelve miles, when I noticed a splendid team of double horses attached to a light wagon, in which were seated four men, evidently of the higher-strung order. They swept past as if to show how easily they could do it. They shortened in and allowed me to come up with them and, hailing me, asked me to "wet," or in other words, diminish the contents of a jug of old rye they had aboard, but I excused myself, with the plea that I had plenty on board. They asked me how far I was going. I told them as far as Mount Vernon, if my horse didn't tire out. They mentioned a pleasant tavern ten miles ahead as a nice stopping place and then drove on.

I did not like the looks of those fellows nor their actions. But I was bound to go ahead. I had a brace of revolvers and a nice knife; my money was not in a valise or my sulkey, but in my belt around my body. I drove slow in hopes they would go on and I should see them no more. It was nearly dark when I saw their wagon standing at the door. I would have passed on but my horse needed rest. I hauled up, and a woman came to the door. She turned pale as a sheet when she saw me. She did not speak, but with a meaning look she put her finger on her lip and beckoned me in. She was the wife of my late client.

When I entered the party recognized me, hailed me as an old traveling friend, and asked me to drink. I respectfully but firmly declined to do so.

"But you shall drink or fight!" said the noisiest of the party.

"Just as you please, drink I shall not?" said I, purposely showing the butt of a Colt, which kicks six times in rapid succession.

The others interposed and very easily quieted my opponent. One offered me a cigar, which I should not have received, but a glance of the woman induced me to accept it. She advanced and proffered me a light, and in doing so slipped a note into my hand, which she must have written with a pencil the moment before. Never shall I forget the words—they were: "Beware—they are members of the gang. They mean to rob and murder you. Leave soon. I will manage to detain them."

I did not feel comfortable just then, but tried to look so.

"Have you any room to put up my horse?" I asked turning to the woman.

"What, are you not going on tonight?" asked one of the men. "We are."

"No!" said I. "I shall stay here tonight."

"We'll all stay, then, I guess, and make a night of it," said one of the cut-throats.

"You'll have to put up your own horse—here's a lantern," said the woman.

"I am used to that," I said. "Gentlemen, excuse me a minute, I'll join you in a drink when I come in."

"Good on your head! More whiskey, old gal," shouted they.

I went out and glanced at their wagon: it was old-fashioned, and linchpins secured the wheels. To take out my knife and pry one from the fore and hind wheels was but the work of an instant, and I threw them into the darkness as far as I could. To untie my horse and dash off was but the work of a moment. The road lay down a steep hill, but my lantern lighted me somewhat.

I had hardly got under full headway, when I heard a yell from the party I had so unceremoniously left. I put whip to my horse. The next moment they started. I threw my light away and left my horse to pick his road. A moment later, I heard a crash, a horrible shriek. The wheels were off. Then came the rush of the horses tearing along with the wreck of the wagon. Finally, they seemed to fetch up in the woods. One or two shrieks I heard as I swept on, leaving them far behind. For some time, I hurried my horse— you'd better believe "I rid." It was a little after midnight when I got to Mount Vernon.

The next day I heard that Moore's prairie team had run away, and two men out of four had been so badly hurt that their lives had been despaired of, but I did not cry. My clients got their money, but I didn't travel that road anymore.

SURPRISED BY GUERILLAS:
AN INCIDENT OF THE MEXICAN WAR

It was while our army was in quiet possession of the city of Monterey, that one morning I had made my regular visit to my almost vacated hospital and, returning to my quarters in the *calle del obispo*, had ordered my horse with the intention of joining a friend in a ride to Arista's Garden and the heights of the Bishop's palace. My gallant little "Hacaneo," a native of the mountain breed, from Durango and one of the finest animals I had met with in the country, was giving expression to his impatience of restraint by furiously pawing the pavement of the court and making the place ring with his loud neighing.

As I was about to throw myself into the saddle, having my hand upon the mane of my restless steed and one foot in the stirrup, I felt a hand laid gently on my shoulder, and as I turned my head, the good-natured face of my friend and frequent guide, Jose Maria Luna, met my eye.

"A very good day, Señor Doctor," said he, displaying in his cheerful smile a mouth full of regularly arranged and brilliantly white teeth, a feature for which his countrymen are remarkable.

"Where do you ride?" continued he, while his earnest countenance expressed a good deal of interest in the question.

"Only for a *pasear* (pleasure ride)," I replied. "What can I do for you, Jose?"

"Oh! much, Señor," he answered, and then turning to a tall countryman of the *poblano* class, who stood by his side: "Señor Doctor," said he, "this is my cousin and *compadre*, who comes from the village of Guajuca (pronounced *Wahukah*), which is the home of my old father. He now lies dangerously sick and has dispatched Gabrielo to me to beg the attendance of my good friend, the American Medico."

"What is the distance, Jose?" I inquired.

"Oh! Señor, it is only a short ride with that noble little fellow of yours—just a pleasant *pasear*—no more than ten leagues."

As I was under some heavy obligations to Jose, who had twice saved my life, I consented to accompany him, and we were soon dashing away over the country.

We had passed a number of considerable villages, and I observed that contrary to my usual experience, there were no men to be seen, and the women, on our application for refreshments for ourselves and horses, invariably met us with a shrug of the shoulder and the cold and repelling reply: "*No hai nada, nadita, Señores* (We have nothing, not anything, sirs)!" at the same time making a significant motion with the forefinger toward me—a motion intended only for the eyes of my companions. This unfriendly conduct, so different from what I had been accustomed to, was explained by a printed proclamation which Jose slipped into my hand, and on reading which I saw, to my great surprise, that the blood-thirsty Canales had ordered every Mexican to join the native army and commanded that no quarter should be shown to any American who should in any manner fall into their hands.

"How is it," said I to Jose, as I finished reading this precious document, "that you and Gabrielo are not also enrolled in the troop of this cut-throat governor?"

"Oh! Señor, you don't know our little general as we do. Very few well-disposed people will be governed by this terrible proclamation. The rancheros will be kept out of sight for a few days, and everybody will be a little shy. But, though our fighting governor will take the field with his guerillas, his forces will not be much increased. He is more robber than soldier or statesman, and more coward than either. I should pity the poor Americano, however, who might fall into his hands. But here, Señor Doctor, is Guajuca." And spurring up our horses, a turn in the road brought us into the now deserted streets of the village. Halting before a respectable looking building, having a long, low verandah in front, the Mexican dismounted, and taking my bridle, welcomed me with the usual Spanish compliments to his father's house. We were kindly received at the door by two dark-eyed, smiling senoritas, the sisters of Jose. Within we found the invalid for whose sake we had performed the journey. He was lying upon a cowhide cot, surrounded by a little group of sympathizing women. On our entrance, however, they respectfully withdrew from the side of the sick man to make room for Jose and myself.

I had examined my patient, who was afflicted with a chronic disease of the stomach, had made my prescriptions, and given the necessary directions for his after-treatment, when I was invited to another apartment, where was prepared an excellent dinner, of which at this advanced hour, I greatly felt the need, having eaten nothing since previous to leaving my quarters early in the day. The long and rapid ride, together with the pure mountain air, had sharpened my appetite to a keen edge, but, as I was sitting down to the fragrant meal, the outer door was suddenly thrown open and Jose, panting with excitement and unable to articulate, made his appearance. Grasping me by the arm and pointing toward a door opening to the rear of the house, he hurried me into the garden beyond, and with rapid strides, pushing me before him, entered a thick grove of pomegranate and lime trees at the farther end of the enclosure.

Not till we were completely screened from sight by the luxuriant foliage did he attempt to speak and then in a hurried and agitated whisper informed me that a party of guerillas had just encamped in the village and had been made aware of the presence of an American officer in the place.

The words had scarcely escaped his lips when we perceived that the house and garden were filling with armed men.

"They are already on our track," exclaimed the excited Mexican. Then, laying his hand upon my arm as I was about to draw my revolver from my belt, he continued, "We had better surrender at discretion, for if we attempt to defend ourselves, they will kill us upon the spot."

"At all events," I replied, "they shall not have my life without taking with it the contents of this revolver."

While we were speaking, I could perceive that the yelling crew had encircled the spot, where like hunted beasts, we had taken cover, and were closing in upon us with their carbines directed toward the grove, as if fearful that, like lions at bay, we might spring upon them and dash them to the earth.

Closer and closer those hunters of human prey gathered around us, when my companion, seeing there was no possibility of escape, motioning me to remain quiet, stepped boldly out from the cover of the thickets and, hailing the guerillas, proposed to surrender and begged for quarters.

"Kill the traitor! Death to the friend of the *maldito Americanos* (accursed Americans)!" shouted a score of bloodthirsty throats, and at the same time the thicket was torn and riddled by carbine shots. I remained unhurt, but turning toward my poor friend, I saw him stretched upon the ground, his white camisa stained with a purple flood gushing from his shoulder.

This sight heated my own rapidly pulsating blood, and regardless of the crowd now rushing toward me, I sprang from the friendly shelter, and standing over the insensible body of the Mexican, I poured into the cowardly rabble shot after shot from my revolver. Three or four of the foremost fell bleeding to the ground, and the others, like wolves frightened from their prey, rushed in confusion toward the house.

At this moment I perceived entering the garden from the dwelling, a dark-faced, villainous-looking Mexican, gaudily dressed in a suit of blue uniform, covered with gold lace and tinsel. He advanced pompously toward his retreating crew and, waving a heavy saber, shouted to them to renew the attack.

"*El Jefe! El Jefe!* (General! General!)" exclaimed the guerillas, and rallying again, discharged another volley of bullets into the thicket, to which I had retired to reload my weapon. As before, I remained uninjured, for stooping in the hurried act of recharging my pistol, the shots all passed over me, having no other effect than to shower down upon my head a little tempest of leaves and severed twigs.

"Give him another round! And fire low, d'ye hear! Show the rascally American no quarter—kill him!" yelled the cowardly and black-hearted Canales—for it was he.

Seeing my hopeless and desperate condition, surrounded as I was by the murderous crowd, I determined to take advantage of the brief interval while they were engaged in reloading their carbines and rush upon their cowardly leader and revenge the death of my faithful Jose, as well as that of my own, in advance, by blowing out his dastardly heart. I had, in fact, advanced several steps for that purpose, when my attention was attracted by a crowd of females, who led on by the two dark-eyed sisters of my poor friend, forced their way through the guerillas and, motioning me back to the cover of the grove, placed themselves between the Mexicans and the body of Jose and myself. They formed around us a strong cordon of women's sympathizing hearts.

The sisters threw themselves upon the ground by the body of their brother and gave vent, in wild cries, to the bitterness of their grief and in imprecations upon his cowardly murderers. They had seen him fall by the shot of the guerillas and hastened to cover his body from further indignities. They also knew that I had been his friend, and it was in consequence of that friendship that I had visited their sick parent and thus, for them, had put myself into this desperate position. They therefore determined, if possible, to save me from that rabble thirsting for my blood. Aware of the savage and cowardly character of their leader—the author of that murderous proclamation—these true women had thrown them-selves as a wall between me and inevitable death.

The other women had gathered close around me, while the two sisters were staunching the still bleeding wounds of Jose.

"He lives! He lives! Oh! thanks to the Blessed Virgin, he lives!" whispered one to the other, as she felt the throbbing of his heart and watched the regular but rapid heaving of his breast. "But for the love of Heaven, let not yonder miscreants suspect it. Oh! Juana, we may yet save him!"

Then whispering a few hurried words to her sister, she rose from the side of the wounded man and entered the thicket, back to which the women had forced me.

In the meantime, seeing this, the guerillas, who with all their savage natures were by no means devoid of gallantry, threw up their carbines and, turning to their chief, awaited his further orders.

That individual, with all the vanity of gold lace and gaudy feathers, was pacing pompously up and down the garden path and impatiently trying the edge of his saber upon the plants and flower stems within his reach. But seeing the eyes of his men turned toward him inquiringly, he exclaimed, with a vulgar oath, "Let those fools yonder have their own way for a moment, but keep a close watch on the American. Let him not escape for your lives. He shall leave this place only with a lariat about his throat! I have sworn to give quarter to no enemy of our glorious republic!" And the pompous ruffian recommenced his strides.

Meanwhile, the elder sister approached within the cover of the thicket and began, to my surprise, to hastily disrobe herself, and in a moment more, she stood before me covered only with her undergarments.

"There, Señor," said she, "you must for once in your life become a Mexican Señorita and put on my dress. I can save you, but you have not a moment to lose. The guerillas yonder will soon be upon us. You must assist my sister in bearing off my poor, wounded brother, who yet lives. But be careful, and remember you are now Carlota," continued she, as having thrown off my coat, I mechanically obeyed her instructions and donned the girl's dress.

"There now," as she displaced my cap, and in room of it fastened her long *manta* over my head and face, completely covering my features, "even poor Jose, could he see you, would be cheated by the change. You make a very pretty woman, Señor," said she, smiling at the transformation she had made in my appearance. "Now, Señor, follow my directions and you are safe. The shadows of night now gathering about us will favor your disguise. You must assist my sister Juana to the house with our wounded brother, as if you were carrying his dead body. Under my father's bed you will find a loose plank; raise it, and descend into the vault you will find below, and wait patiently for my return. And now, Señor, no awkwardness, and may the holy saints protect you!"

"And you?" I asked.

"Oh, give yourself no thought of me! I shall be soon with you." And she gently pushed me from the thicket.

I followed Carlota's directions to the letter. I assisted Juana in conveying the wounded man through the broken circle of guerillas, keeping my features hid by the close folds of the *manta*, and whatever awkwardness of gait or manner I might have exhibited was covered by the friendly twilight which had now come on. We entered the house and deposited the still insensible Jose upon a cot; then creeping beneath the sick man's bed, I descended into the little vault below while Juana carefully replaced the planks and pushed a heavy trunk over the spot.

In a few moments I heard the voices of the women, who, having returned, were surrounding the wounded man and filling the place with lamentations for his death. They accused the guerilla chief of being his murderer and called upon his head the vengeance of heaven. From my hiding place I also heard the voices of the guerillas as they searched every nook and corner of the garden for the *maldito Americano.*

Canales raved and stormed and swore that unless I was found before morning, some of them should pay with their lives for their carelessness.

I know not how many hours I had been in the narrow vault, for the fatigue of my ride, my deprivation of food, and the subsequent excitement together had exhausted my strength and I had fallen asleep. I was aroused by a hand laid gently on my head, and Carlota, with a lamp in her hand, looked down upon me from the aperture in the floor above.

"Come, Señor," said she, "you must away. The rising sun must find you well on your way toward Monterey."

And giving me her hand, she assisted me out of my cramping confinement.

"You require food," continued the kind-hearted girl. "Eat in haste, for Gabrielo awaits you with your horse beyond the village. He will also accompany you on your way."

"But how is my poor friend?" I asked.

"He is alive, has asked after you, and the knowledge that you are safe will hasten his recovery, but we have removed him beyond the reach of that bad man, who yet thinks him dead." And she handed me my coat and cap in exchange for the disguise which I had left in the vault.

Having hastily satisfied my hunger, the generous and brave Carlota hurried me from the house. She led me through gardens and over walls to the outskirts of the village where we found Gabrielo, who mounted on his own horse, was holding by the bridle my gallant little Hacaneo. The faithful animal welcomed my approach with a low whinny of recognition, and after kissing the hand of my brave, noble-hearted deliverer, and acknowledging the immense debt I owed her, I bounded into the saddle and rode rapidly away from the place.

The sun was high when we reached the city, and many weeks elapsed before my faithful Jose and myself had an opportunity to congratulate each other upon our almost miraculous escape from death at the hands of the blood-thirsty Canales.

WONDERFUL ESCAPE OF TOM HIGGINS

During the War of 1812, Tom Higgins, as he was called by his comrades, enlisted in the Rangers—a company of mounted men organized expressly for the purpose of protecting the inhabitants of the western frontier. He was one of a party of twelve men commanded by Lieutenant Journey and posted at Hill's Station, a small stockade fort about three miles south of where the village of Greenville, Illinois, now stands and about twenty miles from Vandalia, neither of which towns were then settled, the whole country, for miles around, being nothing but a vast wilderness.

On the 30th of August, 1814, signs of Indians were seen about half a mile from the fort, and at night the savages were discovered prowling around, but no alarm was given. Early on the following morning, Lieutenant Journey, with a part of his men, started in pursuit of the Indians. Passing around a field of corn which adjoined the fort, they crossed the prairie and had proceeded but a short distance, when, in crossing a ridge closely covered with a hazel thicket, in full view of the fort, they fell into an ambush of a large party of Indians, numbering some seventy or eighty, who suddenly rose around them and fired, killing four of the party, among whom was Lieutenant Journey, and badly wounding another; the rest fled, with the exception of Higgins.

The morning of a sultry day was just beginning to dawn. A heavy dew had fallen the preceding night, and the air was still humid, causing the smoke from the guns to hang in heavy clouds over the spot, and under cover of these clouds the remaining companions of Higgins had escaped, believing that all who were left were dead, or that at any rate it would be useless to attempt to rescue them from such superior numbers. Tom's horse had fallen upon his knees several times, and believing him to be severely wounded, he dismounted, but upon examination he found he was only shot in the neck and not seriously disabled. He still retained his hold on the bridle, and as he now felt sure of being able to retreat in safety, he determined to have one more shot at the savages to avenge his comrades. He looked around for a shelter but could see only one small elm, for which he started; just at that moment the smoke lifted, disclosing to his view a number of Indians, who had not yet discovered him. One of them stood only a few paces from him, loading his gun. Tom instantly raised his gun to his shoulder and, taking deliberate aim, fired and brought him to the ground. Being still concealed by the smoke, he reloaded his gun, mounted his horse, and turned to fly when a faint voice hailed him with, "Tom, you won't leave me, will you?"

On looking round to see from whom the voice proceeded, he discovered it to be one of his comrades named Burgess, who was wounded, lying on the ground and unable to move; he instantly replied, "No, I'll not leave you; come along and I'll take care of you."

"I can't come," replied Burgess, "my leg is smashed all to pieces."

Higgins sprang from his saddle and, finding his ankle bone broken, took him in his arms and attempted to put him on his horse, telling him at the same time to make the best of his way to the fort. But the horse taking fright at the same instant, started off, leaving Tom and his wounded comrade behind. Still, Tom's coolness and bravery did not desert him, and setting Burgess down, he said, "Now, my good fellow, you must hop off on three legs, while I stay between you and the Indians to keep them off," giving him instructions at the same time to get into the highest grass and keep as close to the ground as possible.

Burgess followed his advice and escaped unnoticed to the fort.

The clouds of smoke still hung thick around Higgins, hiding him from the enemy, and as he plunged through it, he left it, with the ridge and the hazel thicket between him and the Indians. He was retreating unobserved by them and, if he had taken a direct course toward the fort, might easily have effected his escape. But his friend was slowly crawling away in that direction, and the noble fellow, after coolly surveying the whole ground, saw that if he pursued the same course and should be discovered, his friend, being unable to defend himself, would most likely be sacrificed. He therefore determined to take a circuitous route and, by drawing attention to himself, save his friend.

Carrying out his design, he moved stealthily through the bushes, intending, when he emerged, to run at full speed. But as he left the thicket, he discovered a large Indian near him and two others between himself and the fort. Tom stood coolly surveying his foes and considering the best course to pursue under existing circumstances. Although confident in his own powers, but surrounded with enemies, he still considered it necessary to act with caution, and wishing to separate them, he started at full speed for a ravine not far off, but soon found he should be unable to reach it, from the effect of the wound in one of his legs, which until now he had scarcely noticed. The largest Indian was close upon his heels, and Tom turned several times to fire, but the Indian would stop and dance about to spoil his aim. Tom was aware he could not afford to lose a shot by firing at random. The other two were now fast coming up with him, and he found that unless he could dispose of the larger one, he must inevitably be overpowered. He therefore stopped, determined to receive a fire. Facing his foe, he watched his eye, and the Indian, raising his gun, fired, but Tom, cool and wary, just as he thought his finger touched the trigger, suddenly threw his side to him, and by this means probably saved his life, for the ball, which would otherwise have entered his body, was lodged in his thigh.

Tom fell, but instantly rose again and ran, and the largest Indian, now certain of his prey, loaded again, and with the two others started in pursuit. They soon came up with Tom, who had again fallen, and as he rose, they all fired, lodging three balls in his body. Being now weak from loss of blood and great exertions, he fell and rose again several times, when the Indians, throwing away their guns, rushed upon him with spears and knives, but at his presenting his gun at one or the other of them, they fell back until the largest, probably thinking from Tom's reserving his fire so long that his gun was unloaded, boldly rushed up to him, when Tom, with a steady aim, fired and shot him dead.

Almost any other man, under like circumstances, with four bullets in his body and an empty gun in his hands, would have given up in despair. But Tom Higgins had not the slightest idea of it. The largest and most formidable of the three was now out of his way, and of the other two he had but little fear, having seen from their eyes that he was their superior in courage and coolness. He therefore faced them and began loading his rifle. They raised their whoop and rushed on him. In telling the story, Tom said, "They kept their distance as long as my rifle was loaded, but when they knew it was empty, they were braver soldiers."

A fierce and bloody conflict now ensued. The Indians, rushing upon Tom, stabbed him in many places, but, fortunately for him, their spears were nothing but small green poles, cut hastily for the occasion, and bent whenever the point came in contact with Tom's ribs or one of his tough muscles. In consequence of his continued exertions with his hands and rifle in warding off their thrusts, the wounds were not deep, but his chest, and indeed his whole front, was covered with gashes, the scars of which always remained in proof of his courage and skill.

At last, one of them threw his hatchet, the edge of which struck him in his cheek, passing through the ear, which it severed, laying bare his skull to the back of his head and stretching him on the ground. The Indians rushed in, but Tom, cool as ever, was still enough for them and kept them off with his feet and hands until he at length succeeded in grasping one of their spears, which, as the Indian attempted to withdraw, aided him to rise, and clubbing his rifle, he struck the nearest of his foes and dashed out his brains, in doing which he broke the stock, leaving nothing in his hands but the barrel. The other Indian, having until now fought with much caution—probably considering his character as a warrior at stake, and that to run from a man badly wounded and almost entirely disarmed, or to suffer him to escape, would subject him to the ridicule of his tribe—uttered a horrid yell, rushed on, and attempted to stab the almost exhausted soldier, but Tom was again too quick for him and, warding off the spear with one hand, raised his rifle barrel with the other.

The Indian, not being wounded, was physically much stronger

than his adversary, but the moral courage of Tom was too much for him, and quailing beneath the fierce glance of his eagle eye, he began to retreat slowly toward the place where he had dropped his rifle. Tom, feeling that if the Indian recovered his rifle, it would be a hopeless case with him, threw away his rifle barrel and, drawing his hunting knife, rushed upon him. A desperate struggle ensued, and several deep cuts were inflicted, but the Indian finally succeeded in casting Tom from him and ran to the spot where he had thrown his gun, while Tom searched for the gun of the other Indian, thus both, bleeding and almost exhausted, were searching for arms to commence anew the battle.

The smoke that hung between them and the main body of Indians had now cleared away, and some of them having passed the thicket were in full view, and seemingly there was no chance of escape for Tom, but notwithstanding, relief was close at hand.

The little garrison at the fort, now numbering six or seven, had witnessed the whole of this desperate conflict. Among them was a Mrs. Pursley, a woman long familiar with deeds of daring, from having passed much of her time on the borders and in association with the Rangers who, seeing Tom bravely fighting with such odds against him, urged the men to go to his rescue, but they, considering the attempt useless, the Indians so far outnumbering them, refused to go. The brave woman, declaring that so fine a fellow as Tom should not be scalped for want of help, snatched a rifle out of her husband's hand and, jumping on a horse, sallied out to the rescue. The men, ashamed to be outdone by a woman, followed at full speed toward the place of combat.

An exciting scene ensued: the Indians at the ridge having just discovered Tom were rushing toward him, swinging their tomahawks and yelling like very devils, and his comrades, urging their horses to the utmost, were trying to reach him first. Tom, exhausted with the loss of blood, had fallen fainting to the earth, while his adversary, too intent on his prey to notice the approach of the Rangers, was searching for his rifle. The Rangers were the first on the ground.

Mrs. Pursley, knowing Tom's spirit, thought he had thrown himself down in despair at the loss of his rifle and the fearful odds against him. She offered him the one she carried, but Tom was past using it for the present. His friends hastily lifted him up before one of their number and turned to retreat just as the main body of the Indians came up. They made good their retreat, and the Indians retired without molesting them further.

After being carried into the fort, Tom remained insensible for some days, and for some time, his recovery was doubtful. His friends extracted two of the bullets, leaving two in his thigh, which they were unable to extract, one of which continued to give him much pain for several years, although the wound was healed. At length, hearing that a surgeon had settled within a day's journey of where he was, he went to see him. The surgeon told him he could extract the ball but charged the enormous sum of fifty dollars for the operation. This Tom considered exorbitant and refused to give, as it was more than one half of his yearly pension. On his way home, he thought the matter over and concluded he could do it himself and save the expense. Accordingly, on reaching home, he requested his wife to hand him his razor. The ride home had so irritated the parts that the ball, which at other times could not be discovered, could now be felt. With the assistance of his wife, he deliberately laid open his thigh until the edge of the razor touched the ball, and then inserting his two thumbs into the gash, he, as he termed it, *"flirted it out without costing a cent."* The other ball still remained in his thigh, but caused him no pain, except when he used violent exercise.

He continued to be one of the best hunters in the country, and it still took a strong man to handle him.

History nowhere records a nobler and more disinterested act than the one here related. Higgins, having the sure means of escape from what would be considered by most men as almost hopeless peril, unhesitatingly gave them up to a wounded comrade by offering his horse and, when that intention was defeated by the flight of the horse and there was still a chance of retreat for himself, remained at the hazard of his own life to protect his wounded friend. Were not the facts corroborated, they could hardly be believed.

ADVENTURES OF A NAVY OFFICER
IN THE CANADIAN REBELLION:
HOW HE OUTWITTED GENERAL SCOTT

The long pent-up fires of Canadian discontent had at length burst forth throughout the whole extent of the two provinces, from Quebec to Penetanguishene, in many acts of open rebellion, which threatened before long to grow into a popular and successful revolution. Thirty thousand American sympathizers, possessing as a general thing as little character as true courage, and less capital than either, responded to the call of McKenzie, Papeneau, and other equally patriotic Canadian demagogues and were rallying their forces at various points along the whole American frontier, preparing, in defiance of all law, human or divine, to invade Canada, crush the galling yoke of Britain from off her enslaved colonies, revolutionize British America, and establish a model republic, under which every American liberator was to hold an office of trust and profit.

Commissions of generals, colonels, commodores, and army and navy captains were as plenty and common among the vagabond crusaders in Western New York, Ohio, and Michigan as were the floods of worthless "wild cat" bank notes of the same period in the latter state.

I had taken a very active interest in the brigand crusade, and the "Canadian Congress" assembled in an obscure cellar in Cleveland, Ohio, had rewarded my zeal by making me a captain in the Canadian navy, with the present command of a little fore-and-aft schooner and that of a first-class line-of-battle ship in prospective.

It was late in the season (1838), when I was sent to Buffalo with my vessel for the purpose of receiving six old brass six-pounders, which were to constitute the schooner's battery when the war fairly begun, and a considerable quantity of ammunition, together with three hundred muskets, dragoons' cutlasses, and pistols *ad infinitum*, which were to be used by the patriot army in the west to commence the war with.

By the exercise of some little tact on my part, and a combination of lucky circumstances on the part of providence, I succeeded in accomplishing my mission so far as to get the arms and munitions of war on board and escaping from the harbor of Buffalo in a snowstorm, while the half dozen United States Marshals were overhauling a harmless Canadian schooner to which I had directed their attention for my own benefit.

My instructions were to touch at Cleveland for the purpose of taking in a quantity of arms which had been collected there, and then to stop at Huron, where I would be met by Gen. McLeod of the patriot army, who would give me definite instructions as to my final destination.

I got into Cleveland without any trouble and out again by carrying off two deputy marshals who came down to search the schooner and landing them on the lake shore in the woods, some ten miles to the westward of the harbor.

My six "sixes" were buried under the ballast alongside the keelson, the powder stowed in flour barrels bored full of holes and oysters all around the kegs, while the balls were packed in real red lead casks and the pistols, muskets, and swords in long boxes with lots of hay showing through the joints, all marked "Bedsteads." So that I had little fear of being caught in Huron, particularly as the people there, to a man and to a woman too I think, were favorable to the piratical revolutionary movement.

It was very nearly dark, on a cold, boisterous evening in the month of December, when I arrived at Huron, and as the crew were all out on the long wooden pier which forms the western side of the harbor, bent on to a long tow-line "tracking" the schooner up toward the piers, I saw a tall, military-looking man come along down the pier, point toward the vessel when he came near the men, and after making, as I judged, some hurried inquiries of them about her, came toward me, and the moment he stopped opposite where I was standing at the helm, I recognized him past all doubt as Gen. McLeod, the commander-in-chief of the patriot army in the west. I had never seen the general, but he had been described so minutely that I could not be mistaken in him; besides, the moment he stopped, he passed word which served as the "grand hailing sign" among the "hunters," a secret organization, of which nearly every vagabond was a member, so that there could be no mistake in the matter the man was no other than the veritable General McLeod himself.

"Good evening, Captain," he said, as soon as I had replied to the hail. "What luck, Captain?"

"Good! All right, General. But come aboard, sir," and I gave the schooner a sheer in alongside the pier, so that he could step on deck.

A moment later, and he stood there beside me at the helm, a real Hercules in stature, enveloped in a stout, gray overcoat with a fur turned down about his ears, while I gazed for a few seconds in mute admiration upon the stalwart form of one of the "Iron Duke's" favorite veterans of the peninsula and Waterloo. The general gave me the regular "hunter's grip" and then asked again, "Well, Captain, what success?"

"Beautiful, sir," I answered. "Got 'em all right down there, fooled Uncle Sam's officers in Buffalo, gave two more of 'em a free passage for nine miles out of Cleveland, and set them ashore in the woods, and here I am, General, all square by the lifts and braces, ready to fool 'Old Lundy's Lane,' Gen. John E. Wool, and all the other epauletted 'preventatives' that I expect will be here in Huron before I get away."

"Good!" exclaimed the general, laughing heartily, "Very good, Captain. There is nothing like confidence in helping one out of a tight place. But you say you have got everything safe?"

"Ay, General, so nicely stowed away that even the Argus-eyed Scott himself might ransack the schooner for a whole day and fail to discover anything wrong. I've got the cannon buried under the ballast, the powder stowed in oysters, bullets in red lead barrels, and the small arms packed in furniture boxes; so you see we're all safe, General."

"Yes, it would seem so, but look out that 'Old Lundy's Lane,' as you call him, don't get at your secret. He's in town, I believe, and there's the steamer *Constitution* lying up there, from which he has this very afternoon taken a large quantity of arms and ammunition; so look out for him."

"I will, General, and if the old seven-foot hero of Chippewa gets to wind'ard of me, I'll ship second mate of a limekiln and use my commission as captain in the Canadian navy to light the fire with."

"Bravo, Captain! That's the right sort of spirit. But come up and see me as soon as you get fast. Come and take supper with me. I'm *incog.*, you know, this evening—stopping at Jenkins' Hotel—come up, will you?" and the moment I answered "yes," the general leaped ashore and went off with a true military stride along up the wharf toward the big hotel.

As I entered the hotel, half an hour later, I was shown into the dining-room where the company were already seated at supper, and there, at the head of the table, sat the head of the patriot army in a suit of plain clothes, while ranged along down on either hand were several officers of the United States army, and one of them, a stout, hard-featured man, in a brilliant uniform, I set down at once as Major-General Scott. General McLeod smiled and nodded familiarly to me as I entered, and the seats near him being all filled, he pointed with his knife to one near the foot of the long table into which I introduced myself without further ceremony and commenced playing knife and fork with the others.

I observed during supper that the officers toward the head of the table eyed the patriotic general and myself very suspiciously, but no word was spoken to either of us, and I had very nearly finished my supper in silence, when a doctor who was seated next to me, and with whom I was intimately acquainted, asked me in a low tone what I thought of the general.

"What general?" I asked.

"Why, General Scott, of course."

"Well, then, I don't know, doctor, for I have never seen him, but one thing I *do* know, and that is, if he is half as noble-looking an officer as our commander-in-chief up there at the head of the table is, the American people will be proud of him as the head of their army."

"Why, what in the name of nonsense do you mean, Captain?"

"Just this, doctor—that General Donald McLeod there, at the head of the table, looks more like a hero than forty General Scotts."

"Captain, are you drunk or crazy? Why, man, that is *General Winfield Scott himself!*"

Down went my up-raised tea-cup with a clash that shivered it to atoms on the table at this startling announcement and, leaping to my feet, I darted from the room, through the hall, out into the street, and away down toward the wharf like a locomotive, determined to get the schooner under way and be off, somewhere—I didn't care where—much so that I escaped from "Old Lundy's Lane."

But I was too late, for I found the vessel in possession of some fifty United States soldiers, who were all working away like beavers discharging my contraband cargo of patriot arms and ammunition.

I wandered about the streets for nearly an hour, feeling myself as completely sold as ever a man was, and was so thoroughly ashamed of myself that I didn't want to go where anyone could see my face, till I was finally picked up by a Lieutenant who informed me that General Scott wished to see me at the hotel.

I was like a dog going to be hung, and being ushered into the presence of the hero of Chippewa, General Wool, and about a dozen other United States officers, I received in the first place a great deal of good advice from General Scott and then a most pressing invitation to join the party in an oyster supper prepared from the bivalves which, only an hour previously, had served as overcoats to our patriot powder. I remained, and before the party broke up, I made a public and most positive declaration that if I ever engaged in another piratical expedition, it should be in some country where Major-General Winfield Scott would not be likely to interfere with my sailing orders.

A DESPERADO'S THRILLING ADVENTURE

In the autumn of 1777, when Lord Howe had possession of Philadelphia, the situation of the Americans who could not follow their beloved commander was truly distressing, subject to the everyday insults of cruel and oppressive foes. Bound to pay obedience to laws predicated on the momentary power of a proud and vindictive commander, it can be better pictured than described. To obtain the common necessaries of life, particularly flour, they had to go as far as Bristol, a distance of eighteen or twenty miles, and even this indulgence was not granted them until a pass was procured from Lord Howe, as guards were placed along Vine Street, extending from the Delaware to the Schuylkill, forming a complete barrier; beyond these, through the woods extending as far as Frankford, were stationed the picket guards, thus rendering it in a manner impossible to reach the Bristol mills unless first obtaining a pass.

The American forces were then encamped at Valley Forge, suffering from cold, hunger, and the inclemency of the season. The British rolled in plenty, and spent their days in feastings, their nights in balls, riots, and dissipation, thus resting in supposed security, while the American chief was planning a mode for their final extirpation. A poor woman, with six small children, whose husband was at Valley Forge, had made frequent applications for a pass. Engagements rendered it impossible for her cruel tormentors to give her one. Rendered desperate from disappointment and the cries of her children, she started alone without a pass, and by good luck eluded the guards and reached Bristol.

About this time, there were six brothers of the name of Doale renowned for many acts of heroic bravery, but which were in the character of marauders rather than soldiers. They were men full six feet high, stout and active, a fearless intrepidity characterizing their deeds, and they always succeeded in making their escape. A marked partiality to the Americans rendered them obnoxious to the British and always welcome to the former, to whom they conveyed what information they could glean in their adventures.

Our adventurous female, having procured her flour in a pillow-case, holding about twenty pounds, was returning with a light heart to her anxious and lonely babes. She had passed the picket guards at Frankford and was just entering the woods a little this side when a tall, stout man stepped from behind a tree and, putting a letter in her hand, requested her to read it. She grasped with eager joy the letter bearing the character of her husband's handwriting. After a pause, he said, "Your husband is well, madam, and requested me to say that in a short time he will be with you; money is a scarce article among us—I mean among them—but on account of your husband's partiality to the cause of liberty, I am willing to become his banker." So saying, he handed her a piece of money. "My means, madam, are adequate, or I would not be thus lavish," seeing she was about to refuse it.

"You said, sir, my husband would see me shortly; how do you know that which seems so impossible? And how did you know me, who never—"

"Hush, madam, we are now approaching the British guard; suffice it to say, the American commander has that in his head which, like an earthquake, will shake the whole American continent and expunge all these miscreants, but hark! Take the road to the left—farewell." So saying, he departed. She gave one look, but vacancy filled the spot where he stood. With slow and cautious steps, she approached Vine Street. Already her fire burned beneath her bread, when the awful word "Halt!" struck her to the soul. She started and found herself in the custody of a British sentinel.

"Your pass, woman?"

"I have none, sir, my children are—"

"Curse the rebel crew! Why do you breed enemies to your king? This flour is mine—off, woman, and die with your babes."

A groan was her only answer. The ruffian was about departing when the former messenger appeared; his whole demeanor was changed: humble simplicity marked his gait—he approached the guard with a seeming fearfulness and begged him, in a suppliant voice, to give the poor woman her flour.

"Fool! Idiot!" exclaimed the guard. "Who are you? See yonder guard house—if you interfere here, that shall be your quarters."

"Maybe so, sir, but won't you give the poor woman the means of supporting her little family one week longer? Recollect the distance she has walked, the weight of the bag, and recollect—"

"Hell and fury, sirrah! Why bid me recollect, you plead in vain—begone, or I'll seize you as a spy."

"You won't give the poor woman her flour?"

"No."

"Then by my country's faith and hopes of freedom you shall!" And with a powerful arm he seized the guard by the throat and hurled him to the ground. "Run, madam, run—see the guard house is alive—secure your flour, pass Vine Street, and you are safe."

'Twas done. The guard made an attempt to rise when the stranger drew a pistol and shot him dead. The unfortunate man gazed around him with fearless intrepidity. There was but one way of escape: through the woods. Seizing the dead man's musket, he started like a deer pursued by the hounds. "Shoot him down! Shoot him down!" was echoed from one line to another. The desperado was lost in the woods, and a general search commenced; the object of their pursuit, in the meantime, flew like lightning; the main guard was left behind, but the whole picket line would soon be alarmed—one course alone presented itself, and that was to mount his horse, which was concealed among the bushes, and gallop down to the Delaware; a boat was already there for him. The thought was no sooner suggested than it was put into execution. He mounted his horse and, eluding the alarmed guards, had nearly reached the Delaware.

Here he found himself headed and hemmed in by at least fifty exasperated soldiers. One sprang from behind a tree and demanded immediate surrender. "'Tis useless to prevaricate—you are now in our possession."

"Son of a slave! Slave of a king! How dare you to address a

freeman! Surrender yourself—a Doale never surrendered himself to any man, far less to a blinded poltroon—away, or die," and attempted to pass. The guard leveled his gun, but himself was leveled in the dust; the ball of Doale's pistol had been swifter than his own. His case was now truly desperate; behind him was the whole line of guards—on the north of him, the Frankford pickets, and on the left of him, the city of Philadelphia, filled with British troops.

One way and only one presented itself, and that was to cross the river. He knew his horse; he plunged in—a shout succeeded, and before he reached half the distance, twenty armed boats were in swift pursuit. His noble horse dashed through the Delaware; his master spurred him on with double interest, while the balls whistled around him. The tide was running down, and when he reached the Jersey shore, he found himself immediately opposite the old slip at Market Street. On reaching the shore he turned round, took out a pistol, and, with a steady aim, fired at the first boat; a man fell over the side and sank to rise no more. He then disappeared in the wood. The angry, harassed, and disappointed pursuers gave one look, one curse, and returned to the Pennsylvania shore, fully believing that, if he was not the devil, he was at least one of his principal agents.

THE GAMBLERS OF THE SOUTH AND WEST

The entire world cannot produce such a collection of unmitigated scoundrels as are to be found in the South and West, some spending their time upon the rivers, some passing for planters and tavern-keepers, scattered through the country at convenient distances, making a chain of posts for the accommodation of their brethren, and others prowling about under various guises, as horse-dealers, Negro drovers, and peddlers, but carrying on the more profitable trades of Negro stealing, robbery, and murder. Commencing in most cases with gambling, the western scamp seldom pauses in his career until he has reached the topmost round in the ladder of crime.

No boat ever travels over the Mississippi, Ohio, or their tributaries without the accustomed freightage of "Chevaliers d'Industrie," as much superior in audacity and villainy to their congeners of the old world as is an incarnate demon of hell to a common, every-day rascal.

Boats are owned by associations of these scoundrels, run to facilitate gambling and robbing operations, and I would here warn all tyros in Western travel to inquire well into the character of both boat and captain before embarking, and when on board, to be reduced into no game of chance even for amusement with a stranger.

Some few years since, I think in 1842, a man was hung in Cincinnati who, although but twenty-four years of age, confessed to twenty-two murders.

According to his own story, he had been for three years of his career a nominal barkeeper upon a Western boat in order that he might have a better chance to commit and conceal crime.

Traveling as a solitary gambler, while a mere boy, he had marked one of the passengers for his prey under the idea that he carried with him a large amount of money. He engaged a part of the same state-room and, not succeeding in his efforts to inveigle the man into a game of cards, determined to murder him in the night and leave the boat with his booty.

He succeeded in the commission of the crime, but as he was searching for the supposed money, the door opening upon the guards was unlocked, and the captain of the boat entered.

Both were astonished, and the murderer paralyzed, until the captain, the older adept in guilt, informed him that he had only forestalled his intentions and proposed a division of the spoil.

For three years he remained upon the boat, engaged in gambling and, when a fair opportunity presented itself, murder.

When all or a great portion of this tribe of villains were united by that arch-fiend Murrel, they presented a phalanx of crime that seemed almost impregnable to the law, and could only have been checked, for entirely uprooted they were not, by the ultra means adopted for this purpose in Mississippi.

THRILLING ADVENTURE IN THE NORTHWEST:
HOW A BRAVE MAN SAVED DETROIT

The 16th of August, 1812, was a day that will be long remembered by the people of Detroit, for it was on that day that the old and imbecile Hull, in his capacity of Governor of the Michigan Territory, shamefully surrendered this important post, then garrisoned by two thousand brave and efficient troops, to the British and Indians.

As soon as the articles of capitulation were signed, the enemy crossed the river from Malden and took possession of the place, followed by a rabble of vile camp followers and all the savages that for some weeks had been attached to the English camp. Of course, the citizens were thrown into the utmost dismay at the sight of the painted Indians swarming their streets, and the knowledge that they might at any hour, when maddened by whisky and encouraged by their no less savage allies among the Whites, make an indiscriminate plunder of the town. But the influence of the British general for some days was sufficient to keep them from acts of open violence, and by degrees the townspeople became accustomed to their presence and strove by all means in their power to ingratiate themselves into the good graces of their captors.

When the news of the surrender reached the tribes of the southwest, they gathered from far and near and poured down upon the frontier to share in the plunder, which, in consideration of their being allies of the British, they deemed themselves justly entitled to. Detroit was filled and surrounded with savages, and the town became a scene of drunken orgies and terror, which the English were altogether unable to control. Scarcely an hour passed without an act of violence upon the unprotected citizens, and night was rendered sleepless by the fierce yells and whoops of these drunken fiends.

One day during this fearful period, a small party of Indians, restless for want of plunder and scalps, went to a store kept by a Frenchman named De Quindre, and two of them entered with the pretense that they wished to purchase something while their comrades remained without. There were lying on the counter several pieces of cloth. The Indians, seeing them, each snatched a roll and turned to leave the place. De Quindre called to them to stop, as they had not paid for the goods. But the savages were passing out of the door to rejoin their laughing companions with the cloth under their arms, when the Frenchman, leaping over his counter, jerked the goods from them and, being a powerful man, pitched the two Indians into the street.

Instantly the war-whoop was raised by the party, which was replied to from all parts of the town, and the savages, drawing their knives, made a rush upon the imprudent store-keeper. But the latter, immediately perceiving the terrible storm he had incautiously invoked, sprang back again to his store and, locking the door, ran into an upper room from which, by a window, he made his escape and ran through a back alley out upon the common and on to the fort where he begged the British commanding officer to protect himself and property from destruction. But that officer could and would do nothing, although he saw that the Indians would probably massacre the entire population if they once got a going, under such a state of excitement.

"It is not my property alone that is in danger from their violence," persisted the Frenchman, "but the lives of the entire population are in the hands of the savages, and unless you exert your authority to quiet them, our streets will flow with blood!"

"I am sorry for you, sir," coolly replied the Briton, "but the truth is, my troops are too few in number to control the warriors, and I can do nothing for you!"

De Quindre therefore abruptly left the fort and ran to the quarters of Colonel McKee, then the British agent, who he knew was not only popular among the savages but had always exerted over them unbounded influence.

On his way he could see that the Indians were gathering in

hundreds from every direction, armed with war-clubs and tomahawks, prepared for a general massacre of the inhabitants while their fierce war-cries were ringing with piercing tones upon the air. A mob of at least a thousand of the painted demons had assembled in front of his house and were demolishing his doors and windows, while his goods were being thrown out to the crowd waiting impatiently for the owner to be dragged forth and delivered to their murderous knives. This sight gave fleetness to his feet and, rushing into the colonel's quarters, he found that officer to whom he briefly, and as distinctly as his excitement would permit, related what had occurred and begged him to interfere, if possible, and prevent the threatened massacre.

McKee, well versed in the Indian character, instantly perceived the imminent danger that menaced the place, and requesting De Quindre to remain where he was, lest the Indians, so greatly exasperated against him, might kill him, hastened to the scene of excitement.

He was a tall, straight, athletic, noble-looking man, with a voice like thunder, and from his long intercourse with the Indians of the frontier had an intimate knowledge of their language. Pushing his way through the savages, now excited to madness at not finding the Frenchman, he mounted to the top of a low building, waved his sword, and in loud tones shouted, "Ho! Who are the cowards in this crowd?"

The sound of his well-known voice arrested the attention of the yelling rabble, and, after a brief silence, one of the Indians replied, "There are no *cowards* here! We are all braves!"

"It's *a lie*," returned the colonel, stamping his foot with pretended rage. "I tell you, warriors, there are cowards, craven cowards among you!"

This insulting accusation was received with astonishment by the Indians at first, and then they turned toward the bold man who had dared to utter it, with eyes burning with passion, and a yell of defiance broke simultaneously from them. But, without moving a muscle, the courageous agent met their fiery glances unquailingly. He had changed the tide of feeling and thus far had gained a very important point.

"I repeat it," continued the colonel, straightening his tall, commanding figure to its utmost stretch, "there are cowards, sneaking wolves, in this crowd, that I am ashamed to see among my brave Indians! Now, let my brave warriors separate themselves from them and stand on this side of the path, while the cowards remain about the Frenchman's doors—they are perfectly welcome to plunder his worthless goods!"

The powerful voice of the White man now struck upon the ears of the savages with an electric effect, and once more a revulsion of feeling took place among them. The tempest of angry passion was instantly subdued, and the loud yells sank to low murmurs, while the entire mass, as if impelled by one common sentiment, moved together to the other side of the street and, raising their faces to where the brave officer was standing, seemed to await his further orders.

"That is well, my friends," cried he. "Now let every brave man follow me. The cowards may remain behind and secure their plunder."

So saying, the colonel descended from his elevated position and then led them to the common beyond the town, where, mounting a stump, he detained them with a good-natured harangue while he sent off to the commissary's store for a barrel of whisky. When it arrived, he invited the Indians to drink. The barrel was soon emptied and another and another still were sent for, till under the mellowing influence of the strong waters, the fiery warriors forgot their late excitement and, by the prompt and determined action of this brave White man, were restrained from further violence.

Throughout the night, however, there were frequently heard, amid the drunken sounds, the threatening words of "fire, blood, scalps, and plunder."

But Colonel McKee had provided against further trouble from the discontented spirits among the Indians by selecting the sober warriors and dispatching two to each of the dwellings of the citizens who had been most strongly threatened. These fellows, wrapping themselves in their blankets, stretched themselves on the doorsteps as a guard to protect the inmates from any sudden outbreak of savage fury.

Thus, the energetic conduct of this brave officer, on that critical occasion, saved the city of Detroit from the torch of the savages, and its people from indiscriminate slaughter. In a great crisis, one brave, clear-headed man is worth many timid statesmen or cowardly rhetoricians.

JACOB WETZEL AND HIS FAITHFUL DOG:
A LEGEND OF CINCINNATI

The Wetzels were among the bravest of the brave hunters who ranged the forests when Ohio was the Far-West and Cincinnati a mere collection of cabins; when the smooth waters of the majestic river which gave its name to the state were disturbed only by the prow of the bark canoe or the flat boat, as it leisurely floated down upon its tide; and the Miamis, the Pottawatomies, and the Shawnees contended with the White man for the right to these beautiful hunting grounds. Many and thrilling are the incidents related of Jacob Wetzel, the most fearless of the brothers. He hated the Red man with a mortal hatred and reveled in the hand-to-hand contest in which life was the stake.

On one occasion he was returning from a very successful hunt, in which he had secured a large amount of game, to procure a horse on which to pack his booty. He had reached a spot near the banks of a water-course which ran into the Ohio, in the immediate vicinity of the collection of cabins which occupied the site where now stands "The Queen City of the West," and had sat down upon a log to wipe away the perspiration which his exertions in pressing through the thickets of underbrush had started upon his face, notwithstanding the season, when his attention was awakened by a rustling of the leaves and cracking of dry twigs under the feet of some heavy animal or more dangerous foe. His dog, too, which till now had sat quietly at his side, was startled by the sound and gave utter to a low growl which betokened his consciousness of the proximity of an enemy. Silencing the animal by a gesture, Wetzel seized his rifle and, springing behind a tree, peered through the leaves to discover his antagonist. The swaying of a bough caught his eye, and he at once became conscious of the fact that an Indian was likewise endeavoring to make out the whereabouts of the enemy, whose presence had been certified by the growling of the dog. The moving of the bough had also attracted the dog's eye, and he broke out into a long and continuous barking.

The moment Wetzel made out the form of the Indian, which was partially exposed to his aim, he brought his rifle to the shoulder. The movement was not lost upon the warrior, who, with equally rapid movement, brought his piece to a present; in doing so he altered his position so as to compel Wetzel to change his aim, and both rifles exploded simultaneously but with different effect. The Indian's aim had been too rapid to be sure, and his ball whizzed by the hunter's head without injury. Wetzel's aim, on the contrary, although hasty, had been more certain, and his ball crashed through the elbow joint of his antagonist's left arm, rendering it useless, and in much less time than I have taken to describe it, they found themselves face to face, prepared for the deadly hand-to-hand struggle in which the life of one or the other was to be the sacrifice.

Wetzel, thinking the other was disabled, concluded to decide the affair with the knife and had dropped his rifle, drawn his blade, and rushed forward to give his opponent the *coup-de-grace*, as he supposed. But the other was no child in the art of warfare and was prepared to meet him. He was a powerful, muscular, and athletic fellow, naked to his waist, and his chest and upper limbs were beautifully proportioned, exhibiting great force, combined with agility and endurance. All this was observed by Wetzel, as they stood for a moment, measuring each other's strength. The next instant they had closed in deadly combat. The skillful blows of the White man were as skillfully parried by the Indian warrior, and for a few moments the contest appeared doubtful, notwithstanding the Indian's wound.

At length, however, he parried his opponent's blows with such force and dexterity as to knock his weapon out of his hand and throw it to a distance of thirty feet among the leaves and bushes. Weaponless, but undaunted, the hunter had no other resource but to close with his antagonist and endeavor to wrench away his knife or to escape by running. The latter he was not at all disposed to try, and quick as thought he adopted the former expedient. As he rushed in and seized the Indian, he clasped his arm around his body in such a manner as to encircle his right arm, so that he could not use his knife, and in this way they struggled for a few moments until their feet becoming interlocked, they both came to the ground together. So great was the shock that the Indian's arm was released, and he prepared to strike his antagonist a fatal blow. Wetzel was not so easily finished, however, and by rolling the Indian over on his right side, prevented him from using the knife and prolonged the contest. This was repeated two or three times, until, at length, the Indian, by a powerful effort in which he concentrated his whole strength, threw the hunter underneath and, planting his knee upon the other's breast, raised his arm with an exulting shout of victory to give the final stroke. Wetzel saw the impending blow and closed his eyes in expectation of its immediate descent.

A new antagonist appears upon the scene, however, in the shape of his faithful dog, who although he had not been an idle spectator of the contest, had done but little more than bark and snap at the Indian's leggings. Roused now to the highest pitch of rage at his master's predicament, he came to the rescue at the critical moment by rushing at the Indian's throat, which he seized between his fangs and tore without mercy, causing him to drop his knife and fall backwards in such a manner as to release his master somewhat from his unpleasant situation. Collecting all his remaining strength, Wetzel threw the Indian from him, sprang to his feet, seized the other's knife, and in another instant, it was planted to the hilt in his heart, and he expired almost without a groan. Rightly judging that there might be other Red-skins in the vicinity, Wetzel lost no time in gathering up his own and the Indian's weapons and making good his escape.

He had proceeded but a short distance before he heard behind him the shouts of quite a large party of Indians, who speedily gathered around the body of their fallen comrade, and as they recognized in his distorted lineaments the features of one of their bravest chiefs, they sent up a yell which made the forests resound again. An immediate pursuit was commenced, but the hunter had fortunately found a canoe in the creek, which he had availed himself of, and when the Indians came to the opposite bank, he was safe upon the other side and out of their reach.

A DESPERADO AMONG THE MAIL BAGS:
THE STAGE DRIVER'S STORY

Fourteen years ago, I drove from Littleton, a distance of forty-two miles, and, as I had to wait the arrival of two or three coaches, did not start until after dinner, so I very often had a good distance to drive after dark. It was in the dead of winter, and the season had been a tough one. A great deal of snow had fallen, and the drifts were plenty and deep. The mail that I carried was not due at Littleton, by the contract, until one o'clock in the morning, but that winter the postmaster was very often obliged to sit up a little later than that for me.

One day in January, when I drove up for my mail at Danbury, the postmaster called me into his office.

"Pete," said he, with an important, serious look, "there's some pretty heavy money packages in that bag," and he pointed to the bag as he spoke. He said the money was from Boston to some land agents up near the Canada line. Then he asked me if I'd got any passengers who were going through to Littleton. I told him I did not know, but "suppose I haven't?" said I.

"Why," said he, "the agent of the lower route came in today, and he says that there have been two suspicious characters on the stage that came up last night, and he suspects that they have an eye upon the mail so that it will stand you in hand to be a little careful."

He said the agent had described one of them as a short, thick-set fellow, about forty years of age, with long hair and a thick, heavy clump of beard under the chin, but none on the side of his face. He didn't know anything about the other. I told the old fellow I guessed there was not much danger.

"Oh, no, not if you have got passengers through, but I only told you this so you might look out for your mail and look out when you change horses."

I answered that I should do so and then took the bag under my arm and left the office. I stowed the mail under my seat a little more carefully than usual, placing it so that I could keep my feet against it, but beyond this I did not feel any concern. It was past one o'clock in the afternoon when I started, and I had four passengers, two of whom rode on to my first stopping place. I reached Gowan's Mills at dark, when we stopped for supper and where my other two passengers concluded to stop for the night.

About six o'clock in the evening I left Gowan's Mills alone, having two horses and an open pung.

I had seventeen miles to go, and a hard seventeen it was too. The night was quite clear, but the wind was sharp and cold, the loose snow flying in all directions while the drifts were deep and closely packed. It was slow, tedious work, and my horses soon became leg weary and restive. At the distance of six miles, I came to a little settlement called Bull's Corners, where I took fresh horses. I'd been two hours going that distance. Just as I was going to start, a man came up and asked me if I was going through to Littleton. I told him I should go through if the thing could be possibly done. He said he was very anxious to go, and as he had no baggage, I told him to jump in and make himself comfortable as possible. I was gathering up my lines when the hostler came up and asked me if I knew that one of my horses had cut himself badly. I jumped out and went with him and found that one of the animals had got a deep cork cut on the off forefoot. I gave such directions as I considered necessary and was about to turn away when the hostler remarked that he thought I came alone. I told him I did.

"Then where did you get that passenger?" said he.

"He has just got in," I answered.

"Got in from where?"

"I don't know."

"Well, now," said the hostler, "that's kind o' curious. There ain't no such man been at the house, and I know that there ain't been none at any of the neighbor's."

"Let's have a look at his face," said I. "We can get that much at any rate. Go back with me, and when I get into the pung, just hold your lantern so that the light will shine into his face."

He did as I wished, and as I stepped into the pung, I got a fair view of such portions of my passenger's face as were not muffled up. I saw a short, thick frame, full, hardy features, and I could see that there was a heavy beard under the chin. I thought of the man whom the postmaster had described to me but I didn't think seriously upon it until I had started. Perhaps I had got half a mile when I noticed that the mail-bag wasn't in its old place under my feet.

"Hallo!" says I, holding up my horses a little. "Where's my mail?"

My passenger sat on the seat behind me, and I turned toward him. "Here is a bag of some kind slipped back under my feet," he said, giving it a kick, as though he'd shoved it forward.

Just at this moment my horses lumbered into a deep snow-drift, and I was forced to get out and tread the snow down ahead of them and lead them through it.

This took me all of fifteen minutes, and when I got in again, I pulled the mail-bag forward and got my feet upon it. And as I was doing this, I saw the man take something from his lap, beneath the buffalo, and put it in his breast pocket. At this I thought it was a pistol. I had caught the gleam of the barrel in the star-light, and when I had time to reflect, I knew I could not be mistaken.

About this time, I began to think somewhat seriously. From what I had heard and seen, I soon made up my mind that the individual behind me not only meant to rob the mail, but he was prepared to rob me of my life. If I resisted him, he would shoot me, and perhaps he meant to perform that delicate job at any rate. While I was pondering, the horses fell into another deep snowdrift, and I was again forced to get out and tread down the snow before them. I asked my passenger if he would help me, but he said he didn't feel very well—wouldn't try it; so, I worked alone, and was all of a quarter of an hour getting my team through the drift. When I got into the sleigh again, I began to feel for the mail-bag with my feet and found it where I had left it, but when I attempted to withdraw my foot, I discovered that it had become entangled in something. I thought it the buffalo and tried to kick it clear, but the more I kicked, the more closely was it held. I reached down my hand, and after feeling about a few minutes, I found that my foot was in the mail-bag! I felt again and found my hand in among the packages of letters and papers! I ran my fingers over the edges of the opening and became assured that the stout leather had been cut with a knife.

Here was a discovery. I began to wish I had taken a little more forethought before leaving Danbury, but as I knew that making such wishes was only a waste of time, I quickly gave it up and began to consider what I had best do under the existing circumstances. I wasn't long in making up my mind upon a few essential points. First, the man behind me was a villain; second, he had cut open the mail-bag and robbed it of some valuable matter. He must have known the money letters by the size and shape; third, he meant to leave the stage on the first opportunity; and fourthly, he was prepared to shoot me if I attempted to arrest or detain him.

I revolved these things over in my mind, and pretty soon I thought up of a course to pursue. I knew that to get my hands safely upon the rascal, I must take him unawares, and this I could not do while he was behind me—for his eyes were upon me all the time—so I must resort to stratagem. Only a little distance ahead of us was a house. An old farmer named Lougee lived there, and directly in front of it was a huge snow-bank stretched across the road, through which a track for wagons had been cleared with shovels.

As we approached the cot, I saw a light in the front room, as I felt confident I should, for the old man generally sat up until the stage went by. I drove on and, when nearly opposite the dwelling, stood up, as I had frequently done when approaching difficult places. I saw the snow-bank ahead and could distinguish it. I urged my horses to a good speed and, when near the bank, forced them into it.

One of the runners mounted the edge of the bank, after which the other ran into the cut, thus throwing the sleigh over about as quick as if lightning had struck it. My passenger had not calculated on any such movement and wasn't prepared for it, but I had calculated and was prepared. He rolled out into the deep snow with a heavy buffalo robe about him, while I lighted upon my feet directly on the top of him. I punched his head in the snow, and then sang out for old Lougee. I did not have to call a second time, for the farmer had come to the window to see me pass, and as soon as he saw my sleigh overturn, he had lighted his lantern and hurried out.

"What's to pay!" asked the old man, as he hurried out.

"Lead the horses into the track, and then come here," said I. As I spoke, I partially loosened my hold upon the villain's throat and he drew up a pistol from his bosom, but I saw it in season and jammed his head into the snow and got the weapon away from him. By this time Lougee had led the horses out and came back, and I explained the matter to him in as few words as possible. We hauled the rascal out into the road, and upon examination we found about twenty packages of letters that he had stolen from the mail-bag and stowed away in his pockets. He swore and threatened and prayed, but we paid no attention to his blarney. Lougee got some stout cord, and when we had securely bound the villain, we tumbled him into the pung. I asked the old man if he would accompany me to Littleton, and he said "of course." So, he got his overcoat and muffler, and before long we started.

I reached the end of my route with my mail all safe, though not as snug as it might have been, and my mail-bag a little worse for the game he had played upon it. However, the mail robber was secure, and within a week he was identified by some officer from Concord as an old offender, and I'm rather inclined to the opinion that he's in the state prison at the present moment. At any rate, he was there the last I heard of him.

BRADY AND THE DUTCHMAN

Captain Brady had returned from Sandusky, perhaps a week, when he was observed one evening by a man of the name of Phouts, sitting in a solitary part of the fort, apparently absorbed in thought. Phouts approached him unregarded and was pained to the bottom of his honest heart to perceive that the countenance of his honored captain bore traces of deep care, and even melancholy. He accosted him, however, in the best English he had and soothingly said, "Gabtain, was ails you?"

Brady looked at him a short time without speaking; then resuming his usual equanimity, replied, "I have been thinking about the Red-skins, and it is my opinion there are some above us on the river. I have a mind to pay them a visit. Now, if I get permission from the general to do so, will you go along?"

Phouts was a stout, thick Dutchman of uncommon strength and activity. He was also well acquainted with the woods. When Brady had ceased speaking, Phouts raised himself on tip-toe and, bringing his heels hard down on the ground by way of emphasis, his eyes full of fire, said, "By dunder und lightnin, I would rader go mit you, Gabtain, as to any of te finest weddins in tis guntry." Brady told him to keep quiet and say nothing about it, as no man in the fort must know anything of the expedition except General Broadhead, bidding Phouts call at his tent in an hour. He then went to the general's quarters, whom he found reading.

After the usual topics were discussed. Brady proposed for consideration his project of ascending the Alleghany with but one man in company, stating his reasons for apprehending a descent from that quarter by the Indians. The general gave his consent and, at parting, took him by the hand in a friendly manner, advising him how to proceed and charging him particularly to be careful of his own life and that of the men or man whom he might select to accompany him. So affectionate were the general's admonitions and so great the emotion he displayed, that Brady left him with tears in his eyes and repaired to his tent, where he found Phouts in deep conversation with one of his *pet* Indians.

He told Phouts of his success with the general, and that, as it was early in the light of the moon, they must get ready and be off betimes.

They immediately set about cleaning their guns, preparing their ammunition, and having secured a small quantity of salt, they lay down together and slept soundly until about two hours before day break. Brady awoke first and, stirring Phouts, each took down the "deadly rifle," and while all but the sentinels were wrapped in sleep, they left the little fort and in a short time found themselves buried in the forest. That day they marched through woods never traversed by either of them before; following the general course of the river, they reached a small creek that put in from the Pittsburg side; it was near night when they got there, and having no provision, they concluded to remain there all night.

Phouts struck a fire, and after having kindled a little, they covered it up with leaves and brush to keep it in. They then proceeded up the creek to look for game. About a mile from the mouth of the creek, a run comes into it; upon this run was a lick apparently much frequented by deer. They placed themselves in readiness, and in a short time two deer came in; Phouts shot one, which they skinned and carried over to their fire, and during the night jerked a great part of it. In the morning they took what they could carry of jerked and hung the remainder on a small tree in the skin, intending, if they were spared to return, to call for it on their way homeward.

Next morning, they started early and traveled hard all day. Near evening they spied a number of crows hovering over the tops of the trees near the bank of the river. Brady told Phouts that there were Indians in the neighborhood, or else the men who were expected from Susquehanna at Pittsburg were there encamped or had been some time before.

Phouts was anxious to go down and see, but Brady forbade him, telling him at the same time, "We must secrete ourselves till after night, when fires will be made by them, be they whom they may." Accordingly, they hid themselves among fallen timber and remained so till about ten o'clock at night. But even then, they could still see no fire. Brady concluded there must be a hill or thick woods between him and where the crows were seen and decided on leaving his hiding place to ascertain the fact; Phouts accompanied him. They walked with the utmost caution down toward the river bank and had gone about two hundred yards when they observed the twinkling of a fire at some distance on their right. They at first thought the river made a very short bend, but on proceeding further, they discovered it was a fork or branch of the river, probably the Kiskeminetas.

Brady desired Phouts to stay where he was, intending to go himself to the fire and see who was there, but Phouts refused, saying, "No, by George, I vil see too." They approached the fire together, but with the utmost care, and from appearances judged it to be an Indian encampment, much too large to be attacked by them. Having resolved to ascertain the number of the enemy, the captain of the spies and his brave comrade went close up to the fire and discovered an old Indian sitting beside a tree near the fire, either mending or making a pair of moccasins.

Phouts, who never thought of danger, was for shooting the Indian immediately, but Brady prevented him. After examining carefully around the camp, he was of the opinion that the number by which it was made had been large but that they were principally absent. He determined on knowing more in the morning, and forcing Phouts away with him, who was bent on killing the old Indian, he retired a short distance into the woods to await the approach of day. As soon as it appeared, they returned to the camp again, but saw no living thing, except the old Indian, a dog, and a horse.

Brady wished to see the country around the camp and understand its features better; for this purpose, he kept at some distance from it and examined about till he got on the river above it. Here he found a large *trail* of Indians, who had gone up the Allegheny; to his judgment it appeared to have been made one or two days before. Upon seeing this, he concluded on going back to the camp and taking the old Indian prisoner.

Supposing the old savage to have arms about him, and not wishing to run the risk of the alarm the report of a rifle might create if Indians were in the neighborhood, Brady determined to seize the old fellow single-handed without doing him further "scathe" and carry him off to Pittsburg. With this view both crept toward the camp again very cautiously. When they came so near as to perceive him, the Indian was lying on his back with his head toward them.

Brady ordered Phouts to remain where he was and not to fire at all, unless the dog should attempt to assist his master. In that case he was to shoot the dog but by no means to hurt the Indian. The plan being arranged, Brady dropped his rifle and, tomahawk in hand, silently crept toward the "old man of the woods" till within a few feet; then, raising himself up, he made a spring like a panther and, with a yell that awakened the echoes round, seized the Indian hard and fast by the throat. The old man struggled a little at first, but Brady's was the grip of a lion; holding his tomahawk over the head of his prisoner, he bade him surrender, as he valued his life. The dog behaved very civilly; he merely growled a little. Phouts came up, and they tied their prisoner. On examining the camp, they found nothing of value except some powder and lead, which they threw into the river. When the Indian learned that he was to be taken to Pittsburg and would be kindly treated, he showed them a canoe, which they stepped into with their prisoner and his dog, and were soon afloat on the smooth bosom of the Allegheny.

They paddled swiftly along for the purpose of reaching the mouth of the run on which they had encamped coming up, for Brady had left his wiping-rod there. It was late when they got to the creek's mouth. They landed, made a fire, and all laid down to sleep.

As soon as daylight appeared, the captain started to where their jerk was hanging, leaving Phouts in charge of the prisoner and his canoe. He had not left the camp long, till the Indian complained to Phouts that the cords upon his wrists hurt him. He had probably discovered that in Phouts' composition there was a much larger proportion of *kindness* than of *fear*. The Dutchman at once took off the cords, and the Indian was, or pretended to be, very grateful.

Phouts was busied with something else in a minute and left his gun standing by a tree. The moment the Indian saw that the eye of the other was not upon him, he sprung to the tree, seized the gun, and the first Phouts knew was that it was cocked and at his breast, whereupon he let out a most magnificent *roar* and jumped at the Indian. But the trigger was pulled, and the bullet whistled past him, taking with it a part of his shot-pouch belt. One stroke of the Dutchman's tomahawk settled the Indian forever and nearly severed the head from his body.

Brady heard the report of the rifle and the yell of Phouts, and supposing all was not right, ran instantly to the spot where he found the latter sitting on the body of the Indian, examining the rent in his shot-pouch belt. "In the name of Heaven," said Brady, "what have you done!"

"Yust look, Gabtain," said the fearless Dutchman, holding up to view the hole in his belt. He then related what has been stated with respect to his untying the Indian and the attempt of the latter to kill him. They then took off the scalp of the Indian, got their canoe, took in the Indian's dog, and returned to Pittsburg, the fourth day after their departure.

The captain related to the general what he had seen and gave it as his opinion that the Indians whose camp he had discovered were about making an attack upon the Susquehanna settlement. The general was of the same opinion and was much affected by the information, for he had just made a requisition upon the country for men and had been expecting them on every day. He now feared that the Indians would either draw them into an ambush and cut them off or fall upon their families, rendered defenseless by their absence.

MAJOR STOUT, THE REGULATOR

As late as the year 1852, there lived in the state of Kentucky a man who presented in his traits of character the most marked contrast ever, perhaps, exhibited in one individual. A murderer by his own confession, a brute in all his instincts, he entertained the most bitter and malignant spirit of revenge against everyone who did him an injury, however trivial, which invariably resulted in the sudden and violent death of the offending individual. His address was such, however, that the crime could never be fastened upon him, and although there were many who were ready to swear that he was the murderer, yet no legal proof could be obtained sufficient to base an indictment upon, and he died in his bed at the age of eighty-two. Notwithstanding his murderous proclivities, he was an exemplary man in his family and had a great regard for the gentler sex, whose champion he was on all occasions, constituting himself a "Regulator" of all wrongs inflicted upon them. The following instance of his decision "in equity" is characteristic.

There lived in the neighborhood the widow of a man with whom he had a slight acquaintance and who had left to his family a tract of three hundred acres of land and a few Negroes. There was a slight mortgage of two or three hundred dollars on the property, however, which in time became due, and the widow, inexperienced in such matters, began to fear the loss of her comfortable home. A near neighbor, professing a deep sympathy in her distress, offered to loan her the necessary amount to redeem her property, which offer was accepted and a new mortgage given to the *kind neighbor* bearing interest at the rate of *60 percent per annum*. Thus it stood for several years, the interest being added up every ninety days, made principal, and a note taken from the widow to be tacked to the mortgage, until the whole amounted to more than the land would sell for under foreclosure, when the kind neighbor obtained a bill of sale of her Negroes.

The position of matters became known, and Stout, having satisfied himself by a look at the records, shouldered his rifle one morning without saying a word to anyone and went to look after the money-lender, whom he discovered in his cornfield at a distance from his own or any other dwelling engaged in shooting squirrels—those busy depredators upon his roasting ears.

He was suddenly confronted by Stout, the man whom of all others he dreaded and least of all wished to see with his rifle cocked and presented to his breast, who commanded him in a threatening tone to "throw down that gun."

The affrighted usurer obeyed and, in trembling accents, exclaimed, "My God! Uncle Bill, what is the matter, what harm have I ever done you?"

"Oh, none that I know of," said Stout, "but old Master," turning his eyes upwards, "has sent me for you. He says you are not fit to live among men and has told me to kill you and throw you into that sink hole."

"Oh! Major Stout, have mercy upon me," said Avery—as we shall call him—throwing himself upon his knees, "oh, have mercy upon me."

"Well, now," replied Stout, "don't pray to me! Pray to old Master, for he says you must die. If you want, I'll give you time to pray to him, but you must be quick about it. Maybe he'll help you; I can't."

Fully believing in the certainty of approaching death, the usurer engaged in earnest supplications to God for mercy, and among other ejaculations was, "Oh, Lord! Have mercy on my poor wife and children."

As these words were uttered, a demoniac scowl passed over the face of Stout, who still stood with his rifle at the other's breast, and said, "Aye, now that's a good prayer, and while you pray for your wife and children, pray also for King's widow and orphans, whom you have ruined. Maybe old Master will then do something good for you."

"Oh!" said Avery, "I'll do anything you say I must for Mrs. King and her poor little children—only spare my life, Major."

"I cannot spare your life unless old Master tells me to," said Stout, and the poor trembling wretch again addressed his prayers to Heaven, praying for the widow and her children, each by name.

And while in the fervor and earnestness of his petition in their behalf, he was interrupted by Stout, who said, "Ah! that's the right way to pray! Didn't you say a while ago that you was willing to do anything I said you ought for Mrs. King and her children?"

"Oh! yes," replied Avery, as the tears streamed down his pallid cheeks, "I'll do anything for them you say."

"Well, old Master has told me if you will do what I tell you I may spare your life. Now, you must give up her Negroes, for whom you have her bill of sale, and execute and record a release of the mortgage you hold on her land."

"Oh! I'll do it. Major, I'll do it now—anything you require."

"Well," said Stout, "we'll see," and taking a sheet of paper from the crown of his hat, a penful of ink from his ink-vial, which he carried suspended by a piece of string to a button of his vest, he seated himself upon a fallen log—a position he was accustomed to, and would have preferred to the most convenient desk in a merchant's counting-room—and began to write out a bill of sale for the Negroes and a release of the mortgage upon the widow's property. Both being finished were read over to the kneeling supplicant slowly and distinctly, and Stout then said, "This," presenting the bill of sale, "you must now sign, and I will witness it and keep it for Mrs. King, and this," presenting the release, "you must also sign, but as it has to be recorded in the county clerk's office, you must go tomorrow morning to the clerk and acknowledge it for record before him, as it is best not to have to call in two witnesses. This is a matter between us alone, and I want no witnesses.

"And now, upon two conditions, old Master tells me I may spare your life. Now, you know I will kill you, go where you will, if you fail to comply, if you do not meet me tomorrow morning at the clerk's office in Russellville, between nine and ten o'clock, to acknowledge the release. This is one condition. And if you raise a talk or fuss about it, now or hereafter, I will assuredly kill you. Nothing but death shall save you from my vengeance."

The usurer solemnly engaged to comply with all the major required of him. He then signed his name to the papers. Stout attested them and put them in his pocketbook, when, as it was near night, after again admonishing Avery to be prompt to his engagement, he started for his home at Russellville, a distance of thirteen miles, while his humbled victim gathered up his gun and hat and started for his house, not a little nervous from the scene he had passed through. It may be questioned whether he slept much that night. Nevertheless, he appeared at Russellville punctually at the hour named and, repairing to the clerk's office, acknowledged the release to be his own act and deed, and it is not known to this day that he ever complained in any way or even whispered the affair to anyone. Stout did, however, more than once, and triumphantly referred to the record as proof of the truth of the story.

The reader may doubt whether the threats of Stout were more than a mere hoax. He is assured, however, that they were not so intended. Avery knew the indomitable will and energy of the man, and knowing of similar affairs that had ended more tragically, he was well aware that Stout's threats would be executed if he had not compiled with his demands. He thought it better, therefore, to lose the land than his life.

DESPERATE ADVENTURE OF COLONEL MCLANE

Colonel Allen McLane, who died at Wilmington, Delaware in 1829, at the patriarchal age of eighty-three, was distinguished for his personal courage and for his activity as a partisan officer. He was long attached to Major Lee's famous legion of horse. While the British occupied Philadelphia, McLane was constantly scouring the upper ends of Bucks and Montgomery counties to cut off the scouting parties of the enemy and intercept their supplies of provisions. Having agreed for some purpose to rendezvous near Shoemakertown, Colonel McLane ordered his little band of troopers to follow at some distance and commanded two of them to precede the main body but also to keep in his rear and, if they discovered an enemy, to ride up to his side and inform him of it without speaking aloud.

While leisurely approaching the place of rendezvous in this order, in the early gray of the morning, the two men directly in the rear, forgetting their orders, suddenly called out, "Colonel, the British!" Faced about and putting spurs to their horses, they were soon out of sight. The colonel, looking around, discovered that he was in the center of a powerful ambush, into which the enemy had silently allowed him to pass without his observing them. They lined both sides of the road and had been stationed there to pick up any straggling party of Americans that might chance to pass.

Immediately on finding they were discovered, a file of soldiers rose from the side of the highway and fired at the colonel, but without effect, and as he put spurs to his horse and mounted the roadside into the woods, the other part of the detachment also fired. The colonel miraculously escaped, but at a shot striking his horse upon the flank, he dashed through the woods, and in a few minutes reached a parallel road upon the opposite side of the forest. Being familiar with the country, he feared to turn to the left, as that course led to the city and he might be intercepted by another ambush. Turning therefore to the right, his frightened horse carried him swiftly beyond the reach of those who had fired upon him. All at once, however, on emerging from a piece of woods, he observed several British troops stationed near the roadside and, directly in sight ahead, a farmhouse, around which he observed a whole troop of the enemy's cavalry drawn up. He dashed by the troops near him without being molested, they believing he was on his way to the main body to surrender himself. The farmhouse was situated at the intersection of two roads, presenting but two avenues by which he could escape.

Nothing daunted by the formidable array before him, he galloped up to the crossroads, on reaching which he spurred his active horse, turned suddenly to the right, and was soon fairly out of reach of their pistols, though as he turned, he heard them call loudly to surrender or die! A dozen were instantly in pursuit, but in a short time they all gave up the pursuit except two. Col. McLane's horse, scared by the first wound he had received and being a chosen animal, kept ahead for several miles while his two pursuers followed with unwearied eagerness. The pursuit at length waxed so hot, that as the colonel's horse stepped out of a small brook that crossed the road, his pursuers entered it at the opposite margin. In ascending a little hill, the horses of the three were greatly exhausted, so much so, that neither could be urged faster than a walk.

Occasionally, as one of the troopers pursued on a little in advance of his companion, the colonel slackened his pace, anxious to be attacked by one of the two, but no sooner was his willingness discovered, then the other fell back to his station. They at length approached so near, that a conversation took place between them, the troopers calling out, "Surrender you rebel, or we'll cut you in pieces." Suddenly, one of them rode up on the right side of the colonel, and, without drawing his sword, laid hold of the colonel's collar. The latter, to use his own words, "had pistols *which he knew he could depend on.*" Drawing one from the holster, he placed it to the heart of his antagonist, fired, and tumbled him dead on the ground. Instantly the other came upon his left, with his sword drawn, and also seized the colonel by the collar of his coat. A fierce and deadly struggle here ensued, in the course of which Col. McLane was desperately wounded in the back of his left hand, the sword of his antagonist cutting asunder the veins and tendons of that member.

Seeing a favorable opportunity, he drew his other pistol, and with a steadiness of purpose, which appeared even in his recital of the incident, placed it directly between the eyes of his adversary, pulled the trigger, and scattered his brains on every side of the road! Fearing that others were in pursuit, he abandoned his horse in the highway, and apprehensive from his extreme weakness, that he might die from loss of blood, he crawled into an adjacent mill-pond, entirely naked, and at length succeeded in stopping the profuse flow of blood occasioned by his wound.

THE BACKWOODSMAN AND THE TURKEY

"What are you doing with that gun, Jim?" said a tall, spare man to a young lad, who was sitting on a stump in the open space of a "station," repairing the lock of an old rifle that was somewhat out of order.

"I am going to shoot that turkey," said the youth.

"What turkey? I don't see any turkey."

"Don't you hear that turkey gobbling on the hillside yonder?" replied the youth. "I've heard him this half hour, and I'm going to have a shot at him as soon as I get this gun fixed."

"I don't believe there's any turkey there, youngster; I haven't heard one, and I reckon my ears are about as good as yours."

"You haven't, eh! Just listen—there, did you hear that? Ain't that a gobbler?"

The man listened until the noise was again repeated and then remarked, "I reckon you'd better not try to shoot that turkey; more'n likely he'd shoot you."

The lad did not understand the drift of his meaning and persisted in his intention of "trying a shot at him anyway," and the other, thinking, doubtless, that it would be useless to persuade him of the true state of the case, remarked, "I'll go shoot it."

"No, you shan't," said the lad, "I heard it first, and I've the best right to it; it's mine, and I'm going to shoot it."

"Well! But you know I'm the best shot," said the man, "and maybe you might miss him. A wild turkey's a mighty scary bird, and it ain't every youngster that knows how to fire a rifle that knows how to shoot one; I reckon you'd better let me shoot him. I've know'd many a feller go out to shoot a gobbler that never cum back agin, and it ain't judgmatical for a youngster like you to be skirting out through the woods when there's so many Red-skins about."

"I don't care," persisted the lad. "That's my turkey, and I'm going after him; I ain't afraid of Red-skins."

"Well, boy, I don't want the turkey, but as I'm a better shot than you are, I'll go get him, and you may have him for all I care."

These terms were agreed to, for the lad knew that the hunter was not excelled as a marksman in the country round about and also knew him to be a man of his word.

The station where the above conversation occurred had been built for the protection of the early settlers in the neighborhood of Clarksburg, Harrison County, Virginia, and at the time was occupied by many of their families, who had been driven to take shelter therein from an alarm caused by the discovery of Indian "sign" in the vicinity. The alarm had somewhat subsided, and most of them were preparing to return to their homes. The lad was a member of one of the families and, like the rest, had become restless at the confinement of the station; it was therefore with considerable reluctance that he consented that the hunter should go after the turkey, but there was something in his tone and words, as well as in his pertinacity, which struck the lad as singular, and his fears were aroused without knowing why, hence his assent.

Jesse Hughes, the hunter, was one of those noble woodsmen whom a life in the forest, and constant strife with the Red men, had made proficient in all the arts of woodcraft, and having been brought up from infancy in the hot-bed of Indian warfare, and having associated with most of those brave pioneers who had been the first to enter the domain of the Indian west of the Alleghanies, he had become an expert in all those arts and practices of the Red men, which added to the superior sagacity of the White man, has made the former succumb to the latter, and yield up, step by step, his hunting grounds, his homes, and the graves of his sires. Of a cold, taciturn disposition, it was not his wont to give his reasons for anything he did, preferring to convince by the force of example than to explain the whys and wherefores of his actions. On the present occasion he wished to give the lad a striking lesson in woodcraft and impress upon his mind the necessity of caution and watchfulness, especially when "the Red-skins were around."

To the ear of Hughes, trained as it had been in the severe school of Indian warfare, there was something in the sound of the gobbling on the hillside that convinced him that the turkey who made it wore a scalp lock and carried a rifle. Saying nothing of his suspicions, however, he made his exit from the fort on the opposite side to that from whence the sound appeared to come and, with the stealthy tread of a cat, made his way along the river, which ran on that side, taking advantage of every shrub, bush, and tree to shelter himself from view.

After proceeding for nearly a quarter of a mile in a direction which led him away from the sound, he struck off to his left into the woods and began to ascend the hill. He was not sure but that he might find an enemy when he least expected to, and hence his progress was very slow and guarded by all the finesse of an experienced scout. At times, when the wood was open, he would trail his body along on the ground, taking advantage of every old log and stump and shrub to screen his movements, and when a thicket or clump of underbrush offered its friendly shelter, he would make use of it to study his ground and listen for the sound that directed his next advance. In this cautious manner he proceeded, making his way always up, but always with a noiseless tread, not a twig being broken nor a leaf rustled under his moccasined feet until he had reached a point considerably above the spot where the supposed turkey ought to be.

Here he stopped to listen for the sound again and was surprised to hear it repeated somewhat nearer than he had counted upon. Drawing himself back, he lay quietly down upon his face, and slowly dragging his rifle with him, moved with a gradually undulating motion forward. Just in front of him, at the distance of one hundred yards or a little more, was an open space from whence the sound appeared to proceed and where he felt sure of finding his game. Between him and this open space was a thicket of hazel bushes that effectually sheltered his approach but at the same time would prevent his getting close enough to fire without some little noise. This he knew would not answer, and he carefully looked about him for an opening.

At length, observing a space on his left where a tree had been cut down, he dragged himself carefully toward it and, using the stump as a shield to his person, gradually drew himself up behind it. Here he cautiously raised his head and discovered what he had expected to find: an Indian, sitting on a chestnut-stump, surrounded by the young sprouts that had started up around it, gobbling in imitation of a turkey and watching to see if anyone came from the fort to shoot it. In much less time than it requires to tell it, there was a flash and a report, and the turkey lay quivering in the agonies of death.

Darting into the hazel bushes, Hughes lay quiet for at least a quarter of an hour, during which time he reloaded his rifle, and then, satisfied that there were no other Indians in the immediate neighborhood, he took the scalp and rifle of the poor fellow he had shot and made his way to the fort. On reaching it, he was accosted by the lad who had anxiously waited to hear the report of Hughes's rifle and was now equally as anxiously awaiting the coveted prize.

On beholding the hunter returning without the turkey, he exclaimed, "There now! I knew you would let the turkey go. I would have killed him if I had gone."

"Don't be so sure of that, youngster; it might have taken two to make that bargain. I didn't let him go."

"Where is he then?" said Jim.

"There's your turkey, Jim; take it, I don't want it," said Hughes at the same time throwing down the scalp.

The lad looked at it for a moment, and when he appreciated the danger he had escaped, purely through the foresight, keen perception, and management of the hunter, he was so overcome that he nearly fainted away.

THE INDIANS AND THE HOLLOW LOG

In the fall of 1781, a man was captured in the vicinity of Fort Plain by seven Indians and hurried off into the wilderness. At night, the party halted at a deserted log tenement. The Indians built a fire and after supper gathered around it discussing the misfortunes of their expedition, which thus fur had resulted in but a few scalps and one prisoner. They therefore resolved to kill and scalp their captive in the morning and return toward the Mohawk with the hope of better success. Upon this conclusion they stretched themselves upon the floor for sleep, with their prisoner between two of them, who was bound by cords, which were also fastened to the bodies of his keepers. The whole of the discussion carried on by the savages was understood by the captive, who in the greatest alarm at his approaching fate, began to tax his ingenuity for some way to escape. The Indians were soon in a sound slumber, but their White companion kept wide awake, vainly striving to devise a plan for his escape and beginning to despair and to yield himself to his doom, when as he accidentally moved his hand upon the floor, it rested upon a fragment of broken window glass.

No sooner did the prisoner seize the glass than a ray of hope entered his bosom, and with this frail assistant he instantly set about regaining his liberty. He commenced severing the rope across his breast, and soon it was stranded. The moment was one of intense excitement; he knew that it was the usual custom for one or more of an Indian party to keep watch and prevent the escape of their prisoners. Was he then watched? Should he go on, with the possibility of hastening his own doom, or wait and see if some remarkable interposition of Providence might save him? A monitor within whispered, "Faith without works is dead," and after a little pause in his efforts, he resumed them and soon had parted another strand, and as no movement was made, he tremblingly cut another; it was the last, and as it yielded, he sat up.

He was then enabled to take a midnight view of the group around him, in the feeble light reflected from the moon through a small window of a single sash. The enemy appeared to sleep, and he soon separated the cords across his limbs. He then advanced to the fire and raked open the coals, which reflected their partial rays upon the painted visages of those misguided heathen, whom British gold had bribed to deeds of damning darkness, and being fully satisfied that all were sound asleep, he approached the door.

The Indians had a large watchdog outside the house. He cautiously opened the door, sprang out, and ran, and as he had anticipated, the dog was yelling at his heels. He had about twenty rods to run across a cleared field before he could reach the woods, and as he neared them, he looked back and, in the clear light of the moon, saw the Indians all in pursuit. As he neared the forest, they all drew up their rifles and fired upon him, at which instant a strong vine caught his foot and he fell to the ground. The volley of balls passed over him, and bounding to his feet, he gained the beechen shade. Not far from where he entered, he had noticed the preceding evening a large hollow log, and on coming to it, he sought safety within it. The dog, at first, ran several rods past the log, which served to mislead the party, but soon returned near it and ceased barking without a visit to the entrance of the captive's retreat.

The Indians sat down over him and talked about their prisoner's escape. They finally came to the conclusion that he had either ascended a tree near or the *devil* had aided him, which to them appeared the most reasonable conclusion. As morning was approaching, they determined on taking an early breakfast and returning to the river settlements, leaving one of their number to keep a vigilant watch in that neighborhood for their captive until afternoon of the following day, when he was to join his fellows at a designated place. This plan settled, an Indian proceeded to an adjoining field where a small flock of sheep had not escaped their notice and shot one of them. While enough of the mutton was dressing to satisfy their immediate wants, others of the party struck up a fire, which they chanced, most unfortunately for his comfort, to build against the log *directly opposite their lost prisoner.*

The heat became almost intolerable to the tenant of the fallen basswood before the meat was cooked; besides, the smoke and steam that found their way through the small wormholes and cracks had nearly suffocated him, before he could sufficiently stop their ingress, which was done by thrusting a quantity of leaves and part of his own clothing into the crannies. A cough, which he knew would ensure his death, he found most difficult to avoid; to back out of his hiding place would also seal his fate, while to remain in it much longer, he felt conscious, would render his situation, to say the least, not enviable.

After suffering most acutely in body and mind for a time, the prisoner, who was again such by accident, found his miseries alleviated when the Indians began to eat, as they then let the fire burn down and did not again replenish it. After they had dispatched their breakfast of mutton, the prisoner heard the leader caution the one left to watch in that vicinity, to be wary, and soon heard the retiring footsteps of the rest of the party. Often during the morning, the watchman was seated or standing over him.

Not having heard the Indian for some time, and believing the hour of his espionage past, he cautiously crept out of the log, and finding himself alone, being prepared by fasting and steaming for a good race, he drew a beeline for Fort Plain, which he reached in safety, believing, as he afterward stated, that all the Indians in the state could not have overtaken him in his flight.

THE TRAVELER AND THE ARKANSAS BULLY

ome years ago, when horse thieves, Negro stealers, gamblers, *id est omne genus,* were much more common in the Arkansas country than they are today, a party of six or eight borderers were one cool evening in November collected around the bar-room fire of the Jefferson House, in a place well known, but which it suits our purpose not to name. They were rather a rough-looking set of fellows, take them all in all, and at the moment we introduced them, were attentively listening to the wonderful exploits of one Kelser, who was known in those parts as the leader of a gang of bullying scoundrels, though the persons to whom he was talking, being comparative strangers, permitted him the rare enjoyment of telling his story, spreading his fame, and making himself a hero in a new quarter.

Winding up the detail of his sixth bloody duel and rencounter with an oath, he added, by way of a climax: "I'm one of them as is never afeard of anything—White, Black, or Red—and all I want is (displaying the hilt of his bowie knife) for anybody to show me the fellow as says I is."

As he spoke, he straightened himself up, bent his round, bullet-head forward, and brought his face, with its pug nose, thin, sneering lips, and small, black, somewhat bloodshot eyes, to bear upon each of those present, and with a defiant expression, which seemed to say as plainly as words, "Who dares contradict me?"

No one made any answer, and each eye, if it did not quail, at least fell before the contemptuous glance of the braggadocio.

"Yes," he repeated, with another oath, "I'm one of them as is never afraid of anything, as I said afore, and to prove it, I'll tell ye of my fight with Dexter—Rash Dexter, as we used to call him."

And then, with the air of one perfectly satisfied that he was a hero, which no man dared dispute, he was proceeding with his story, when a tall, slender individual, in the dress of a northern traveler, somewhat dusty and with a pair of saddle-bags thrown across his arm, quietly entered the inn.

Approaching the bar—whither the landlord, who was one of the party at the fire, immediately repaired—the stranger mildly inquired if he could be entertained for the night.

"Certainly, sir," returned Boniface, with a cheerful air. "A horse, I reckon, sir?"

The traveler nodded, and while he proceeded to divest himself of his overcoat and deposit his traveling equipment with the host, the latter called to a Black servant and ordered him to attend to the gentleman's beast.

"Supper, sir?" pursued the landlord, with an eye to business.

Again, the traveler nodded, and perceiving the fire was surrounded by the party already mentioned and evidently not wishing to intrude himself among strangers, he quietly took his seat by a table near the wall.

Meantime he had not escaped notice as no newcomer in such a place does, but while most of the company scanned him somewhat furtively, Kelser, the egotistical hero of his own bloody exploits, angered by the interruption, stopped his narration and regarded him with a savage scowl.

"Another dang Yankee, I'll bet high on't!" he said, in a sneering, grating tone, intended to disconcert, irritate, and insult the traveler.

The latter, however, seemed to take no notice of the remark, but turning to the table upon which there chanced to be lying an old paper, he picked it up, as it were, mechanically, and soon appeared to be deeply absorbed in its contents.

This quiet, inoffensive proceeding served to irritate the ruffian still more, but contenting himself for the time by muttering something about all Yankees being cowards, he turned to the others and proceeded with his story speaking somewhat louder than usual, especially when he came to the bloody details of his narrative as if to arrest the attention of the stranger and impress him unfavorably.

Finding the latter was not in the least disturbed, however, Kesler closed with a tremendous oath, and then, turning to the landlord, who had once more joined the party, he inquired, in a loud tone, if he thought there were any "cussed thieves amongst 'em from abroad?"

"Hush!" returned the host, in a low, cautious tone. "Don't go for to make a muss here, I beg of you, for such things ruin a man's house!"

"Do you want to take up on that fellow's side?" sneered the bully, fixing his black, snaky eyes upon the host with an expression that made the latter quail.

"Oh, no, Kelser—I don't want to take anything up, and so I beg you won't say nothing to him. Come, let's take a drink all round, and call it quits."

"In course we'll take a drink," returned the other, with a coarse laugh, "and as it's to be all round, why, we'll have it all round."

Saying this, and rising as he spoke, he walked over to the inoffensive traveler with a swaggering air and, slapping him somewhat heavily on the shoulder, said roughly, "How d'ye do, stranger?"

The man looked up with something like a start and displayed features in striking contrast with those of his interrogator. He seemed about five-and-twenty years of age; had a smooth, broad, high forehead; a rather German, slightly effeminate, and almost beardless face; and mild, pleasant blue eyes, the general expression of the whole countenance denoting one of a naturally timid, retiring, and unobtrusive disposition. Fixing his eyes upon the bully—rather with the air of one who did not exactly comprehend the cause of being so rudely disturbed, than with anything like anger or resentment at the harsh, unceremonious interruption—he seemed to wait for the latter to volunteer some explanation of his uncivil proceeding.

"I said, how d'ye do, stranger?" repeated Kesler. "But you don't seem to understand the civil thing."

At this the crowd, in expectation of a quarrel, at once started up and silently gathered around the bully and the traveler. This seemed to startle the latter a little, and glancing quickly from one to the other, he replied, "I am very well, if that is what you wish to know, but really, I do not comprehend why you should be so solicitous about my health."

"There's a great many things that you dang Yankees don't comprehend!" rejoined Kesler, with a chuckling laugh.

"What does this mean, gentlemen?" inquired the traveler, turning a little pale—his mild, blue eyes beginning to gleam with a strange, peculiar light—at the same time rising and glancing from one to the other, till his gaze rested upon the troubled visage of his host. "What have I done that anyone here should seek to insult me? Do you permit this, sir?" he added, addressing the innkeeper.

"He can't help himself," interposed the bully. "If there's anybody as wants to insult you, it's me, and Bill Kelser always does what he likes—anywhere and with anybody!"

"And why do *you* seek to quarrel with a man that never saw or exchanged a word with you before?" quietly asked the stranger, his lips slightly quivering, either with fear or suppressed anger—a soft glow diffusing itself over his whole face and the pupils of his eyes seeming to expand, and grow dark, and gleam even more strangely than before.

"Because I hate all you cussed Yankees, and whenever I see one of your tribe, I always feel like cutting his heart out! For I'm one of those as never knowed what it was to fear either man or devil!"

"Come!" interposed the landlord, taking the bully by the arm. "We was going to take a drink, you know!"

"Yes, I'm in for that too!" said Kelser. "Always good at either a drink or a fight, I am. You hear, stranger?" he continued, taking hold of the latter's arm somewhat roughly. "You hear, don't you? We're going to take a drink with the landlord, and if you can prove you're a decent White man, we'll *honor* you by taking another with you afterward."

"I shall have no objection to treat, if the gentlemen here think I ought to do so," returned the traveler, drawing himself up with dignified firmness, and speaking in a more positive manner than he had yet done, "but as for drinking myself, that is something I never do."

Nothing at that moment could have pleased the bully better than to hear the stranger refuse to drink, for he had long since resolved upon a quarrel with him: first, from natural malice;

secondly, because he believed him one to be easily disposed of; and thirdly, because he might thus make a grand display of his fighting qualities with little or no risk to himself—a very important consideration, when we bear in mind that all such characters are utter cowards at heart.

"So you don't drink, eh?" he said to the stranger. "D'ye hear that, gentlemen?" appealing to the crowd. "Now everybody round here has to drink or fight! And so (walking up to the traveler) you've got to do one or t'other—which shall it be?"

"I do not wish to do either," was the reply, "but drink I will not!"

"Then fight you shall!" cried the other, closing the sentence with a wicked oath and at the same time laying his hand upon the hilt of his bowie knife and partly drawing it from its sheath.

"Do you intend to murder me? Or give me a chance for my life?" inquired the stranger, with a coolness that astonished those who, looking upon his fine, delicate features and slender figure, expected to see him shrink back in alarm and dismay.

"Give you a chance, in course!" returned the bully, in a less confident tone for he too had expected to see the other succumb at once.

"Do you challenge me to a fair combat?" inquired the other.

"In course I does," blustered Kelser. "We don't do nothing else in this country but the fair thing."

The affair now began to look serious.

"Gentlemen," said the traveler, with a polite bow to the company in general, "you know how quietly I came in here and how inoffensively I conducted myself afterward, and you have seen how this man has ventured beyond all rules of good breeding and stepped out of his way to insult and fix a quarrel upon me. Now, then, as I am a stranger here though one who has heard much of southern chivalry, I wish to know how many of you will agree to stand by and see fair play?"

"All! All of us!" was the almost simultaneous response. "You shall have fair play, stranger!"

The bully turned slightly pale and seemed more discomposed and uneasy.

"I thank you, gentlemen, for convincing me by your offer that you are governed by justice and honor!" pursued the traveler.

"And now I will prove to you that this man is a cowardly braggadocio, or else one of us shall not quit this place alive! It is understood that I am challenged to a single fight, is it not?"

There was a general affirmative response.

"The challenged party, I believe, has the choice of weapons, time, and place?"

Another affirmative response, the bully looking still paler and more anxious.

"Well then, gentlemen, not being handy with the bowie knife and wishing an equal chance for life, I propose to leave the result to fate and so test the courage of my opponent. Any man can stand up for a fight if he knows he has the best of it, but only true courage can coolly face uncertainty, and my insulter boasts of fearing nothing. My proposition is this: Let two pistols be selected, one be loaded, and both be concealed under a cloth upon this table. Then my fighting friend and myself shall draw one by lot, point the drawn one at the heart of his foe, and pull the trigger, the unarmed one standing firm and receiving the charge or not as heaven shall will! Is not this fair?"

"Perfectly fair!" coincided all but Kesler, who demurred and swore that nobody but a Yankee would ever have thought of such a heathenish way of doing business.

"Did I not tell you he was a coward, this fellow, who a few minutes ago feared neither man nor devil?" sneered the stranger, thus, drawing a laugh from the company, who now seemed to be all on his side.

The landlord now objected to the affair taking place in his house, but on one of the company taking him aside and whispering in his ear, he made no further opposition.

Accordingly, Kelser reluctantly consenting, one was chosen to prepare the pistols, which were immediately produced, and in less than ten minutes they were placed under a cloth upon the table.

"I waive all right to the first choice," said the stranger, as he and Kelser were brought face to face in their proper positions.

The bully, who was really very much alarmed and who showed it in his pale face, trembling limbs, and quivering muscles, at once seemed to brighten at this concession, and thrusting his hand under the cloth, he drew forth one of the weapons, presented it at the breast of the other, and pulled the trigger.

It did not fire, but the stranger, who knew not that it was unloaded, neither blanched nor changed expression. The crowd applauded, and the bully grew ghastly pale.

"It is my turn now!" said the traveler, in a quiet, determined tone, fixing his blue eye steadily upon the cowering form of Kelser.

This was more than the latter could stand.

"No, I'll be damned if it is!" he shouted, and instantly drawing the other pistol, he presented it and pulled the trigger also.

But with a like result—for neither pistol was loaded—the company having secretly resolved to test the courage of both without bloodshed.

Throwing down the pistol with a bitter curse, amid a universal cry of "Shame! Shame!" Kelser whipped out his knife and made a rush for his antagonist. But the latter, gliding quickly around the table, suddenly stopped and exclaimed, "Three times at my life and now once at yours!"

And with these ominous words he raised his arm quickly; the next instant there was a flash, a crack, and the bully fell heavily forward, shot through the brain.

The verdict of the jury who sat upon the case was justifiable homicide, and the blue-eyed stranger resumed his journey as if nothing had happened.

Would you know who he is? If we named him, we should name one who now holds a high official position, and for many reasons we prefer he should be known only by those who are already cognizant of the incident we have recorded.

A RACE FOR LIFE

Among the members of that celebrated rifle corps that was composed of such splendid material and commanded by Daniel Morgan, was a man by the name of Elerson, who in deeds of daring and intrepidity, was almost a match for Murphy, whose frequent companion he was when on an expedition against their mutual enemies, the Tories, red-coats, and Indians. Quick of perception, rapid in his conclusions and actions, light of foot, and brave as a lion, he was an enemy whom the Indians feared and a friend whom all ranked as second only to the renowned Murphy himself.

The corps to which these celebrated marksmen belonged was attached to the expedition of Generals Clinton and Sullivan against the Six Nations in 1779. Elerson was with Clinton when that officer halted at Otsego Lake to await the coming of his superior, from the direction of Wyoming. While the army lay at this place, Elerson rambled off from the main body in search of adventure and pulse for the dinner of the mess to which he belonged. Regardless of the danger and risk he ran, he wandered about until he had procured a quantity of the latter, sufficient for his purpose, when he prepared to return to camp.

It seems that he had been discovered and tracked by a party of Indians, who determined upon his capture, and as he was adjusting his burden to retrace his steps, he thought he heard a rustling of the leaves near him. Looking in the direction from whence came the sound, he discovered a band of six or eight Indians who had stationed themselves between him and the camp, so as to cut off his retreat in that direction, and were in the act of springing upon him. Becoming immediately conscious of their

object—for he might have been shot down with ease—he determined to foil them if in his power, for he knew full well the fate of
a prisoner in their hands. Seizing his rifle, he dropped his bundle
and fled through the only avenue left open for his escape, followed
by the whole pack, hooting and yelling at his heels. As he started
to run, half a dozen tomahawks were hurled at him and came
whizzing and flying through the air, but fortunately only one
reached its object, and that cut the middle finger of his left hand,
nearly severing it. With the agility of the hunted stag, he bounded
over an old brushwood fence that stood in his path and darted into
the shades of the forest, followed by his no less swift and rapid
pursuers.

He was aware that the course he had taken was away from the
camp—so also were his enemies—and while they anticipated a
speedy capture, he prepared himself for a mighty effort, trusting
that an opportunity might offer to double and find his way back.
Vain hope! The Indians, aware that such would naturally be his
aim, took care to prevent it by spreading themselves somewhat in
the form of a crescent to prevent the consummation of such an
end, but in so doing, they nearly lost sight of their prey. Fearful
lest he might escape, they discharged their rifles at him, hoping to
wound or kill him, but with no effect. The brave fellow tried every
nerve to outstrip, and every stratagem and device, to mislead and
misdirect the Indians, but they were too cunning to be deceived
and pursued him with the ardor and determination of blood-
hounds.

Four long hours the chase continued thus, until overtasked
nature threatened to give way and yield him to the tomahawks and
scalping-knives of his pursuers. Like some powerful engine, his
heart was forcing the blood through his distended and throbbing
veins, which threatened to burst with the mighty efforts of the
man. His breath came short and rapid and betokened a speedy
termination to the race, unless a breathing-spell was afforded him.
An opportunity at last was offered, when having, as he thought,
outstripped his pursuers for a moment, he halted in a little lonely
dell to recover his waning strength and regain his almost
exhausted breath. His hope was destined to disappointment,
however, for the circle closed in upon him, and the bust of an

Indian presented itself at a height opening in front. He raised his rifle to fire, and in the same moment a shot from his rear admonished him that danger was all around; another took effect in his side and warned him of the danger of delay. The Indian in front had disappeared, and he hastened forward with the love of life and liberty still strong in his breast, although his powers of endurance had been sadly, fearfully tested. The wound in his side bled freely, although only a flesh wound and therefore not dangerous nor painful. It served, however, to track him by, and conscious of the fact, he managed to tear a strip from his hunting-shirt and stanch the blood.

On, on went pursuer and pursued—over hill and dale, brook, streamlet, and running stream, through briar and bramble, through field and wood—until the parched and burning tongue of the fugitive protruded from his mouth, swelled to such detention as almost to stop his breathing. Exhausted, nature could do no more, and he threw himself prostrate on the bank of a tiny brook, resolved to yield the contest for the sake of a hearty draught of its clear, sparkling waters. He bathed his brow in the cool element and drank deeply of its reviving virtues. Raising his head, he discovered the foremost of the now scattered and equally exhausted enemy, crossing the brow of a ridge over which he had just passed. The instinct of life was awakened afresh in his bosom at the sight, and he started to his feet and raised his rifle to his shoulder, but his failing strength would not allow of a certain aim, and an empty weapon might ensure his death. Another moment, and he would be at the mercy of his enemy, without hope or chance of life.

Again, he raised his trusty rifle, and steadying its barrel against a sapling, he secured his aim, fired, and the Indian fell headlong in death. Before the echoes of the report had died away in the neighboring hills, he beheld the remainder of the band of eager, hungry pursuers coming over the ridge, and he felt that his hold of life was short and his minutes numbered. Hidden partially by the tree behind which he stood, they did not discover him, however, and while they paused over the body of their fallen comrade, he made another attempt to fly from their pursuit. He staggered forward, fell, rose again, and exerting his failing powers to the utmost, he managed to reach a clump or thicket of young trees, overgrown with wild vines, into which he threw himself with the energy of desperation. Fortune favored him, and he discovered the rotten, moldering trunk of a fallen tree, whose hollow butt, hidden and screened by the deep shadow of the surrounding foliage, offered an asylum from the impending death that seemed so near.

The approaching steps of the savages quickened his movements, as he crawled headfirst into the recess caused by decay, which was barely large enough to admit his person. Here he lay within hearing of the efforts made to discover his hiding-place, until they died away in the distance. Conscious, however, that the Indians would search long and anxiously for him, he lay in this situation for two days and nights before he ventured to crawl from his hiding-place. When he did so he knew not which way to turn, but striking off at a venture, he soon emerged upon a clearing near Cobleskill, a distance of twenty-five miles from his place of starting.

DESPERATE FIGHT WITH A PANTHER:
A KENTUCKIAN'S STORY

I never was downhearted but once in my life, and that was on seeing the death of a faithful friend who lost his life in trying to save mine. The fact is, I was one day making tracks homeward after a long tramp through one of our forests—my rifle carelessly resting on my shoulder—when my favorite dog, Sport, who was trotting quietly ahead of me, suddenly stopped stock still, gazed into a big oak tree, bristled up his back, and fetched a loud growl. I looked up and saw upon a quivering limb a half-grown panther, crouching down close and in the very act of springing upon him. With a motion quicker than chain lightning, I leveled my rifle, blazed away, and shot him clean through and through the heart.

The varmint, with teeth all set and claws spread, pitched sprawling head foremost to the ground, as dead as Julius Caesar! That was all fair enough, but mark, afore I had hardly dropped my rifle, I found myself thrown down on my profile by the old she-panther, who that minute sprung from an opposite tree and lit upon my shoulders, heavier than all creation! I feel the print of her teeth and nails now! My dog grew mighty loving; he jumped atop and seized her by the neck, so we all rolled and clawed, and a pretty considerable tight scratch we had of it.

I began to think my right arm was about chawed up, when the varmint, finding the dog's teeth rather hurt her feelings, let me go altogether and clenched him. Seeing at once that the dog was undermost, and that there was no two ways about a chance of a choke-off or let up about her, I just out jackknife, and with one slash, perhaps I didn't cut the panther's throat deep enough for her to breathe the rest of her life without nostrils. I did feel mighty savagerous, and big as she was, I laid hold of her hide by the back with an alligator grip and slung her against the nearest tree, hard enough to make every bone in her body flash fire. "Thar," says I, "you tarnal varmint, root and branch, you are what I call used up!"

But I turned round to look for my dog, and—and—and tears gushed into my eyes as I see the poor affectionate creature: all of a gore of blood, half raised on his fore legs, and trying to drag his mangled body toward me. Down he dropped; I ran up to him, whistled loud, and gave him a friendly shake of the paws, for I loved my dog. But he was too far gone; he had just strength enough to wag his tail feebly, fixed his closing eyes upon me wistfully, then gave a gasp or two, and all was over!

LA FAYETTE AND THE JERSEYMAN

Charles Morgan was a shrewd private of the Jersey brigade, a good soldier, and had attracted the notice of the Marquis de la Fayette. In the course of the movements on James River, the marquis was anxious to procure exact information of the force under Cornwallis and, if possible, to penetrate his lordship's designs; he considered Charles as a proper agent for the accomplishment of his purposes and proposed to him to enter the British camp in the character of a deserter, but in reality, as a spy. Charles undertook the perilous enterprise, merely stipulating that, if he were detected, the marquis should cause it to be inserted in the Jersey newspapers that he was acting under the orders of his commanding officer.

The pretended deserter entered the British lines and was conducted into the presence of Cornwallis. On being questioned by that nobleman concerning his motives for desertion, he replied "that he had been with the American army from the beginning of the war, and that while under General Washington, he was satisfied, but now that they had put him under a Frenchman, he did not like it and therefore had deserted." Charles was received without suspicion, was punctual in discharging his duty as a soldier, and carefully observed everything that passed. One day while on duty with his comrades, Cornwallis, who was in close conversation with some of his officers, called him and asked, "How long will it take the marquis to cross James River?"

"Three hours, my Lord," was the answer.

"Three hours!" exclaimed his lordship. "Will it not take three days?"

"No, my Lord," said Charles, "the marquis has so many boats,

263

each boat will carry so many men, and if your lordship will take the trouble of calculating, you will find he can cross in three hours."

Turning to his officers, the earl said, in the hearing of the American, "The scheme will not do."

Charles was now resolved to abandon his new friends, and for that purpose plied his comrades with grog till they were all in high spirits with the liquor. He then began to complain of the wants in the British camp, extolled the plentiful provision enjoyed by the Americans, and concluded by proposing to them to desert; they agreed to accompany him and left it to him to manage the sentinels. To the first he offered, in a very friendly manner, a draught of rum from his canteen, but while the soldier was drinking, Charles seized his arms and then proposed to him to desert with them, which he did through necessity. The second sentinel was served in the same way, and Charles hastened to the American camp at the head of seven British deserters. On presenting himself before his employer, the marquis exclaimed "Ah, Charles! Have you got back?"

"Yes sir," was the answer, "and have brought seven more with me." The marquis offered him money, but he declined accepting it and only desired to have his gun again. The marquis then proposed to raise him to the rank of a corporal or sergeant, but Charles' reply was, "I will not have any promotion; I have abilities for a common soldier and have a good character; should I be promoted, my abilities may not answer, and I may lose my character." He, however, generously requested for his fellow soldiers, who were not so well supplied with stockings, shoes, and clothing as himself, the marquis' interference to procure a supply of their wants.

THRILLING ADVENTURE OF TWO SCOUTS

As early as the year 1790, the blockhouse and stockade above the mouth of the Hockhocking River was a frontier post for the hardy pioneers of that portion of our state from the Hockhocking to the Scioto, and from the Ohio River to our northern lakes. Then nature wore her undisturbed livery of dark and thick forests, interspersed with green and flowery prairies. Then the axe of the woodman had not been heard in the wilderness, nor the plough of the husbandman marred the beauty of the green prairies. Among the many rich and luxuriant valleys, that of the Hockhocking was preeminent for nature's richest gifts, and the portion of it whereon Lancaster now stands was marked as the most luxuriant and picturesque and became the seat of an Indian village at a period so early that the "memory of man runneth not parallel thereto."

On the green sward of the prairie was held many a rude gambol of the Indians, and here, too, was many an assemblage of the warriors of one of the most powerful tribes, taking counsel for a "war path" upon some weak or defenseless frontier post.

Upon one of these *war-stirring* occasions, intelligence reached the little garrison above the mouth of the Hockhocking that the Indians were gathering in force somewhere up the valley for the purpose of striking a terrible blow on one of the few and scattered defenses of the Whites. A council was held by the garrison, and scouts were sent up the Hockhocking in order to ascertain the strength of the foe and the probable point of attack.

In the month of October, and on one of the balmiest days of our Indian summer, two men could have been seen emerging out of the thick plum and hazel bushes skirting the prairie and stealthily climbing the eastern declivity of that most remarkable promontory, now known as Mount Pleasant, whose western summit gives a commanding view to the eye of what is doing on the prairie. This eminence was gained by our two adventurous and hardy scouts, and from this point they carefully observed the movements taking place on the prairie.

Every day brought an accession of warriors to those already assembled, and every day the scouts witnessed from their eyrie the horseracing, leaping, running, and throwing the deadly tomahawk by the warriors; the old sachems looking on with indifference; the squaws, for the most part, engaged in the useful drudgeries; and the papooses manifesting all the noisy and wayward joy of childhood. The arrival of any new party of warriors was hailed by the terrible war whoop, which striking the mural face of Mount Pleasant, was driven back into the various indentations of the surrounding hills, producing reverberation on reverberation, and echo on echo, till it seemed as if ten thousand fiends were gathered in their orgies. Such yells might well strike terror into the bosoms of those unaccustomed to them.

To our scouts these were but martial music strains that waked their watchfulness and strung their iron frames. From their early youth had they been on the frontier, and therefore well practiced in all the subtlety, craft, and cunning, as well as knowing the ferocity and bloodthirsty perseverance of the savage. They were therefore not likely to be circumvented by the cunning of their foes and, without a desperate struggle, would not fall victims to the scalping knife.

On several occasions, small parties of warriors left the prairie and ascended the mount, at which times our scouts would hide in the fissures of the rocks or, lying by the side of some long prostrate tree, cover themselves with the sear and yellow leaf and again leave their hiding places when their uninvited visitors had disappeared. For food they depended on jerked venison and cold corn bread, with which their knapsacks had been well stored. Fire they dared not kindle, and the report of one of their rifles would bring upon them the entire force of the Indians. For drink they depended on some rain water, which stood in excavations of the rocks, but in a few days this store was exhausted and M'Clelland and White must abandon their enterprise or find a new supply.

To accomplish this most hazardous affair, M'Clelland, being the elder, resolved to make the attempt. With his trusty rifle in his grasp and two canteens strung across his shoulders, he cautiously descended to the prairie, and skirting the hills on the north as much as possible within the hazel thickets, he struck a course for the Hockhocking River. He reached its margin, and turning an abrupt point of a hill, he found a beautiful fountain of limpid water, now known as the Cold Spring, within a few feet of the river. He filled his canteens and returned in safety to his watchful companion.

It was now determined to have a fresh supply of water every day, and this duty was to be performed alternately. On one of these occasions, after White had filled his canteens, he sat a few moments, watching the limpid element as it came gurgling out of the bosom of the earth; the light sound of footsteps caught his practiced ear, and upon turning round, he saw two squaws within a few feet of him; these upon turning the jet of the hill had thus suddenly come upon him. The elder squaw gave one of those far-reaching whoops peculiar to the Indians.

White at once comprehended his perilous situation, for if the alarm should reach the camp, he and his companion must inevitably perish. Self-preservation impelled him to inflict a noiseless death upon the squaws, and in such a manner as to leave no trace behind. Ever rapid in thought and prompt in action, he sprang upon his victims with the rapidity and power of a panther, and grasping the throat of each, with one bound, he sprang into the Hockhocking and rapidly thrust the head of the elder woman underwater and made strong efforts to submerge the younger, who, however, powerfully resisted.

During the short struggle, the younger female addressed him in his own language, though almost in inarticulate sounds.

Releasing his hold, she informed him that ten years before, she had been made a prisoner on Grave Creek flats, and that the Indians in her presence butchered her mother and two sisters, and that an only remaining brother had been captured with her who succeeded on the second night in making his escape, but what had become of him she knew not. During the narrative, White, unobserved by the girl, had let go his grasp on the elder squaw, whose body soon floated where it would not, probably, soon be found. He now directed the girl hastily to follow him and, with his usual energy and speed, pushed for the mount.

They had scarcely gone two hundred yards from the spring before the alarm cry was heard some quarter of a mile down the stream. It was supposed that some warriors returning from a hunt struck the Hockhocking just as the body of the drowned squaw floated past. White and the girl succeeded in reaching the Mount where M'Clelland had been no indifferent spectator to the sudden commotion among the Indians, as the prairie parties were seen to strike off in every direction, and before White and the girl had arrived, a party of some twenty warriors had already gained the eastern acclivity of the Mount and were cautiously ascending, carefully keeping under cover.

Soon the two scouts saw the swarthy faces of the foe, as they glided from tree to tree and rock to rock, until the whole base of the Mount was surrounded and all hopes of escape cut off.

In this peril, nothing was left, other than to sell their lives as dearly as they could; this they resolved to do and advised the girl to escape to the Indians and tell them she had been made a captive to the scouts.

She said, "No! Death, and that in the presence of my people, is to me a thousand times sweeter than captivity—furnish me with a rifle, and I will show you that I can fight as well as die. This spot I leave not! Here my bones shall lie bleaching with yours! And should either of us escape, you will carry the tidings of my death to my remaining relatives."

Remonstrance proved fruitless; the two scouts matured their plans for a vigorous defense, opposing craft to craft, expedient to expedient, and an unerring fire of the deadly rifle.

The attack commenced in front, where from the narrow backbone of the Mount, the savages had to advance in single file but where they could avail themselves of the rocks and trees. In advancing, the warrior must be momentarily exposed, and two bare inches of his swarthy form was enough for the unerring rifle of the scouts. After bravely maintaining the fight in front, and keeping the enemy in check, they discovered a new danger threatening them. The wary foe now made every preparation to attack them in flank, which could be most successfully and fatally done by reaching an insulated rock lying in one of the ravines on the southern hillside. This rock once gained by the Indians, they could bring the scouts under point blank shot of the rifle and without the possibility of escape.

Our brave scouts saw the hopelessness of their situation, which nothing could avert but brave companions and an unerring shot—them they had not. But the brave never despair. With this certain fate resting upon them, they had continued as calm and as calculating and as unwearied as the strongest desire of vengeance on a treacherous foe could produce. Soon M'Clelland saw a tall and swarthy figure preparing to spring from a cover so near the fatal rock that a single bound must reach it and all hope be destroyed.

He felt that all depended on one advantageous shot, although but one inch of the warrior's body was exposed, and that at a distance of one hundred yards. He resolved to risk all; coolly he raised his rifle to his eye, carefully shading the sight with his hand, and drew a bead so sure that he felt conscious it would do. He touched the hair trigger with his finger, the hammer came down, but in place of striking fire it crushed his flint into a hundred fragments! Although he felt that the savage must reach the fatal rock before he could adjust another flint, he proceeded to the task with the utmost composure, casting many a furtive glance toward the fearful point.

Suddenly he saw the warrior stretching every muscle for the leap, and with the agility of a deer he made the spring; instead of reaching the rock, he sprung ten feet in the air, and giving one terrific yell, he fell upon the earth, and his dark corpse rolled fifty feet down the hill. He had evidently received a death shot from some unknown hand. A hundred voices from below re-echoed the terrible shout, and it was evident that they had lost a favorite warrior, as well as been foiled for a time in their most important movement.

A very few moments proved that the advantage so mysteriously gained would be of short duration, for already the scouts caught a glimpse of a swarthy warrior cautiously advancing toward the cover so recently occupied by a fellow companion. Now, too, the attack in front was resumed with increased fury, so as to require the incessant fire of both scouts to prevent the Indians from gaining the eminence, and in a short time M'Clelland saw the wary warrior behind the cover, preparing for a leap to gain the fearful rock. The leap was made, and the warrior turning a somerset, his corpse rolled down toward his companion; again a mysterious agent had interposed in their behalf.

This second sacrifice cast dismay into the ranks of the assailants, and just as the sun was disappearing behind the western hills, the foe withdrew a short distance for the purpose of devising new modes of attack. The respite came most seasonably to the scouts, who had bravely kept their position and boldly maintained the unequal fight from the middle of the day.

Now, for the first time was the girl missing, and the scouts supposed that through terror she had escaped to her former captors or that she had been killed during the fight. They were not long left to doubt, for in a few moments the girl was seen emerging from behind a rock and coming to them with a rifle in her hand. During the heat of the fight, she saw a warrior fall, who had advanced some fifty yards before the main body in front. She at once resolved to possess herself of his rifle, and crouching in undergrowth, she crept to the spot and succeeded in her enterprise, being all the time exposed to the crossfire of the defenders and assailants. Her practiced eye had early noticed the *fatal rock*, and hers was the mysterious hand by which the two warriors had fallen, the last being the most wary, untiring, and bloodthirsty brave of the Shawanese tribe. He it was, who ten years previous had scalped the family of the girl and been her captor.

In the west, dark clouds were now gathering, and in an hour the whole heavens were shrouded in them; this darkness greatly embarrassed the scouts in their contemplated night retreat, for they might readily lose their way, or accidentally fall on the enemy—this being highly probable, if not inevitable. An hour's consultation decided their plans, and it was agreed that the girl, from her intimate knowledge of their localities, should lead the advance a few steps.

Another advantage might be gained by this arrangement, for in case they should fall in with some outposts, the girl's knowledge of the Indian tongue would perhaps enable her to deceive the sentinel, and so the sequel proved, for scarcely had they descended one hundred feet, when a low "whist" from the girl, warned them of present danger.

The scouts sunk silently to the earth, where by previous agreement they were to remain till another signal was given them by the girl, whose absence for more than a quarter of an hour now began to excite the most serious apprehensions. At length she again appeared and told them that she had succeeded in removing two sentinels who were directly in their route to a point some hundred feet distant. The descent was noiselessly resumed, the level gained, and the scouts followed their intrepid pioneer for half a mile in the most profound silence, when the barking of a small dog, within a few feet, apprised them of a new danger. The almost simultaneous click of the scouts' rifles was heard by the girl, who rapidly approached them and stated that they were now in the midst of the Indian wigwams, and their lives depended on the most profound silence and implicitly following her footsteps. A moment afterward, the girl was accosted by a squaw from an opening in a wigwam. She replied in the Indian language and, without stopping, pressed forward.

In a short time, she stopped and assured the scouts that the village was cleared and that they were now in safety. She knew that every pass leading out of the prairie was safely guarded by the Indians and at once resolved to adopt the bold adventure of passing through the very center of their village as the least hazardous. The result proved the correctness of her judgment.

They now kept a course for the Ohio, being guided by the Hockhocking River, and after three days' march and suffering, the party arrived at the blockhouse in safety. Their escape from the Indians prevented the contemplated attack, and the rescued girl proved to be the sister of the intrepid Neil Washburn, celebrated in Indian history as the renowned scout to Captain Kenton's bloody Kentuckians.

THE BRAVO OF TEXAS

"Lem M'Guire" was known throughout Texas as a thorough-paced villain and black-leg. Accustomed from infancy to the most infamous companions, as he increased in years, so did he grow old in crime, and at the age of twenty was deemed by his companions worthy of the front rank in their columns.

One of the first acts that made his name well known was his participation—while yet a mere child—in an affray in which a friend and protector of his was shot and most deservedly by a tavern-keeper, upon whom he had made a murderous attack.

M'Guire fought like a young tiger—as he was—clinging to the landlord with his hands and teeth, and though crying with rage and grief at the death of his patron, seemed perfectly regardless of the danger to himself.

I have no intention of writing the history of his career, but shall merely note an incident or two to give our readers an idea of the man.

He had been brought up by a man of his own kind, named Johnson, who furnished him with a home—such as it was—until by his practices the latter had become possessed of sufficient property to awaken M'Guire's cupidity and a determination to become possessed of it by foul means, as he could not by fair ones.

He accordingly laid his plans and caused Johnson to become involved in a quarrel in which his life was taken at the instigation of the serpent he had nourished, who immediately after married his widow—a woman twice his age—and thus accomplished his designs.

A few months before his death, he paid a very characteristic visit to Houston, where he succeeded, as usual, in bringing himself into speedy notice. Entering one of the bar-rooms of the place in a state of semi-intoxication, and taking offense at a simple German who presided over the bottles and whose imperfect knowledge of the language prevented him from understanding correctly what was required, M'Guire struck him in the face with a heavy cut-glass decanter, breaking it in the act and severely injuring the man.

Among the crowd that collected, M'Guire spied a judge of one of the courts and, turning upon him, immediately knocked him down; then crossing the street where stood the mayor, "spectator of the fight" as he supposed at a safe distance, the gentleman prostrated *him* also at a blow.

He then retreated, walking up the main street of the town in triumph, and no more was seen of him—although warrants were issued for his apprehension—until the second day, when he rode down the street, stopped his horse at the scene of his late disturbance, and calling out the proprietor, told him he had traveled some distance out of his way to bid him goodbye, and then rode out of town.

At this time, he resided not far from the town of Crocket, and soon after his return from his Houston exploit, he determined, for reasons of his own—whether from enmity, to remove a troublesome witness or a partner in crime, I know not—to have one of his neighbors "put out of the way."

Not being willing to take the trouble himself, he hired another, a journeyman at the trade of blood, to do the business for him. For some time the bravo deferred the murder, until at length M'Guire imagined that he had turned traitor and betrayed his designs to his enemy, which belief was strengthened by the ultimate refusal of the man to have anything to do with it.

So far, M'Guire had only gained the necessity of removing two persons in the place of one, and perhaps agreeing with Dr. Franklin's adage, "If you wish a thing done, *go*; if you do not, *send*," determined *this* time to do his own work.

To murder his accomplice, he had a double motive, fear and revenge. Having secured the aid of one or more persons upon whom he could depend, he rode over to the house of the supposed traitor and, calling him out into the yard in front of the house, in full sight of his wife and family, shot him down like a dog; then the party turned their horses toward the house of the one whom he had marked before for his victim and killed him in precisely the same manner.

All this happened in broad daylight, nor did his audacity cease here, but knowing that a magistrate lived nearby, the party again mounted and rode to his plantation.

M'Guire was probably deceived in the man, whom he must either have supposed to have been a reckless being like himself or one who might be influenced by fear or money, to subserve his ends.

The magistrate was very coolly informed that they came to be tried, that he must go through some form, no matter what, and give them a certificate of acquittal, which although the magistrate's court was only a preliminary one, they imagined, combined with the known and certain danger of meddling with them, would be sufficient to prevent any further inquiry.

As the reader may well imagine, the magistrate, who was almost alone in the house, was extremely alarmed, but had sufficient presence of mind to conceal his feelings and put the villains off, upon the plea that it was necessary to have some other persons present and also to prepare certain papers, which could not be done at a moment's notice. It was Saturday, and he promised them that if they returned on Monday morning, he would have everything fixed for them, which he certainly did.

On Monday, M'Guire appeared with a reinforcement, making in all five or six, and found the magistrate sitting at the farther end of the hall. For the information of those who are not skilled in the houses of a new county, I would say that a double log cabin, such as the magistrate's, consists usually of two large rooms separated by a wide hall, which in pleasant weather, serves the family for a dining and sitting room, but being generally open at both ends, is not used in inclement days.

From all appearances, they found that the trial was to be an affair of more detail than they admired, and M'Guire, considering himself now to be in a condition to dictate his own terms, insolently demanded if the justice intended to do as he was ordered, adding that if he did not, and that immediately, he would cut him to pieces with his knife. The justice replied that he intended to proceed according to law and in no other way, but hardly had he spoken when M'Guire, knife in hand, followed by his friends, rushed upon him.

At this critical moment, the side doors were dashed open and on either side a volley from six rifles was poured upon them. M'Guire and two others fell dead; the rest, more or less injured, were seized and bound with cords.

It was like a "*coup de théâtre*," except that it exceeded one, as reality ever does fiction. I am sure that no melodramist ever invented or got up a more perfect or successful affair, and who may say that it was not pure, even-handed justice?

JOHN DEAN AND THE INDIANS

About the year 1780, an Indian had been murdered in West-moreland County, New York, by some unknown White man. The chiefs met in council at Oneida to determine what was to be done. One of the early settlers in the county was a Mr. John Dean, who feeling curious, perhaps alarmed, at the proceedings around him, continued through the friendship of an Indian to obtain knowledge of their consultations. It by no means satisfied him, since from the office he held (judge of county courts) and his high standing among the White men, the chiefs urged that he was the proper one to make atonement. But he had been adopted by them as a son, and many of the warriors argued that this circumstance would nullify the virtue of the sacrifice.

For several days the matter was debated without being decided. His friendly informant apprised him of all that was done, and he continued to hope for the best. An effort to escape would have exposed him, with his wife and children, to certain destruction. He adopted the precaution of concealing from his family all knowledge of his situation, and as the council remained in session, his hopes of escape brightened. They were vain.

One night after retiring to rest, he heard the war-whoop, and then for the first time intimated to his wife that he feared a party was approaching to take his life. After exhorting her to remain quiet with the children, he went to an adjoining chamber, admitted the Indians, and seated them in the outer room. They numbered eighteen and were the principal men of the tribe.

After a short interval, the senior chief arose and informed the judge that they had come to sacrifice him for their dead brother, and that he must prepare to die. To this disagreeable piece of information he replied at length, affirming that as he was an adopted son of the tribe, it would be wrong to require his blood for the wrong committed by a wicked White man, that he was not ready to die, and that he could not leave his wife and children unprovided for. The council listened with profound gravity and attention, and after he had finished, one of the chiefs replied. The debate continued a long while, but evidently little to the judge's favor.

When about resigning himself to his doom, the noise of footsteps was heard, and suddenly a squaw entered. She was wife to the senior chief and the foster parent of the unfortunate White man. Though her entrance into the solemn council was entirely repugnant to all Indian notions of propriety, she was permitted to take her place in silence. Immediately after, another squaw entered, and she was soon followed by another.

Each of the three stood closely wrapped in a blanket, but said nothing. After a long pause, the presiding warrior bade them be gone. The wife replied that the council must change its determination and leave her adopted son, the good White man, alone. The command was repeated. Suddenly each of the women, throwing off her blanket, brandished a knife and declared that if the sentence was executed, she would plunge it into her bosom.

So strange a scene amazed even Indians; they regarded the unheard-of procedure of a woman's interfering with a national council as an interposition of the Great Spirit. The will of their deity was implicitly obeyed, the decree reversed on the spot, and the judge dismissed with honor.

THE MURDERER'S ORDEAL:
A CALIFORNIAN'S STORY

I was always fond of the science of physiognomy. From my youth up, I was noted for my proclivity for reading the character of a man from his face, and I finally became such an adept in the art that I could occasionally guess the very thoughts of the individual whose countenance I was studying.

Soon after the gold fever broke out, I went to California, and there, I must confess, among what else there was to interest me, I had a grand opportunity of exercising my skill upon all sorts of faces, seen under all sorts of circumstances, from the highest triumph of success to the deepest despair of failure. I first tried my luck at digging gold myself, but soon tired of that, and believing I could make money faster and with less labor, I opened a kind of grocery and provision store and went regularly into the business of trade, buying most of my articles at Sacramento, getting them hauled to my quarters, and disposing of them at a fair advance to the miners and others.

My store, as I dignified my place of trade, consisted of a rude skeleton of poles, with a sufficiency of cheap muslin drawn over them and pinned down to the earth, and was stocked only with the most saleable articles, of which flour, pork, and whiskey found the ready market, especially whiskey. In the dry season it was dusty, and everybody seemed to be dry with a thirst that water could not quench. If a man was successful, he wanted to bring his body up to the altitude of his spirits; if unsuccessful, he wanted whiskey to bring his spirits up to the altitude of his body; if it chanced to be a little cool, he wanted a little whiskey to warm him; if it was very hot, he wanted whiskey to cool him; he needed whiskey in the morning to make him bright and active; he needed whiskey at night to rest him and make him sleep well; he wanted it when he bought and when he sold, when he stood up and when he sat down; in short, whiskey was the great regulator of all human feelings—the genuine *elixir vitae*—and consequently I had an immense business in whiskey.

Now this, though somewhat irrelevant, brings me to my story.

My store being the headquarters of that locality for whiskey and provisions, I was brought in contact with nearly every specimen of the *genus homo* that ventured into that region, and such another conglomeration of White, Black, and Red—such another mixture of gentlemen, laborers, mountaineers, gamblers, thieves, and assassins—it would be hard to find outside the limits of California. Of course I had a chance to study all sorts of faces to my heart's content, but having, as I have said, become an adept in the art, an ordinary countenance or a man governed by ordinary passions, whether brutish or gentle, did not interest me. I wanted to get hold of what is termed a character, or one whose external would give no indication of his internal to any but a connoisseur, or one who would really puzzle you to tell what to think of him.

Among the many, such a one I at length found. At first, I did not notice him. At a casual glance there was nothing to distinguish him from the herd. He came in quietly, unobtrusively, purchased a quantity of flour, pork, and tea, paid for it in gold dust, and went out about his business. He repeated his visits, at different intervals, perhaps some half a dozen times, before he attracted my attention to anything peculiar in his appearance, and then I should have been at a loss to say what I saw more in him at last than at first.

He was apparently about twenty-five years of age, of medium height and slender figure, of a dark complexion, regular features, with dark straight hair, dark eyes, and a beard that covered the lower part of his face—in all of which there was nothing remarkable, nothing striking. He was quiet, not talkative—had nothing to say, except about the business he came on—got what he wanted when I was disengaged, paid for what he got like a gentleman, and generally retired with an ordinary "Good day, sir," or some similar civility. And yet, as I have said, he began to attract my attention at last, and I began to wonder why. Was it because he was so quiet, reserved, and gentlemanly, and did not purchase whiskey like the rest and occasionally get excited and boisterous? Or was it because there was something about him I could not readily fathom? At all events, he had begun to interest me in some way, and the very fact, perhaps, that I could not tell how or why, led into a closer scrutiny, a deeper study of the man.

After this, I prolonged his visits as long as I could without causing him to suspect I did so intentionally. The things that he wanted I generally had some trouble in getting and filled up the interval by remarks about the weather, the country, the mines, the success of some, and the failure of others—in a word, anything I could think of to induce conversation, watching him furtively all the while. He answered easily and readily and yet with that peculiar kind of reserve that was not suggestive or tending toward familiarity. His replies, however, evinced a man of mind and education, and I began to give him credit for being a thinker—perhaps a practical and selfish dreamer, if I may use a paradoxical term that best expresses my idea.

One day, I scarcely know how, I touched upon the general superstitions of mankind, and to my surprise, I saw that at last he was interested. His eyes changed expression, and brightened, and emitted a strange and peculiar gleam, and my attention being thus directed to his eye, I now bethought me that I had never seen one exactly like it—one capable of being so apparently open down to the soul, while concealing so much. It was off its guard now—the door was really open down to the soul of the man—and I looked in at that door, that opening, *and saw that the soul of that man was a dark one.* A nameless fear came over me; a strange thrill passed through me like an electric shock; I felt an internal shudder of dread. No wonder I had not been able to read him before; the man had been wearing an impenetrable mask.

I now had the key to the mystery, and to him, and I used it. He was interested in superstitions—he was superstitions himself. Why? Good men may be superstitious—bad men always are, because they carry a hell of wild fancies within them. Thus it was with this man, as I could see by his eye, and I made his fancies work upon him. I told him stories of sorcery, witchcraft, and magic of ghosts, of hobgoblins, and devils till he became pale with fear, breathed with compressed lips, and trembled in spite of his great nerve and will.

If good men, as I have said, are sometimes superstitious, why, you ask, did I think this man bad for being superstitious also? First, I answer, because I had accidentally thrown him off his guard and had read his soul; and secondly, because he was not naturally nervous and credulous. *Fear* only had made him so, and in one of his iron nature, fear could only arise from his self-convicted knowledge of a past wicked deed. The man was even then a criminal.

But let me hasten to the *denouement.*

It chanced that no other person was present when this conversation occurred about the superstitious fancies of men, and as soon as we were interrupted by the entrance of another customer, my dark visitor left somewhat abruptly. After that he did not come as often as before, and never seemed as much at ease, and never renewed the conversation that had so agitated him, and never, in fact, entered into any other that he could possibly avoid. I kept my thoughts to myself, but made some casual inquiries about him and learned that he had been so fortunate as to secure a capital "lead," from which, with his partner, another young man, he was taking out gold in such quantities as promised to enrich both, and that both had the good will and esteem of all who knew them.

One dark night, about three or four weeks after this, I was startled from my sleep by wild, prolonged shouts and cries of "Murder! Murder! Help! Help!"

I jumped up, seized my revolvers, and darted out into the open air. The cries and screams still continued, coming from a point on the bend of the river about a hundred rods below. In a minute I was joined by five others, all well-armed, and together we ran, as fast as we could, to the place from whence the sound proceeded. When we arrived there, at least thirty men were collected in and about the tent of the dark man I have been describing, and he himself it was who had given the alarm. His partner and companion had been murdered and robbed; he himself had been slightly cut across the face and gashed on the left arm and was all excitement, lamenting his dearest friend and vowing vengeance against the assassin. It was sometime before we could get at the particulars, and then we learned that both had been sleeping side by side when an unknown robber had crawled under the canvass, stabbed one to the heart, and taken a large bag of gold from under his head. With this he was escaping, when the present narrator awoke and seized him and received the wounds that had compelled him to relinquish his hold. Lights were brought, and there, sure enough, was the bloody confirmation of all that had been related.

I shall make no attempt to portray the intense excitement, the wild rage and consternation that this daring murder occasioned. Every man felt that, if the assassin escaped without his just punishment, there would no longer be security for anyone in our thus far quiet and peaceful valley, and solemn oaths were taken to hang the wretch, if found, on the nearest tree. A large reward was offered for his detection, and every gambler that had ever been seen about there was more or less suspected, and I believe that, had any man been arrested on the following day, he would have been hung first and tried afterward. I said less than any, for I had my own suspicions, and I contrived my plot in secret and made a confidant of no one.

The murdered young man was as decently buried as surrounding circumstances would permit, and his companion, my superstitious friend, grew moodier with grief, refused to work his "lead" any more, and proposed selling off altogether. I think he would have gone at once, only that I told him it would not look well to leave without an effort to discover the murderer, as some people might be malicious enough to say he knew something of the matter and so get him into trouble. He turned very pale and declared he would stay a year if he thought by that means he could discover the assassin of his dear friend.

On the second afternoon following the tragedy, almost every individual in the vicinity, the friend of the murdered man among the rest, assembled at my store at my request. I had told them I had something to communicate concerning the foul deed, and I thought it not unlikely I would give them some clue to the assassin.

When all had collected and arranged themselves as I had directed, in a semicircle before my door, eager, expectant, excited,

I came forward, holding in my hand an egg. Then I made them a short speech on the various superstitions of mankind, which I contended had their origin in mysterious facts revealed from the other world by God's good providence, for the protection of the innocent and the punishment of the guilty, and among other things, I mentioned how the ghosts of their victims would often haunt the murderers, compelling them to reveal their crimes, how land and sea had been known to give up their awful secrets, and how it had been asserted, that if the guilty wretch should place his hand upon the body of the man he had secretly slain, the wounds would bleed afresh.

"And now, gentlemen," I continued, "I hold in my hand as sure a test as any I have named. This simple egg, so fair to the view, contains the murderer's secret. Let him but take it in his hand, and the frail shell will crumble to pieces and show to all that it is filled with the blood of his victim. You will excuse me, gentlemen, for putting you all to this test. We do not know each other's secrets; the murderer of the young man we buried yesterday may be among us, but only the *guilty* need *fear* the trial—the *innocent* will surely pass the ordeal unharmed."

As I said this, I fixed my eyes upon my dark visitor, my suspected man. I never saw a more wretched and ghastly countenance, nor a greater struggle in any living being to keep a calm and unmoved exterior.

The egg began its round. Some took it gravely, some lightly, some turned slightly pale, and some laughed outright. But on it went and came nearer and nearer to the man for whom it was intended. I saw that he was trembling—that his very lips were getting white.

"It is your turn now!" I said, at length, in a cold, stern tone.

"Mine?" he answered, with a ghastly attempt at a smile. "Why— why should I take it? Poor Wilson was my—my—friend!"

"Let him prove so now!" I said. "All eyes are upon you. Take the ordeal sent by Heaven, and prove your innocence—*if you can!*"

He glanced hurriedly around. All eyes were indeed upon him, and with looks of awakening suspicion. He made one despairing effort to be calm, gulped his breath like one choking, and seized the fatal egg with trembling hands.

The next moment it was crushed to atoms, and his hands were wet and stained as if with human gore.

A yell burst from the crowd. A despairing shriek came from the lips of the guilty wretch, and falling, rather than sinking down upon his knees, he cried out, "God of mercy, forgive me! I did kill him! I did kill him! For his gold, his gold! His gold! Oh, cursed gold! Oh, God of Heaven, forgive me!"

"And how many before him?" I demanded.

"Three! Three! Oh, God of mercy, forgive me!"

There was another wild yell, or rather a howl of fury—a rush like wolves upon their prey—and the poor wretch was seized, almost torn limb from limb, and dragged furiously away.

In less than ten minutes from his confession, he was dangling from a neighboring tree, swinging by his neck.

So died the murderer, whose name I have suppressed, because he had respectable friends who are still living.

I will only add, that, believing him guilty, I had previously prepared the egg, putting a red coloring fluid in it, expecting to see him crush it through his superstitious fears of a supernatural discovery. They offered me the promised reward for the detection of the murderer—but this I declined. Justice was all I had sought, and this I had obtained.

THRILLING CONTEST WITH A STAG:
A KENTUCKY SPORTSMAN'S STORY

Our Kentucky sportsman had a favorite stag-hound, strong and of first-rate qualities, named Bravo, which he, on one occasion, in going on a hunting expedition, left at home, taking in his stead, on trial, a fine-looking hound that had been presented to him a few days before. Having gone a certain length into the woodlands in quest of game, he fired at a powerful stag, which he brought down after a considerable run and believed to be dead. The animal, however, was only stunned by the shot. On stooping down to bleed him, he was no sooner touched with the keen edge of the knife than he rose with a sudden bound.

Threw me from his body and hurled my knife from my hand. I at once saw my danger, but it was too late. With one bound he was upon me, wounding and almost disabling me with his sharp horns and feet.

I seized him by his wide-spread antlers and sought to regain possession of my knife, but in vain; each new struggle drew us farther from it. My horse, frightened at the unusual scene, had madly fled to an adjoining ridge where he stood looking down upon the combat, trembling and quivering in every limb. My dog had not come up, and his bay I could not now hear.

The struggles of the furious animal had become dreadful, and every moment I could feel his sharp hoofs cutting deep into my flesh; my grasp upon his antlers was growing less firm, and yet I relinquished not my hold. The struggle had brought us near a deep ditch, washed by autumn rains, and into this I endeavored to force my adversary, but my strength was unequal to the effort; when we approached to the very brink, he leaped over the drain. I relinquished my hold and rolled in, hoping thus to escape him, but he returned to the attack and, throwing himself upon me, inflicted numerous severe cuts upon my face and breast before I could again seize him.

Locking my arms around his antlers, I drew his head close to my breast, and was thus, by great effort, enabled to prevent his doing me any serious injury. But I felt that this could not last long; every muscle and fiber of my frame was called into action, and human nature could not long bear up under such exertion. Faltering a silent prayer to Heaven, I prepared to meet my fate.

At this moment of despair, I heard the faint baying of the hound; the stag too heard the sound and, springing from the ditch, drew me with him. His efforts were now redoubled, and I could scarcely cling to him. Yet that blessed sound came nearer. Oh, how wildly beat my heart as I saw the hound emerge from the ravine and spring forward with a short, quick bark, as his eye rested on his game. I released my hold of the stag, who turned upon the new enemy. Exhausted and unable to rise, I still cheered the dog, that dastardly fled before the infuriated animal, which seemingly despising such an enemy, again threw himself upon me. Again did I succeed in throwing my arms around his antlers, but not until he had inflicted several dangerous wounds upon my head and face, cutting to the very bone.

Blinded by the flowing blood, exhausted and despairing, I cursed the coward dog, which stood near, baying furiously, yet refusing to seize his game. Oh, how I prayed for Bravo! The thoughts of death were bitter. To die thus in the wild forest, alone, with none to help! Thoughts of home and friends coursed like lightning through my brain.

At that moment, when hope itself had fled, deep and clear over the neighboring hill came the baying of my gallant Bravo! I should have known his voice among a thousand. I pealed forth, in one faint shout: "On, Bravo, on!"

The next moment, with tiger-like bounds, the noble dog came leaping down the declivity, scattering the dried autumn leaves like a whirlwind in his path. No pause he knew, but fixing his fangs in the stag's throat, he at once commenced the struggle.

I fell back, completely exhausted. Blinded with blood, I only knew that a terrific struggle was going on. In a few moments all was still, and I felt the warm breath of my faithful dog as he licked my wounds. Clearing my eyes from gore, I saw my late adversary dead at my feet, and Bravo, "my own Bravo," as the heroine of a modern novel would say, standing over me. He yet bore around his neck a fragment of the rope with which I had tied him. He had gnawed it in two and, following his master through all his windings, arrived in time to rescue him from a most horrible death.

THE WOLVES AND THE DARKEY FIDDLER

In the early days of the settlement of South Kentucky, there was great trouble with the wolves. The large gray wolf of the more wooded northern and middle districts greatly abounded in the heavy forests of the Green River Bottom, particularly in the neighborhood of Henderson, which is situated on the Ohio not far below the mouth of the Green River. The barnyard suffered to a great extent, in the way of pigs, calves, and poultry, from their depredations, which frequently in mid-winter were even carried to the audacious extreme of attacking human beings. Indeed, it was no unusual thing for the belated footman, at such times, when they were pressed by hunger, to find himself surrounded by a herd of them in the woods. Hence the adventure of old Dick, the fiddler.

Old Dick, who was the property of one of the Hendersons, from whom the town and county take their names, was esteemed by his good-natured and wealthy master as decidedly a privileged character. He was "a good old good-for-nothing darkey," as the word went in the neighborhood, whose sole merit consisted in his fiddling, but, by the way, singular as this merit was, it in reality constituted him by far the most important "gemmen of color" within forty miles around. He had his time pretty much to himself, and no one pretended to interfere with its disposal, as his master humorously styled him a "necessary nuisance" to the neighborhood, because he kept the darkeys in a good humor by his fiddle.

Now Dick had most strongly developed the strongest and most marked traits of the fiddler, the world over, namely punctilious-ness and punctuality. Upon either of these points he was peculiarly irritable, nay even ferocious. With all the proverbial timidity of the "child of genius," old Dick was yet as savage as a hyena at any improprieties of etiquette which might chance to turn up during the sable orgies over which he presided, but nothing caused him to so far forget "*the* proprieties" in his own person, as the intervention of any unusual or accidental causes of delay which prevented his being on hand in time. Poor Dick! But the story will explain.

On the occasion of a grand wedding festival among the colored gentry of a neighboring plantation, some six miles distant, old Dick was, of course, expected to officiate as master of the ceremonies. It had been an unusually severe winter, and a heavy snow lay upon the ground on the eventful evening, when having donned his "long-tailed blue," with its glittering gilt buttons, and mounted the immense shirt collar, by the aid of which the dignity of his official character was properly maintained, the ancient Apollo sallied forth, fiddle in hand, to dare the perils of the distant way alone, for the younger darkeys had all gone to the frolic hours ago, with a haste and eagerness altogether unbecoming his importance.

The moon was out, and the stars twinkled merrily overhead, as the spry old man trudged away over the crisp and crackling snow. The path, which was a very narrow one, led for the greater part of the way through the dark shadows of a heavy bottom forest, which yet remained as wild as when the Indians roamed it and was untraversed by a wagon road for many miles.

The body and soul of the precise old darkey was goaded at every step by the maddening vision of the expectant ranks of sable gentility, rolling the whites of their eyes and stamping their stocking feet upon the puncheon floor, impatient of his delay; for the truth was, that he had lingered a little too long over the polishing of those brass buttons and the setting of that plentitude of collar, and he now first became conscious of it as he had come forth beneath the moon and perceived its unexpected height above the horizon. On he dashed with unrelaxing energy, heedless of the black shadows and hideous night cries in the deep forest. Wolves were howling around him in every direction, but he paid little attention to sounds that were so common. He was soon compelled, however, to give more heed to these animals than was by any means pleasing or expected.

He had now made nearly half of his journey, and the light opening ahead through the trees showed him the "old clearing" as it was called, through which his path led. The wolves had been getting excessively noisy for the last mile, and to the indescribable horror of the old man, he could hear them gathering about him in the crackling bushes on either side as they ran along to keep pace with his rapid steps. The woods very soon seemed to the darkey to be literally alive with them, as they gathered in yelping packs from far and near.

Wolves are cautious about attacking a human being at once, but usually require some little time to work themselves up to the point. That such was the case, now proved most lucky for poor old Dick, who began to realize the horrible danger, as a dark object would brush past his legs every few moments with a snapping sound like the ring of a steel trap, while the yells and patter of the gathering wolves increased with terrible rapidity. Dick knew enough of the habits of the animal to be fully aware that to run would ensure his instant death, as the cowardly pack would be sure to set upon him in a body on the instant of observing any such indication of fear. His only chance was to keep them at bay by preserving the utmost steadiness until he could reach the open ground before him, when he hoped they might leave him, as they do not like to attack in the open ground. He remembered, too, that an old hut still stood in the middle of the clearing, and the thought that he might reach that haven gave him some comfort.

The wolves were becoming more audacious every minute, and the poor old soul could see their green eyes glaring fiery death upon him from all the thickets around. They rushed at him more boldly one after another, snapping as they went past in closer and closer proximity to his thin legs; indeed, the frightened fiddler instinctively thrust at them with his fiddle to turn them aside. In doing so the strings were jarred, and the despairing wretch took on some hope to his shivering soul, when he observed the suddenness of the sound caused them to leap aside with surprise. He instantly drew his hand across the strings with vehemence, and to his infinite relief they sprang back and aside as if he had shot among them. Taking immediate advantage of this lucky diversion in his favor, as he had now reached the edge of the clearing, he made a break for the hut, raking his hand across the fiddle strings at every jump, until they fairly roared again. The astonished wolves paused for a moment on the edge of the clearing, with tails between their legs, looking after him, but the sight of his flying form renewed at once their savage instincts, and with a loud burst of yells, they pursued him at full speed. Alas for the unlucky fiddler, had he been caught now, it would have been all up with him, even had his fiddle continued to shriek more unearthly shrieks than that of Paganini ever gave forth. He had broken the spell by running, for had they caught him now, they would never have paused to listen, had he been an Orpheus in reality.

Luckily the old man reached the hut just as they were at his heels, and slamming the rickety door behind him, he had time to climb out on to the roof where he was comparatively out of danger. I say comparatively, for the perch he now occupied was too rickety to make it anything rather than desirable, except by contrast with the immediate condition from which he had escaped.

The wolves were now furious and, thronging the interior of the hut, leaped up at him with wild yells of gnashing rage. The poor old sinner was horribly frightened, and it required the utmost activity of motion to keep his legs from being snapped by them. Wild with the agonized terror as he was, poor old Dick had managed to cling to his fiddle through it all, and remembering that it had saved him in the woods, he now, with the sheer energy of desperation, drew his bow shrieking across the strings, with a sound that rose high above all their deafening yells, while with his feet kicking out into the open air, he endeavored to avoid their steel-like anger; an instant silence followed this sudden outburst, and Dick continued to produce such frightful spasms of sound as his hysterical condition conceived.

This outbreak kept the wolves quiet for a moment or two, but old Dick soon learned, to his increased horror, that even wolves are too fastidious to stand bad fiddling, for they commenced a renewal of the attack as soon as the first surprise was over, more furiously than ever. This was too much for the poor fiddler, and most especially when the head of a great wolf was thrust up between the boards of the roof, within a few inches of where he sat. He gave himself up now for a gone darkey, and with the horrified exclamation: "Bress God!—who dar?"

He fell to fiddling Yankee Doodle with all his might, unconsciously, as the dying swan is said to sing its own requiem in its closing moments. With the first notes of the air silence commenced, Orpheus had conquered! The brutes owned the subduing spell, and the terror-stricken fiddler, when he came to himself, astonished at the sudden cessation of hostilities, saw he was surrounded by the most attentive and certainly appreciative audience he had ever played before—for the moment there was the slightest cessation of the music, every listener sprang forward to renew the battle and set his pipe-stem legs to flying about in the air again.

But he had now learned the spoil and, so long as he continued to play with tolerable correctness, was comparatively safe. The old fiddler soon forgot his terror now in professional pride, for he was decidedly flattered by such intense appreciation and, entering fully into the spirit of the thing, played with a gusto and effect such as he thought he had never before surpassed or even equaled. Even the wedding, with its warm lights, its sweetened whiskey, was forgotten for the time in the glow of this new professional triumph.

But all pleasures have their drawbacks on this earth, and as time progressed, he began with all his enthusiasm to feel very natural symptoms of cold, fatigue, and even exhaustion. But it would not do; he could not stop a moment before they were at him again, and there they persistently sat, that shaggy troop of connoisseurs, fidgeting on their haunches with lolling tongues and pricked ears, listening to their compulsory charmer for several weary hours, until the Negroes at the wedding, becoming impatient or alarmed about the old man, came out to look for him and found him thus perched upon the roof of the tottering hut sawing away for dear life, while he was ready to drop every instant from sheer fatigue and the freezing cold. They rescued the old man from his comfortless position, while the lingering forms of his late audience told that they most unwillingly surrendered the fruition of their unwonted feast.

THE MURDERER'S CREEK

There is a little stream that runs into that most beautiful of all rivers, the noble Hudson, that still bears the name of the Murderer's Creek, though few perhaps can tell why it was so called. About a century ago, the beautiful region watered by this stream was possessed by a small tribe of Indians, which has long since become extinct or incorporated with some more powerful nation of the west. Three or four hundred yards from the mouth of this little river, a White family of the name of Stacey had established itself in a log house, by tacit permission of the tribe, to whom Stacey had made himself useful by his skill in a variety of arts highly estimated by the savages. In particular a friendship subsisted between him and an old Indian, called Naoman, who often came to his house and partook of his hospitality. The family consisted of Stacey, his wife, and two children, a boy and a girl, the former five and the latter three years old.

The Indians never forgive injuries nor forget benefits.

One day Naoman came to Stacey's log house in his absence, lighted his pipe, and sat down. He looked unusually serious, sometimes sighed deeply, but said not a word. Stacey's wife asked him what was the matter, if he were ill? He shook his head, but said nothing, and soon went away.

The next day he came and behaved in the same manner. Stacey's wife began to think there was something strange in all this and acquainted her husband with the matter as soon as he came home. He advised her to urge the old man to explain his conduct, in case he should come again, which he did the following day. After much importunity, the old Indian at last replied to her questions in this manner: "I am a Red man, and the pale faces are our enemies; why should I speak?”

“But my husband and I are your friends; you have eaten bread with us a hundred times, and my children have sat on your knees as often. If you have anything on your mind, tell it me now.”

“It will cost me my life if it is known, and you white-faced women are not good at keeping secrets,” replied Naoman.

“Try me, and you will find that I can,” said she.

“Will you swear by the Great Spirit that you will tell none but your husband?”

“I have no one else to tell.”

“But will you swear?”

“I do swear, by our Great Spirit, that I will tell none but my husband.”

“Not if my tribe should kill you for not telling?”

“No, not though your tribe should kill me for not telling.”

Naoman then proceeded to tell her, that owing to the frequent encroachments of the White people on their land at the foot of the mountains, his tribe had become exceedingly angry and were resolved that night to massacre all the White settlers within their reach, that she must send for her husband and inform him of the danger and as secretly and speedily as possible take their canoe and paddle with all haste over the river to Fishkill for safety.

“Be quick, and cause no suspicion,” said Naoman, as he departed.

The good wife instantly sought her husband, who was down on the river fishing, told him the story, and as no time was to be lost, they proceeded to their boat, which was unluckily filled with water. It took some time to clear it out, and meanwhile Stacey recollected his gun, which he had left behind. He went to his house and returned with it. All this took a considerable time, and precious time it proved to this poor family.

The daily visits of Naoman, and his more than ordinary gravity, had excited suspicion in some of his tribe, who therefore now paid particular attention to the movements of Stacey. One of the young Indians who had been kept on the watch, seeing the whole family about to take the boat, ran to the little Indian village, about a mile off, and gave the alarm.

Five stout Indians immediately collected and ran down to the river, where their canoes were moored, jumped in, and paddled after Stacey, who by this time, had got some distance out into the stream. They gained upon him so fast that twice he dropped his paddle and took up his gun. But his wife prevented his shooting by telling him that if he fired and they were afterwards overtaken, they would meet with no mercy from the Indians. He accordingly refrained and plied his paddle till the sweat rolled in big drops down his forehead.

All would not do; they reached the opposite shore but were quickly overtaken and carried back with shouts and yells of triumph.

The first thing the Indians did when they got ashore was to set fire to Stacey's house. They then dragged him, his wife, and their children to their village. Here the principal old men, and Naoman among them, assembled to deliberate on the affair. The chief men of the council expressed their opinion that some of the tribe had been guilty of treason, in apprising Stacey, the White man, of their designs, whereby they took alarm and had well-nigh escaped. They proposed that the prisoners should be examined in order to discover who was the traitor. The old men assented to this, and one of them who spoke English began by interrogating Stacey and interpreted what was said to the others.

Stacey refused to betray his informant.

His wife was then questioned while two Indians stood threatening the children with their uplifted tomahawks, in case she did not confess. She attempted to evade the truth, by pretending that she had a dream the night before, which had warned her to fly, and that she had persuaded her husband to do so.

"The Great Spirit never deigns to talk in dreams to the White faces," said one of the old Indians. "Woman, thou hast two tongues and two faces; speak the truth, or thy children shall surely die."

The little boy and girl were then brought close to her, and the two savages stood over them ready to execute their cruel orders.

"Wilt thou name that Red man," said the old Indian, "who betrayed his tribe? I will ask thee three times."

The mother made no answer.

"Wilt thou name the traitor? This is the second time."

The poor woman looked at her husband and then at her children and stole a glance at Naoman, who sat smoking his pipe with invincible gravity. She wrung her hands and wept, but remained silent.

"Wilt thou name the traitor? I ask you for the third and last time."

The agony of the mother was more and more intense; again she sought the eye of Naoman, but it was cold and motionless. A moment's delay was made for her reply. She was silent. The tomahawks were raised over the heads of her children, who besought their mother to release them.

"Stop!" cried Naoman. All eyes were instantly turned upon him.

"Stop!" repeated he, in a tone of authority. "White woman, thou hast kept thy word with me to the last moment. Chiefs, I am the traitor. I have eaten the bread, warmed myself at the fire, and shared the kindness of these Christian White people, and it was I who told them of their danger. I am a withered, leafless, branchless trunk; cut me down if you will; I am ready to fall."

A yell of indignation resounded on all sides. Naoman descended from the little bank of earth on which he sat, shrouded his dark countenance in his buffalo robe, and calmly awaited his fate. He fell dead at the feet of the White woman, by a blow of the tomahawk.

But the sacrifice of Naoman and the heroic firmness of the Christian White woman did not suffice to save the lives of the other victims. They perished—how, it is needless to say, but the memory of their fate has been preserved in the name of the beautiful little stream on whose banks they lived and died, which to this day is called the Murderer's Creek.